598.2942

A Revised List of
Hampshire and
Isle of Wight Birds

A Revised List of
Hampshire and
Isle of Wight Birds

Edwin Cohen and John Taverner

Oxford Illustrated Press 1972

© Oxford Illustrated Press
   Edwin Cohen and John Taverner

SBN 0 902280 15 5
Printed by Blackwells

Contents

List of Plates

List of Illustrations

Foreword

Hampshire, in terms both of breeding and visiting birds, must be one of the richest counties in England. The total of around 326 species recorded on the mainland and in the Isle of Wight is about 70% of the present grand total for Britain and Ireland. Over 130 species, two-thirds of the national total, breed regularly and half a dozen more have bred in the past ten years; and all this without any mountains or true moorland. But there is a wonderful diversity of lowland habitats, which are now assiduously watched and reported on. The task of assembling and summarising so much information about so many birds is formidable and I am not surprised that virtually a new book has emerged from the revision of Edwin Cohen's *Birds of Hampshire and the Isle of Wight* published in 1963. Edwin did not live to complete the task and, in the hands of John Taverner, it has become a fitting memorial to a great naturalist in the tradition of Gilbert White; a great enthusiast for conservation. This book must not be esteemed only for its scientific value; it is a spur to even greater efforts to protect the Hampshire countryside which is facing ever more massive plans for 'development'. Somehow a compromise must be found which allows for human living space and the integrity of the woods, downs, heaths, wetlands and foreshore so that they can continue to be enjoyed and studied. Realisation of their wealth of bird life is an encouragement to us all to carry on the good fight.

BRUCE CAMPBELL

October 1972

Map of Hampshire and Isle of Wight

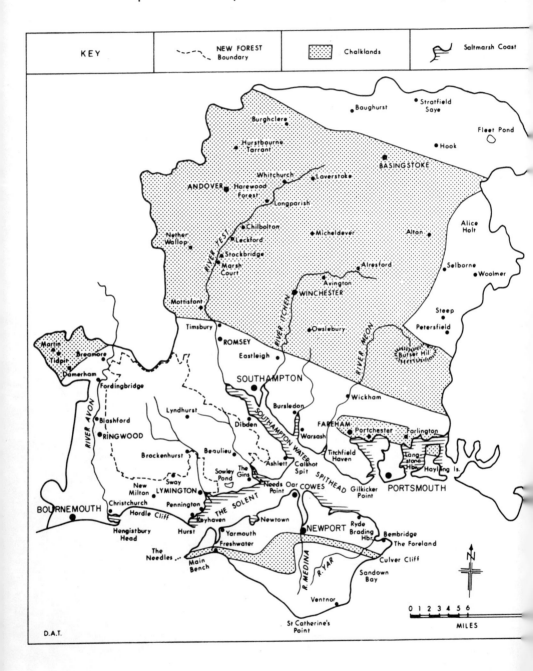

| KEY | - - - NEW FOREST Boundary | Chalklands | Saltmarsh Coast |

D.A.T.

Introduction

IN THE EARLY 1950s, a mini-revolution took place in Hampshire's ornithology. Prior to that date, there were very few active observers in the county and our information on most species was sparse. The resurgence came from Portsmouth where a group of young men began a systematic study of Langstone Harbour and Farlington Marshes, widening their horizon to take in the New Forest, St. Catherine's Point and various parts of the Solent coast. At the same time, E. Cohen and W. H. Dowdeswell provided a vehicle for the organisation of serious ornithology in the county by creating the Ornithological Section of the Hampshire Field Club. Before the end of the 1950s, other observers (myself included) had been inspired by the influence of the Portsmouth Group to set about systematic observation of our bird life, and so developed the body of field workers that has put Hampshire back on the ornithological map.

Through the 1950s, Edwin Cohen was writing *The Birds of Hampshire and the Isle of Wight*. Edwin started writing before the *revolution* had brought to light all the information that is known to us today, and he constantly had to rewrite sections of his book as new data became available. When it was finally published in 1963, the picture was only partly known so that a revised edition soon became a necessity. Edwin had started working on this just before his death, and I was left to see the task through. In fact, it has not been possible to just bring out a second edition. So much new information has come to light that it has meant a completely new book, hence the present volume.

Enough is now known about almost all species in the area to enable a fairly accurate account of their status and distribution to be recorded, but there will be changes as man alters the landscape and there is a great deal of room for detailed work on breeding densities of nearly all our resident species. So that this book will not become out of date as the new data appear, a low-priced paperback Supplement will be prepared every five years outlining changes from — or additions to — the text of this book. Each new Supplement will wholly replace the previous one so that this book plus the latest Supplement will be all that is needed to discover the status of any species in Hampshire. In this way, I trust the present volume will be the foundation of ornithological information in Hampshire to the end of this century, and if all goes to plan, the first Supplement will appear in 1977. This book includes information up to the end of 1971.

Rocketing printing costs mean that a book of this kind, with limited sales, has to be of restricted length. Something had to be cut from Edwin's first book, and since all the changes have occurred in the Systematic List of Species, I have concentrated on this in the present book and dispensed with the early chapters of its predecessor, those dealing with botany, geology and the bird life of a few selected areas. These have not really altered, and although it would be most convenient to repeat them again between these covers, expense dictates that they must be omitted.

No county bird book can be accurate unless the area has been well surveyed, and the real credit for a book such as this should go to all those observers who have spent countless hours in the field and painstakingly recorded and reported all that they have seen. On behalf of Edwin and myself, I acknowledge this prodigious effort by all concerned. I would also like to thank David Thelwell for his text illustrations; Geoffrey Fisher, Norman Orr, Eric Hosking and Aerofilms Ltd. for their photographs; Bruce Campbell for writing the Foreword as he did for *The Birds of*

Hampshire; Miss Mary Allcard for the quite invaluable help she gave; Mrs. Celia Root for her work on the typescript; and the Oxford Illustrated Press for showing faith in this book and for the quality of the finished product. Finally, my thanks to Michael Bryant and David Billett for reading the original text and making valuable observations on how it could be improved.

In the Systematic List, I have presented the species in Wetmore order because this was used in Edwin's original book and is still used in the Hampshire annual bird reports. Similarly, I have used the same scientific names that Edwin used, even though some of these have now been altered, because I think that there should be a degree of continuity between the two books.

John Taverner
Winchester, June 1972.

Abbreviations

[ ]	Claim of species enclosed within square brackets is doubtful.
*	The asterisk after a bird's name means that it is new since K and M.
B.	*Proceedings of the Bournemouth Natural Science Society.*
B.B.	*British Birds.*
B.o.H.	*Birds of Hampshire and the Isle of Wight*, Cohen, 1963.
B.o.M.	*Birds of Milford*, Milford-on-Sea Record Society, Vol. 1, No. 6. August 1913 (Kelsall and Coles).
B.T.O.	British Trust for Ornithology.
Bull. B.O.C.	*Bulletin of the British Ornithologists' Club.*
C.H.O.S.G.	Christchurch Harbour Ornithological Survey Group.
EC	Edwin Cohen, co-author of this book.
H.	Reports of Ornithological Section of Hampshire Field Club and Archaeological Society.
Handbook	*The Handbook of British Birds* (Witherby *et al.* 1938–1941).
I.o.W.	*Bird Report of the Isle of Wight Natural History & Archaeological Society.*
JHT	John Taverner, co-author of this book.
K & M	Kelsall and Munn: *The Birds of Hampshire and the Isle of Wight* (1905).
Kelso	*Notes on Some Common & Rare British Birds* (1912).
N.F.O.C.	New Forest Ornithologists' Club.
P.G.	Portsmouth Group (of bird watchers).
S.P.G.	St. Catherine's Point Group.
W.	Winchester College Natural History Society.

Systematic List of Birds

1.   Black-throated Diver. *Colymbus arcticus*: K & M say: 'An occasional visitor to the coast.' Now, a rather uncommon visitor from October to early May on or near the coast, but one was caught on the River Enborne, the county boundary in the north, on a trimmer baited with dace for pike on 7 March 1935 (Miss Popham in *H.* 13.207). Over the past two decades, these winter birds would typically number fewer than twenty each year, though cold weather *may* bring more for six corpses were found early in 1963 (*H.* 23. Part 1). However, it appears more regularly off St. Catherine's point on spring migration where the following are examples of the numbers recorded flying east, the bulk of them in April: 1958, 14; 1960, 7; 1962, 21; 1966, 9; 1968, 19; 1969, 11. Divers are extremely difficult to identify in flight and most of those seen at St. Catherine's are just recorded as *divers* but some observers believe (and the same idea has been put forward from Sussex and Dorset) that the bulk of these spring divers are Black-throated.

Not reported between 1905 and 1935 except that Kelso (1912) writes: 'it has been obtained off Hayling'.

2.   Great Northern Diver. *Colymbus immer*: K & M say: 'A winter visitor to the coast, rarely occurring inland.' Now, a fairly regularly but rather uncommon visitor to the coast and occasionally nearby waters such as Hatchet Pond between October and May, but one on 1 June 1957 at Lymington (E.L. Jones, *H.* 20 Supplement), and one on 27 September 1958; very rarely, further inland on small lakes. The numbers of winter records would typically be a little higher than those of the previous species and one would expect about thirty records per year. Birds have occurred in full summer plumage.

Occasionally seen off the Island in winter and, like the Black-throated Diver, it is seen regularly flying east off St. Catherine's Point in spring. Examples of such numbers at St. Catherine's are: 1958, 15; 1960, 4; 1962, 8; 1968, 13; 1969, 7. It will be seen that all but one of these counts is smaller than the corresponding count for the Black-throated Diver, though the Great Northern is perhaps easier to identify in flight.

3.   White-billed Diver. *Colymbus adamsii*: One in K & M, winter of 1895/6. Doubt as to the correct identification of this bird is cast by Witherby in *B.B.* 16.11. It may have been *Colymbus immer*; the specimen could not be traced. One found dead on the mainland coast by Keith Shackleton, year uncertain; the bill is in the British Museum (Natural History) and the finding of it is described in *The Field* of 4 October 1962.

Six observers, including Mrs. Miller and N. Pullen, watched a bird which was probably of this species down to 50 yards at Needs Oar on 13 January 1962 in very good light and furnished a full description, the salient point of which was the yellow bill with 'the lower mandible upwardly slanted giving a somewhat up-tilted retroussé appearance to the whole bill'. The Rare Birds Committee were, however, unable to accept it.

4. **Red-throated Diver.** *Colymbus stellatus*: A regular visitor to the coast and occasionally to inland waters. This is usually the commonest diver and although the total number seen each year is typically less than 50, there were over a hundred sightings in 1970. It has occurred in every month except July but May birds are infrequent and are most likely to be seen passing St. Catherine's Point whilst the earliest returns are not usually before October. Like all the divers, records are mostly of single birds, Hengistbury being the locality where a small gathering is most likely, whilst the largest number was 23 in Stokes Bay and off Lee-on-Solent on 2 April 1956 (*H*. 19. Part 3). The remarkable record of 'well over 100 busy diving at sea' off Avon Beach (*H*. 14. p.99) was an error and referred to Great Crested Grebes (Miss Popham *in Litt*.). The occasional inland records have been as far north as Fleet Pond (Donaldson), Ewhurst and Petersfield.

The number identified passing east off St. Catherine's in spring exceeds those of the other divers, examples being: 1957, 40; 1958, 35; 1960, 28; 1962, 20; 1966, 14; 1967, 26; 1968, 12, 1969, 27; 1971, 18.

There is evidence that it has become scarcer lately and a distressingly large number of the reports relate to oiled birds.

Red-throated Diver

Diver species. The numbers given under the previous species are somewhat misleading for the records of unidentified divers in winter and spring are much higher. At St. Catherine's Point, for instance, 341 divers flew east on 14 January 1961 and 134 did likewise the following day. Numbers are also seen passing Hengistbury in winter, some of the largest counts being 116 in January 1967, 103 between 26 and 29 December 1968 and 81 in cold SE winds on 28 December 1969 (many Hengistbury records seem prompted by bad weather). It seems probable that there are considerable numbers of divers off-shore in winter usually out of sight of land, some of which are driven in-shore by bad weather such as gales or fog.

In spring at St. Catherine's, 165 flew east between 9 March and 19 May 1963, 90 flew east between 6 March and 4 May 1966 and 82 did likewise between 24 March and 29 April 1968. Most years produce similar movements.

5.   Great Crested Grebe. *Podiceps cristatus*: K & M give the first breeding record as 'about ten years ago' (i.e. about 1895) on Fleet Pond and describe it as 'a scarce resident in the NE part of the county' by 1905. Meinertzhagen reports successful breeding of one pair at Mottisfont in 1894, the only time he saw them there all through the nineties.

In the 1931 census, thirteen waters held 24 pairs (*B.B.* 26.73). After that the number of breeding pairs declined though the decline seems to have been halted and perhaps reversed. There were only 7 in 1957 and 1958, 12 in 1961, 15 and 5 possibles in 1965, 14 in 1967 and possibly 22 in 1970, but not one of the recent surveys has been complete. Most of the areas used have been in the north of the county but in the south, Alresford Pond, Embley Park, Blashford gravel pits, Timsbury and Winnall have held pairs in recent years.

The inland waters may hold birds outside the breeding season (counts of 20 plus have been made) but they are mainly deserted in favour of the coast. Birds may begin to appear on salt water as early as July and August although the main arrival is from September onwards and they leave for their breeding grounds in March and April, a few remaining until May. During this non-breeding period, they may be seen anywhere along the coast and numbers are sometimes large: e.g., in Langstone Harbour 91 on 2 December 1961 (P.G.); 150—200 off Boscombe in a strong SW wind in December 1942; and a remarkable tight flock of 81 off Alum Chine (Bournemouth) on 28 December 1969 (Peart). See also under Red-throated Diver. The most-used coastal area is Langstone Harbour where birds are likely to b e seen in *all* months with a winter peak of over 50.

From the Island there are reports of some in Osborne Bay in the winter months since 1948 (possibly overlooked previously), of 43 near the Needles on 8 February 1953 and of several on the Solent outside the breeding season similar to the occurrences on the mainland coast.

The first recovery of a British-ringed Great Crested Grebe was of a first-summer bird ringed in July 1964 near Cheltenham and found dead near Basingstoke on 5 December 1965.

Great Crested Grebe

6.   Red-necked Grebe. *Podiceps grisegena*: K & M calling it 'an occasional visitor to the coast in winter', give only some half a dozen records down to 1905. Since then there have been about 100, all save five between November and March, the exceptions being one at St. Catherine's Point on 14 April 1968 (Cheverton), one in summer plumage on 2 April 1970 in Portsmouth Harbour (Bowers), one flying east at St. Catherine's Point on 3 April 1971, and two near Langstone Harbour on 22 and 23 October 1971 (*H.* 1971). All but one of these have been since 1934 and nearly half have been since 1961; either the species is becoming more common or observers more competent. Several of the recent records have been from the Island and all the recent records have been from salt water except for one on Sowley Pond on 29 January 1961 and one on Hatchet Pond from 8/14 February 1970.

The reports from Osborne Bay in *H.* 19. Part 1, p.79 were erroneous (See corrigenda in 1955 report).

7.   Slavonian Grebe. *Podiceps auritus*: Although K & M call it a regular winter visitor to the coast and more common than the Red-necked, they give only about the same number of instances. Since then, however, and particularly since 1947, one or more (maximum together 13, mainly in transitional plumage, on 31 March 1956 in Hayling Bay—Henty) have been recorded on well over a hundred occasions so that it is still more frequent in Hampshire than the Red-necked Grebe. The vast majority of these sightings have been in December, January and February with a few in October, November, March and April. Unusual dates are when a pair was seen three times in the first half of August 1936 at Warren Flats (Troubridge in *H.* 13) and an unusual place was on the Avon above Winkton where one stayed for twenty-three days from 26 March to 17 April 1939 (Jourdain in *H.* 14.379).

There have been several winter records from the Solent coast of the Island and one was in full breeding plumage at Yarmouth from 29 to 31 July 1954 (Adams).

8.   Black-necked Grebe. *Podiceps caspicus*: K & M give seven instances and call it 'an occasional visitor to the coast in winter and spring'. Since then there have been many coastal records but in recent years it has been a *regular* visitor only to Langstone Harbour and Pennington with merely a handful from the rest of the coast. Early and late year maxima in Langstone Harbour are suggested by the following: 1969, 5 and 41; 1968, 7 and 27; 1967, 35 and 36; 1966, 29 and 9. The highest count ever from that locality was 58 in November 1957 (P.G.). Numbers at Pennington are unlikely to exceed 10.

There have been August records but the first returns are usually in September or October. The last winter records are in March or April.

Inland, one was at Frensham Pond from 4 to 12 November 1967 (*H.* 1967) and one was at Winchester Sewage Farm on 21 November 1970 (*H.* 1970).

From the Island there are records of two single birds in February 1954, three in 1957 and 1958, four at Newtown on 4 September 1959 (*I.o.W.* 5.4.149), one from 9 to 14 January 1962 at Newtown (Mrs. Seabroke), one on 8 January 1963 and a group of 10 off Seaview in the cold spell of that year, one at Yarmouth on 10 February 1965 and one on 16 November 1969 at Bembridge.

9.   Little Grebe. *Podiceps ruficollis*: K & M state: 'A common resident, universally distributed in all districts on the mainland; much less common in the Island but resident there also.' By far the largest number of observations since then are outside the main breeding season but it does breed freely on suitable waters all over the mainland; e.g. 150 pairs estimated on the Test system in 1971 (Thelwell). On the Island, it nests occasionally, viz. — near Osborne 1916; Carisbrooke Water Works

1952; Bembridge 1953 and 1955; and near Newtown in 1960 and 1961.

Outside the breeding season, there is a movement to coastal waters where several spots are particularly favoured. On the mainland these are the Portsmouth harbours, Redbridge, the Gins and Needs Oar Point, the Hurst area and Christchurch Harbour. The highest count was 67 in Portsmouth Harbour on 1 December 1956 (Bowers) but any of the above localities may have a winter peak of over 20 and most years produce at least one area with a count of 40 or 50. On the Island, the River Medina seems to be a regularly used water with several counts in excess of 50, the maximum being 60 in 1967. 40 were also reported on the Yar in 1968. The rivers are far from empty in winter however, several hundred probably remaining on the 60 miles of the Test system (Thelwell).

The coastal gatherings disperse in March and April and although the first may return in late July or August, the real build up begins in September.

A bird was reported at St. Catherine's Light on 18 April 1906.

11. Wilson's Petrel. *Oceanites oceanicus*: Two in K & M, 1863 and 1888. None since, the bird claimed at Hengistbury Head on 7 November 1965 having been rejected by *British Birds. The Handbook* says: 'Nov. 1863 *aut* 1888', thus apparently admitting one occurrence only.

12. Leach's Petrel. *Oceanodroma leucorrhoa*: Reports of this species mostly fall into two categories, those found storm-driven and those killed at St. Catherine's Light in September, October and December from 1905 to 1911; single birds were killed at the Light on ten occasions.

Leach's Petrel

Single storm-driven birds were found at various places along the coast or more rarely inland on eight occasions between 1936 (when there was a SW gale from 7 to 9 November) and December 1956. In the last week of October and the first eleven days of November 1952 there was a famous 'wreck' of this species, dead and dying birds being picked up all over the country. Hampshire had its share, at least eight being found dead, three alive but dying and six were seen flying off the coast. Some of the dead and dying were found in the centre of the county round Winchester and Stoke Charity, and even as far inland as Andover and Basingstoke. Some recorders gave no evidence of identification so that perhaps five birds may have been Storm Petrels (*Hydrobates pelagicus*). From the Island six were reported in Freshwater Bay, of which two died and two flew away on 29 October. For a full report of the 'wreck' by H. J. Boyd see *B.B.* 47,137.

One bird, not storm-driven, was seen in the Solent on 15 September 1957, and another on 4 December 1960 (long wings and forked tail seen by five observers). The most recent records have been of singletons at Hurst on 28 October 1962 (Hobby), on 3 November 1962 (Mummery) and on 28 October 1967 (Agland).

13. Madeiran Petrel. *Oceanodroma castro* *: One dead on the beach at Milford-on-Sea, 19 November 1911 (Munn in *B.B.* 5.252).

14. Storm Petrel. *Hydrobates pelagicus*: Some half-dozen examples in K & M. Since then, records have fallen into three categories:

1. Birds killed at St. Catherine's Light. Single birds were killed on thirteen nights in the years 1907 to 1910 between 5 September and 18 December, several were killed on the night of 3/4 December 1910 and one on 17 October, 1971.

2. Birds found dead elsewhere. Singletons were picked up at Hengistbury on 3 January 1947, near Freshwater on 4 April 1948, at Ventnor in August 1954, at Lee-on-Solent in 1957, at Southbourne after gales on 4/6 May 1967, and one long dead at Hengistbury on 28 January 1968.

3. Records of live birds, viz. — one flying west at Warden Point opposite Hurst Castle on 28 November 1954 (Adams); one off Hythe Pier on 9 October 1955 (Kinsey); one at St. Catherine's Light at 0200 hours on 16 November 1958 during easterly winds and driving rain (S.P.G.); one off Gilkicker Point on 26 November 1960 (Terry); one near the Brambles buoy on 1 September 1961 (White); singletons found at St. Catherine's Light on 31 October 1963 (Rattey) and 7 October 1965 (S.P.G.) which flew off when released; two at Hurst on 28 October 1967 (Agland); one flying west' off St. Catherine's Point in south-west gales on 22 June 1968 (Renyard).

16. Manx Shearwater. *Procellaria puffinus*:

(a) *Procellaria p.puffinus*: One killed at St. Catherine's Light on the nights 14/15 May and 17/18 June 1909; one, gale-driven, flying close inshore at Mudeford on 12 November 1936 (Miss Popham in *H.* 13.276); one, which had been dead for several weeks, found on the shore near Warren Farm, Beaulieu, on 21 June 1949 'carefully examined against *The Handbook*' by the finder, Rooke; one found alive at Avington Park on 5 September 1950 died a few days later (Scaife); and one in Spithead between Portsmouth and Ryde on 1 April 1954 (Winterbottom). From then until the end of 1970 the species has been seen on almost fifty occasions, and most of the recent records have been of birds passing St. Catherine's Point, particularly in April/May and less frequently in June/September. The largest of these St. Catherine's movements have been 20 flying east on 20 May 1961, 38 flying west on 6 August 1962, 13 flying east on 4 May 1967, 16 flying east on 31 May 1969 and

45 flying east on 21 May 1970. Complete coverage at St. Catherine's would no doubt reveal that the species is recorded every year in small numbers.

After gales in September 1967 which caused a wreck of this species, Griffiths reported one on 4 September exhausted in the middle of Longstock — it died within a week — another nearby at Houghton was handed to the R.S.P.C.A. and another was found alive at Alton (*H.* 1967).

(b) *Procellaria p.mauretanicus*: The specimen shot in Christchurch Bay in August 1859 (K & M p.344) was, in 1922, in E. Hart's collection (now in the Leicester City Museum) and is of this race (*cf. B.B.* 15.243).

One was seen about ten miles SSE of Ventnor on 21 September 1948 by James Fisher (*B.B.* 45.44); one on 11 September 1955, single birds on 6, 10 and 11 August 1957, and six on 24 October 1959 flew E. past St. Catherine's Point and were seen by several observers — one of whom, Conchie, knew both Manx and Cory's Shearwaters 'and this was neither'. The latest reports are of two flying east there on 24 September 1960 (Wiseman *et al.*), one flying west there on 31 August 1963, five flying east on 1 May 1965 and one flying east on 13 August 1965 — again at St. Catherine's — two more flying east there on 4 May 1966, and one flying west at Pennington on 21 July 1971.

There is also the remark in Kelso (p.415): 'I have twice seen this species off Hayling' (referring to pre-1913).

19. Great Shearwater. *Procellaria gravis*: Two in K & M, 1878 and 1894. None since.

20. Cory's Shearwater. *Procellaria diomedea borealis**: Four flew east past St. Catherine's Point on 23 and 26 April 1965 (Wooldridge, *B.B.* 60.8.334).

21. Sooty Shearwater. *Procellaria grisea**: One at the Foreland (I.o.W.) on 28 September 1963 (Rees, *H.* 23). One to the west off St. Catherine's Point on 14 September 1964 (Wooldridge,*H.* 23. Part 2). One at Ryde Pier on 7 September 1970 (Cheverton, *H.* 1970). Four flying east off St. Catherine's Point on 20 June 1971 (Renyard, *H.* 1971).

26. Fulmar. *Fulmaris glacialis*: K & M give three winter birds 'procured', the last being in January 1880. The next record was on 5 July 1942, and since then the number of sightings increased rapidly so that today the species is seen frequently off the southern coast of Wight — particularly off St. Catherine's Point and at Main Bench — and with increasing frequency from mainland areas such as Hurst, Hengistbury and Gilkicker. It is still rare *in* the Solent. All records since K & M — apart from a dead bird on 5 January 1957 — have been between March and October, the bulk of the records being in April and May.

At St. Catherine's Point, the numbers reported are suggested by the following counts — coverage is by no means complete even at times of peak migration: in 1965, 62 were seen to fly east and 122 west between 13 April and 7 June; in 1966, 61 were seen to fly east and 103 west between 12 March and 21 May; in 1967, 141 were seen to fly east and 74 west between 19 March and 25 June. Numbers there in autumn are very low. Compared with these numbers, the best from any mainland area has been Hengistbury in 1969 when Fulmars were recorded on ten dates (maximum of 3 birds on any date) between 4 April and 24 May.

Breeding has not yet been proved. However, at Main Bench 'prospecting' was first recorded in 1953, and in 1957 a bird was flushed from the same spot on three dates during summer. On 11 June 1967, at least 24 were landing on the cliff face suggesting a colony (Barden, Cheverton, Hunnybun) and up to 13 were on ledges there in 1968, so although breeding has not been definitely established, it is strongly suspected.

A bird was seen prospecting the Hengistbury cliffs in April 1959 (Boys) and another was prospecting at St. Catherine's in 1968.

27.   Gannet. *Sula bassana*: In all months but rarely reported in January, the bulk seen off St. Catherine's Point; has been found dead, oiled, injured or storm-driven far inland — one second-year bird was picked up on 28 August 1933 on Blackmoor golf course near Selborne, which survived in the London Zoo until 3 September of that year (*B.B.* 27.139).

Very occasionally quite large numbers have been seen fishing, notably during a cold spell in December 1941 when there were between 250 and 300 off Mudeford Beach and Highcliffe on the 5th and 7th, and about 50 on the 12th and 22nd. Again, on 12 December 1950 Hollom saw 40 to 50, all adults, off St. Catherine's in half a gale from the SW. About 200 adults and immatures were seen fishing off the shingle bank between Hurst Point and the Needles by Thomas about the last week of August 1953, and between 150 and 200 were seen fishing between the Needles and Hurst on 10 July 1969 (JHT).

Watchers at St. Catherine's Point since 1955 have seen considerable numbers flying past mostly during the two main migrations, rather more going E. than W. in spring and more W. than E. in autumn. The largest total in one day however was 374 going E. on 13 October 1963 (*H.* 23. Part 1).

28.   Cormorant. *Phalacrocorax carbo*:

(a) *P.c. carbo*: K & M say: 'A common resident on the coast; nesting however, only in the Isle of Wight, in some numbers'. Commonly seen away from the Freshwater and Culver Cliffs' breeding colonies, in all coastal areas, occasionally more than 100 together, and once — on 19 September 1955 — as many as 257 on Fawley pier; this is a favourite resting-place for in 1956 there were 148 there on 15 January, 146 on 11 March and 108 on 3 April (all Dennis). Though never seen by Meinertzhagen up the rivers in the nineties, it is now a quite frequent visitor in winter as far as Winchester, Timsbury and Fordingbridge. They have been seen by day up the river valleys as late as May with the first birds returning as early as August; in 1969 two were seen on the Test above Romsey in June. As many as 18 were seen at Timsbury on 14 November 1969, and in that year, birds were seen as far inland as Stratfield Saye in the extreme north of the county (*H.* 1969).

Among the breeding birds in the Island in 1946 and 1950 were some fully as white as *The Handbook's* illustration of *P.c. sinensis* (Hollom and Nicholson).

The size of the Freshwater Cliffs' breeding colony is difficult to estimate; a boat is really required as the nests are hard to see from the cliff top and there is no access at the bottom. Apart from vague statements such as 'still nests plentifully' (1918–19), 'flourish but no increase' (1923), 'assemblage of at least 600 Cormorants and Shags' (18th July 1937) — Shags are much less numerous — and 'breeds in good numbers' (1951), the only definite numbers are 30 plus pairs nesting on 25 April 1937, about 120 pairs with nests on 14 April 1946 (both by Hollom), 95 nests in May 1954 (Rees and Henty), *ca.* 130 nests on 21 May 1955 (Rees and Tubbs), 75 occupied nests in April 1960, *ca.* 60 pairs with nests on 7 May 1966 (*H.* 1966), and 100 plus occupied nests in 1969 (*H.* 1969). On 28 May 1953 about 100, including 15 immatures, were counted in the vicinity of Freshwater Cliffs.

As to breeding on Culver Cliff, Sandown, our only information is 'flourish but no increase' (1923 [lumped with Freshwater Cliffs]), and that breeding occurred there in 1951 (Adams).

Several flight lines were reported in 1957, as follows:

1. Beaulieu Heath SW/NE, flighting all summer at all times of day in both directions, probably birds which breed at the Needles and feed by day in Southampton Water. Numbers seen each month were — March, 16; April, 8; May, 29; June, 12; July, 12; August, 2; September, 1 (Palmer).

2. River Avon at Fordingbridge, where up to 35 were seen each day at dusk from 31 January to 24 March flying S. (Ash).

3. Hill Head to Fawley, up to 55 on six dates between 24 October and 4 November, usually in rough weather (White).

One bird ringed as a nestling on the Farne Islands on 2 August 1919 was recovered in the Island, October/December 1913 (*B.B.* 7.224) and another nestling ringed on Puffin Island on 9 July 1950 was recovered at Binstead, Isle of Wight, 282 miles SE on 1 February 1953.

(b) *Phalacrocorax c. sinensis**: Sight records of this race in breeding plumage (February to May/June) are of doubtful value in view of the statement by Hollom and Nicholson (*antea*) as to the amount of white on some of the breeding birds of the Island — see also 'The Spring Plumage of the Cormorant' (*B.B.* 51.165). Too much reliance therefore cannot now be placed on the record published in *B.B.* of a bird seen by Miss Popham at the mouth of the Avon on 7 February 1944. A well-described bird seen by Miss Diana Newton Dunn four miles up the Avon on 28 March 1952 is equally suspect as are other records in the Solent and in Southampton Water in the spring of 1950, and several at other places on the south coast in November and January to March 1955/57. However, there is one record of proved Continental origin, that of a bird shot at Hengistbury Head in June 1945 which had been ringed as a young bird at Bruges on 19 June 1939 (*B.B.* 41.205), while one from Christchurch (1873) was discovered in the British Museum collection and certified in 1930, being the first occurrence in Britain (*H.* 16.302) of this race.

29. Shag. *Phalacrocorax aristotelis*: All observers from 1907 to the present day agree that the breeding numbers on Freshwater Cliffs are small and certainly much smaller than those of Cormorants. The only reliable figures we have are 15 pairs (5 nests seen) on 25 April 1937, 11 nests on 14 April 1946 — both these from Hollom — 10/12 pairs in 1955, 4 in 1956 and 25 (Bowers) in 1957. In 1923 they were reported as breeding also on the Culver Cliffs where they were said to be 'flourishing but not increasing'. 16 immatures were seen on the sea below in May 1957, which suggests breeding, and 13 adults were seen there on 9 April 1970 so the colony may still be in existence.

From the mainland coast, a typical year would produce fewer than ten records apart from the Hengistbury area where gatherings are a regular feature outside the breeding season. Winter numbers there have exceeded 30 on several occasions and although counts are low whilst the birds are breeding, they have been recorded in all months.

Inland records are rare, an immature on Alresford Pond from 30 October to 7 November 1962 (Winchester College N.H.S., *H.* 22. Part 3) being the last such record. These notes agree closely with the status described in K & M.

One bird ringed as a nestling on the Farnes was recovered in the first year of life off the Foreland, Isle of Wight (*B.B.* 54.230). Another nestling ringed on the Isle of May 10 July 1953 was found, long dead, in the Isle of Wight, 390 miles SSE the following April (*B.B.* 48.471). Another ringed as a nestling on Lundy or the Scillies was recovered at Bournemouth on 14 September 1960, this being the most easterly recovery of a bird ringed in that area (*B.B.* 54.461).

[**Dalmatian Pelican.** *Pelecanus crispus*: Birds such as the one seen at Langstone Harbour, Isle of Wight and Christchurch Harbour between 29 November and 11 December 1967 have almost certainly been escapes (*H*. 1967).]

30. Heron. *Ardea cinerea*: K & M wrote that it was 'certainly on the increase' and the trend seems to have continued until at least 1954. The *British Birds* national census of heronries in 1928 gave over 70 occupied nests at six sites on the mainland and 17 plus in the Island. In the B.T.O's 1954 census, Wickham (37 nests in 1953, 39 in 1957) with 30 was the largest; the total of occupied nests on the mainland was 114 divided among nine heronries. In 1957 the total was 115 divided among seven sites or 126 in nine sites if the two colonies on the Island are included. In 1960, the mainland number was down to 86, the largest being at Tournerbury with 21; Wickham was down to eight. In 1961 the total was 110 with Wickham back to 21 but the species suffered heavily in the cold winter of 1962/3. Heronry counts in recent years have been far from complete, Tournerbury with 20 occupied nests in 1969, Alice Holt with 23 in 1967 and Hinton Admiral with 19 in 1967 being the largest (*H.*).

Heron

Desertion of mainland heronries seems to have been mainly due to tree-felling in both wars and it is also stated that the Wickham heronry used to have nearer 50 nests until Canadian soldiers begain shooting the birds in the last war. That at Mottisfont, which had from 24 to 36 breeding pairs between 1891 and 1899, was wiped out by keepers in 1901 (Meinertzhagen). They are still persecuted; E. L. Jones found 14 together on a gibbet at Laverstoke and found shot birds under the Harewood heronry; the young of two pairs were destroyed by the keeper at Northington in 1963 (*W.* 1963).

They are seen often enough along the coast outside the breeding season and at suitable feeding places inland also, usually well under 10 on any one occasion, but on 30 July 1940 at Stanpit 42 were counted by Miss Popham (*H.* 15.81) and 35 were there on 20 August 1967 (*H.* 1967) so larger post-breeding gatherings occur at some places. From Langstone Harbour observers report that whereas normally there are only two or three, there are sudden peaks between July and December (e.g. 61 on 17 October 1959); during these peaks the birds sometimes appear very restless, often indulging in high-flying evolutions in which most birds present take part.

They are also often to be seen in small numbers on the Island, the largest number together being 15 at King's Quay Creek near Osborne on 2 July 1921. Heronries there now appear to be in only one area — at Wootton — with two occupied nests in 1952; 1953, 10; 1954, four; 1957, 11; 1958/9, 12; 1960, 16; 1961, 17; 1962, 18, and then only four in 1963 following the very severe winter. Numbers built up to eight pairs in 1964 and then from eight to 11 pairs for the next four years. The whole colony is now situated in Briddlesford Copse. Odd nests have occasionally been built and used at other Island localities, as on the mainland, but none have so far given rise to a new colony.

A nestling ringed Pas de Calais on 28 April 1926 recovered Laverstoke Park on 8 November 1926 (*B.B.* 20.250); a bird ringed at Boreham, Essex, on 21 April 1927 recovered at Whitchurch on 23 February 1928; one ringed on the R. Weser (Germany) on 10 August 1929 recovered at Liss on 6 December 1930 (*B.B.* 24.358); one ringed as a nestling at Taplow, Bucks, 18 May 1949 recovered at North Warnborough 23 miles SSW on 14 August 1949 (*B.B.* 43.317); and there is the following evidence of the occurrence of winter visitors from Scandinavia, viz. — ringed as nestling 10 June 1941 at Rogaland (Norway) recovered in the winter of 1941/2 at Winchester; ringed as nestling in Scania (Sweden) 15 June 1941 recovered 24 November 1941 at Highbridge (*B.B.* 38); ringed as nestling Hålta, Bohus (Sweden) 31 May 1954 recovered 2 February 1955 at Burley; and a nestling ringed in Denmark on 22 May 1961 was found dead near Emsworth on 6 February 1963 (*B.B.* 60.67). A nestling ringed at Alice Holt on 26 May 1962 was found dead in the Department of Creuse (Central France) on 16 February 1963 (*B.B.* 57. Ringing Supplement). A nestling ringed in Denmark on 20 May 1965 was found dead at Warnford on 23 October 1967.

Single birds have been seen on a few occasions coming in from far out to sea off St. Catherine's Point and off Hayling Island (once) in spring and late summer.

31. Purple Heron. *Ardea purpurea*: K & M list one in 1875 and another shot at Alverstone in 1890. The next was not until 1957 when one came in at St. Catherine's Point from far out to the SSW on 14 April (Dennis and Bowers). Then recorded almost annually from 1964, the records being:

Immature, St. Catherine's Point, 19 April 1964 (*H.* 23. Part 2).
Adult, Langstone Harbour, 3 August 1964 (*H.* 23. Part 2).
Immature, Bembridge, 18 May 1966 (*H.* 1966).
One, Farlington Marshes, 28 May 1967 (*H.* 1967).

Immature, Keyhaven, 19 May 1968 (*H.* 1968).
One, Cherque Reserve (Near Lee-on-Solent), 5/8 October 1969 (*H.* 1969).
One flying west, Hengistbury, 13 September 1970 (*H.* 1970).
One, Farlington Marshes, 31 August 1971.
All recent records accepted by *British Birds* Rarities Committee.

32.   Little Egret. *Egretta garzetta*: K & M admit one, shot at Christchurch in July 1882 (*B.B.* 1.347). The next was at Hengistbury on 8 May 1956 (Clafton) and from then onwards, most years have produced a record, the list being:
One, Langstone Harbour, 2 June 1957 (*H.* 20 Supplement).
One, Langstone Harbour, 26 July 1959 (*H.* 21. Part 3).
One, Titchfield Haven, 29 May 1960 (*B.B.* 54. 179).
One, Bickton, 21/25 May 1962 (*H.* 22. Part 3).
One, Newtown, 25/28 September 1963 (*B.B.* 57.264).
One, Farlington Marshes, 22 August 1967 (*H.* 1967).
One, Farlington Marshes, 29 May 1968 (*H.* 1968).
One, Keyhaven, 29 May/6 June 1968 (*H.* 1968).
One, Keyhaven, 24 August/12 September 1968 (*H.* 1968).
One, Lymington, 30 May 1970 (*H.* 1970).
One, Beaulieu, 16 May 1971 (*H.* 1971).
All recent records accepted by *British Birds* Rarities Committee.

[**33.   Great White Egret.** *Egretta alba**: One in a case of assorted stuffed birds from the Rev. Mr. Harrison's collection until recently in the possession of Mrs. Strange, Roselands, Millbrook, and stated on her list corresponding to the contents of the case to have been shot at Fawley (no date) was seen by EC on 30 March 1953. It is in winter plumage (scapulars normal and bill yellow). This specimen is not listed in *The Handbook* nor in K & M. Mr. Harrison apparently lived at Droxford and his collection seems to have been sold in 1902.]

34.   Squacco Heron. *Ardeola ralloides*: In Munn's notes for a second edition of K & M (which never appeared) the following correction of the statement in K & M appears:
'The male specimen in the Hart collection at Christchurch was procured on 8 June 1832 by Mr. Saunders and is the one mentioned in Eyton's *Rarer British Birds* as being in the hands of Lord Malmesbury's bird-stuffer at Dewhurst. Another in Lord Malmesbury's collection at Heron Court was killed on the Stour in June 1893. It had been seen several times at Blackwater Ferry by Hart before it was killed. It was obtained about the same time as the Little Bittern, also in Lord Malmesbury's collection, and is set up in the same case'.
The above was based on a letter of 3 December 1905 from Edward Hart. The net result is that there are still only two specimens obtained on the mainland, but that instead of both dating from 1832 one is from 1893.
There have been no subsequent records.

36.   Night Heron. *Nycticorax nycticorax*: K & M mention five, all 'procured'. Since then, the following have been recorded:
One, New Milton on 14 July 1911 had been there since May (*B.B.* 5. 113).
One, Lyndhurst, 14 June 1961 (*B.B.* 55.567).
Immature, Christchurch, early January/28 January 1962 (*H.* 22. Part 3).
Immature, Bucklers Hard area, 8 December 1966 (*H.* 1966).
One adult at Colbury on 16 June 1967 and one near Beaulieu two days later were probably the same bird and possibly the same individual reported in 1966 (*H.* 1967).

One, Alverstone, 25/26 April 1970 (*H. 1970*).

With this species, there is always the possibility of birds originating from the colony at Edinburgh Zoo.

37.   Little Bittern. *Ixobrychus minutus*: K & M list six obtained on the mainland and two on the Island, the last in 1897. The next was one shot on the Island on 3 October 1930 and set up by Jefferies, a Newport taxidermist (*The Field* 30 November 1930 and *B.* 23.42). Since then there have been thirteen, the list being:

Immature, Titchfield Haven, 9 August 1953 (Suffern).

Adult, Titchfield Haven, 13/14 June 1954 (Suffern).

Juvenile found dead, Farlington Marshes, August 1954.

Adult ♂ found at Andover and released by Terry Jones at Leckford, *about* 1954.

Two, Titchfield Haven, 21 May 1960, one staying until 26 May (*B.B.* 54. 180 and *H.* 22. Part 2).

One found on Boscombe Beach, April 1963, lived a day or two. The skin is at Portland Bill observatory (*B.B.* 57.264).

One, Winchester water meadows, 7 May 1964 (*B.B.* 58.356).

One, Titchfield Haven, 3 September 1966 (*H. 1966*).

Adult, Titchfield Haven, 9 June 1968 (*H. 1968*).

One, Alverstone, 28/29 April 1970 (*H. 1970*).

One, Farlington Marshes, 2/6 May 1970 (*H. 1970*).

One, Freshwater, 23 April/4 May 1970 (*H. 1970*).

38.   Bittern. *Botaurus stellaris*: Few winters pass without one or more of this species being reported from the main river valleys, suitable lakes and large ponds. Half a dozen birds in one year would not be at all unusual today, and a possible 14 individuals were recorded in 1970.

As far back as 1918, Munn in his notes for a second edition of K & M says that it occurs 'with increasing frequency in winter but most are killed; would doubtless breed if unmolested'. He has an addendum to the effect that between 1805 and 1834 nine were killed, of which eight are mentioned in the Malmesbury journals but were omitted from K & M. Few are killed today but with one exception there have been no nesting records in recent years although there have been odd reports of booming (e.g. on 4 April 1929 at Titchfield Haven and in the early summer of 1951 near Breamore). Indeed, the only breeding record so far is of a pair near Longparish (near Whitchurch) in 1942 (Waydelin), although an empty nest typical of a Bittern's was found in a dense reed-bed at the same locality on 22 July 1952 (four to five inches high and 18 inches in diameter) by Ash and not far away a Bittern was seen being chased by Black-headed Gulls about 12 July. It seems possible that in these enlightened days of protection the species could start to breed in the county, especially as since 1952 it has been recorded in all the summer months other than June, though records other than winter ones are still very few.

The only reports from the Island since 1905 are of one seen on 9 February 1949 at Newtown Marsh (its tracks were later seen and identified by Dr. Konrad Lorenz), one which flew south over Newport at dusk on 9 April 1954 (Stafford) and one ringed as a nestling on 16 June 1957 on Lake Malaren (Sweden), which was found dead in hard weather on 2 February 1963 at Lake (*B.B.* 57. Supplement).

Incidentally, the local place names of Bitterne and Bisterne do *not* 'point to the bird having once been abundant in the neighbourhood' as thought by K & M. The derivations of the words have nothing whatever to do with the bird. (See: *The Concise Oxford Dictionary of English Place-Names*, 2nd edition, 1940, E. Ekwall).

39.   American Bittern. *Botaurus lentiginosus*: Two in K & M, both shot in 1876. None since.

40.   White Stork. *Ciconia ciconia*: Eight in K & M up to 1905. Since then, the following have been recorded:
   One shot near Southwick in 1931 (*B.B.* 25.362).
   One following the plough, first week of July 1952, near Damerham (*H.* 18.188).
   One flying north, 28 May 1960, Cosham (*B.B.* 54.180).
   One in the Island during November/December 1963 may have been an escape (*H.* 23. Part 1).

41.   Black Stork. *Ciconia nigra* *: One was seen at Godshill on 12 May 1970 (Angliss) and one — probably the same bird — was at Rhinefield between 17 and 19 May 1970 (Duffin, Miss Jones, Gregory, McIntyre). These were accepted by *British Birds* Rarities Committee and are the first county records for the species.

42.   Spoonbill. *Platalea leucorodia*: Although still no more than an occasional visitor it can no longer be called 'a rare occasional visitor' as it is described in K & M who cite only 10 instances up to 1905 and none later than 1893. Needless to say almost all were shot. But in the last 20 years, one or two have turned up somewhere along the coast almost every year, at times staying for some weeks and in 1942 and possibly in 1970 remaining all through summer. It has occurred in every month but in recent years most of the records have been in summer or autumn. Troubridge (*B.B.* 15.20) listed 22 occurrences in which every month except February was included; since then there is a record of two at Hengistbury in February 1942 (*H.* 15.315). Only one record for the Isle of Wight: summer 1949, near Bembridge, one 'for several days'.

43.   Glossy Ibis. *Plegadis falcinellus*: K & M mention seven occurrences. Since then there have been three acceptable records, these being:

Glossy Ibis

Immature, St. Helens, 6 October 1908, the first Island record.
. One shot, Christchurch, 26 October 1929 (*B.B.* 24.168).
One, near Brockenhurst, 24 May/4 August 1965 (*H.* 1965).
A 'possible' was a bird 'very dark, like a black Curlew', which was seen near Bisterne early in 1952.

44.   Flamingo. *Phoenicopterus ruber*: K & M give one instance (shot). Since then there have been others but it is always difficult to say whether they are escapes or genuine wild birds. The records are:
One, flying over the Hampshire corner of Frensham Great Pond (*Country Life*, 15 May 1909) in May 1909, considered by Munn to be a wild bird.
One, Beaulieu River, 21 September 1926 (*B.B.* 20.156 and 228). The bird is said to have been an escape.
One, Stanpit, through June and up to 7 July 1940, in good condition and apparently not quite adult. Fairly tame, it consorted with Cormorants (*H.* 15.81).
One, Farlington Marshes, 17 May 1964 (*H.* 23. Part 2).
One (an escape), St. Helens (I.o.W.), 17 December 1967 (*H.* 1967).

Wildfowl. A whole book (Taverner, J. H., *Wildfowl in Hampshire.* Warren and Son Ltd., 1962) covers this group of birds more fully than space allows here and the reader's attention is drawn to that source. Details of peak numbers for the commonest species at various key localities are given in Appendix I at the end of this book.

45.   Mallard. *Anas platyrhynchos*: K & M call it a resident, generally distributed throughout the mainland and Island and they say that numbers are largely augmented in winter, particularly in severe winters. Today it is plentiful on the mainland throughout the year and common though much less plentiful on the Island, the breeding stock still much reinforced by migrants from late July onwards with some areas showing a marked peak in the autumn months. This is true, for instance, of what in recent years has been the main locality in the county for Mallard — Stratfield Saye — where counts have regularly exceeded 1,000 during September and November since the mid 1960s with 1,700 on 16 October 1966 the maximum. There are very few records from elsewhere of counts over 1,000 — 1,650 in the entrance to Chichester Harbour on 27 February 1932 (Hollom), 1,250 at Northington on 20 August, 1966 (*H.* 1966), 1,000 at Longstock on 13 October 1968 (*H.* 1968) and 1,000 at Sowley Pond on 4 January 1970 (*H.* 1970) — but counts of several hundred occur on many waters outside of the breeding season on the mainland. In the Portsmouth area, the pattern has changed in recent years because of birds released by wildfowlers. From the Island, the highest post-war count is 540 at Bembridge on 14 September 1969.
As a breeding species, it is common and widespread throughout the county. In autumn, large numbers have been recorded flying into stubble from various localities in the north, south and main river valleys.
Ringing recoveries mainly show movement within the county or to adjoining counties. Recoveries involving greater distances are: one ringed as full grown at Overijssel (Holland) on 15 March 1939 recovered at Stockbridge on 27 January 1940 (*B.B.* 38); one hand-reared juvenile ringed at Damerham on 5 July 1955 recovered at Rannu (Estonia) in September 1958; one ♂ ringed at Slimbridge on 6 November 1955 shot at Exbury on 19 September 1959; one adult ♂ ringed at Vermand (France) on 25 January 1963 shot at Petersfield on 21 December 1963 (*H.* 23. Part 2); and one ringed in Denmark on 17 November 1964 shot at Keyhaven on 5 December

1967.
See Appendix I for counts on various waters.

46.   Teal. *Anas crecca*: K & M say: 'A resident nesting in small numbers throughout the county. Next to the Mallard this is the most common duck to breed with us. Its numbers are largely augmented in winter by migrants'. Today it is plentiful in winter on suitable inland waters and sometimes really abundant on sheltered stretches of the coast — post-war maximum 2,300 at Titchfield Haven on 22 January 1962 (*H.* 22. Part 3). Numbers begin to build up in August and to decline towards the end of March. Recorders have been much more active in recent years but as far as one can judge from the scantier notes relating to the earlier part of the century, there is no evidence of any great change in numbers though particular areas may change in their relative importance. At the time of writing, for instance, the main locality away from the coast appears to be the Avon valley between Ringwood and Fordingbridge.

On the Island, between 750 and 800 were at Newtown on 5 November 1966 and 728 were there on 15 December 1968 (*H.* 1968) but they do not often exceed 200 elsewhere; Newtown usually holds the largest flock.

A few pairs are found breeding on the mainland each year from widespread localities but the species is almost certainly overlooked in summer and the few broods reported are probably a poor indication of the real breeding strength. Although in the last few years more breeding pairs of Tufted Ducks and Pochards have been reported than pairs of Teal, the last named could still be our most common breeding duck after the Mallard, as in K & M. On the Island, it has nested at Newtown (*I.o.W.* 1953).

Ringed winter immigrants from Northern Europe have been recovered on seven occasions in the years 1908 to 1968, viz — from Denmark three, Holland two, Finland one and Sweden one, whilst two ringed in the Camargue (France) were shot at Exbury and Fawley in 1959 and 1960 (*B.B.* 53.504: 54.496).

Birds ringed at Abberton (Essex) were recovered as follows: three ringed in October/November 1955 shot in the Island during a cold spell early in 1956 (*I.o.W.* 5.1.22); one adult ♂ ringed 10 January 1959 shot on the Island about 15 January 1960 (*I.o.W.* 5. Part 5); and one juvenile ♂ ringed 15 September 1963 shot at Ringwood on 6 November 1965 (Ash).

See Appendix I for counts on various waters.

Green-winged Teal. *Anas c. carolinensis*: K & M admit one, shot before 1840. Only two since; a drake at Titchfield Haven on 18 March 1956 which remained stationary while being watched for about two hours by six observers who noted vertical lines on the sides of the breast; and a drake at Avington Park from the end of January until at least the third week of March 1962 was seen by many observers including EC and JHT.

47.   Garganey. *Anas querquedula*: K & M call it: 'A scarce spring and summer visitor to a few localities in the county and of occasional occurrence in the Isle of Wight'. Spring records are now moderately numerous, especially since 1945, nearly all in March and April and very occasionally in May and June with very few records north of the group of waters round Winchester. The earliest dates are a pair at Brading on 11 January 1967 (Mrs. Newell, *H.* 1967) and three at Christchurch Harbour on 29 February 1964 (*H.* 23. Part 2). The highest spring count appears to be 11 on a flooded marsh near Pennington on 22 March 1966 which had apparently just arrived and flew off almost at once to ENE (*H.* 1966). A total of 14 flew east past St. Catherine's Point in spring 1962 (*per* Wiseman).

K & M mention only one breeding record. The only other recorded instances have been a pair breeding at Mottisfont in 1894 and 1895 (Meinertzhagen), in SE Hampshire in 1935 (*B.B.* 30.54) and in the Avon valley in 1937 and 1940 (*B.B.* 31.336; Thomas; Brewer).

There are few autumn records before 1955, probably because the birds were overlooked. An immature was shot at Bisterne in the autumn of 1908 (Munn), one was reported at Titchfield Haven in the week ending 2 September 1950 (*per* Suffern), and another was seen at 50 yards range on Warren Flats on 29 November 1953 (Bundy), the latest date ever for Hampshire. In the last few years a late summer/autumn passage has been a regular feature, though numbers involved are low, most of the reports being in July and August with several through September and into October and three records (including the above latest date) in November. The maximum counts were 15 at Pennington on 7 August 1967 (*H.* 1967), and 16 in Christchurch Harbour on 8 August 1971 (*H.* 1971).

49. Gadwall. *Anas strepera*: K & M's description: 'a rather scarce winter visitor', is not quite true today. In addition to the few records of their time can be added a drake shot at Mottisfont in December 1895 (Meinertzhagen).

Most of the records are still outside the breeding season, although they have been reported in all months and in the last five years there have been an increasing number in spring and autumn. Indeed, it seems from the last few years that the species may be experiencing a change in status for Hampshire because far more than usual have been reported in that time and numbers involved have increased. 1961, for instance, saw the first July record for the county and there have been others since. 1962 saw the first definite Island record for this century when two flew past St. Catherine's Point on 14 April, and again there have been others since. The general volume of records has greatly increased, especially since the late 1960s and the highest recorded count at one locality has increased from six in 1961, to 1966, 12; 1969, 16; 1970, 25; and to 27 in 1971. These last three counts came from Marsh Court, the 25 being on 18 October and the 27 on 12 December; at present this is clearly the

Gadwall

18

main water in Hampshire for Gadwall. The build-up at Marsh Court has been quite sudden for the maxima there in 1967 and 1968 were five and eight respectively.

There is no clear reason for this increase. It cannot be wholly connected with birds attracted to the wildfowl collection at Leckford (close to Marsh Court) or to escapes from Leckford because the increase has affected all parts of Hampshire.

50. Wigeon. *Anas penelope*: K & M call it a regular and common winter visitor, particularly to the coast. Today it is an autumn to spring visitor in large numbers to the coast and to the Avon valley between Ringwood and Fordingbridge, and in much smaller numbers (usually below 100) to a few areas well inland. Flocks along the coast gather especially at Needs Oar, Titchfield Haven and Langstone Harbour, and these gatherings, as well as the Avon flock, typically number several hundred at the winter peak whilst several other coastal localities hold smaller regular flocks or large numbers when something has disturbed birds from elsewhere. Four figure counts are unusual, occurring mostly in unusual conditions, the highest counts being 3,350 in the entrance to Chichester Harbour on 27 February 1932 (Hollom) and 2,000 plus at Needs Oar on 9 February 1963 in the very severe cold of that time.

Numbers reported from the Island are usually considerably smaller than those from the mainland but there are reports of 600 together in January (Adams) and February. Newtown is easily the main locality on the Island.

Usually, the last birds are in April and the first returns in August but there have been records in all months. The flocks begin to break up in March and gatherings of a few hundred occur from September onwards.

There are no authenticated cases of breeding.

Some reports indicate an increase in the last twenty to thirty years, although as long ago as 1913 it was stated (*Birds of Milford*) that their feeding grounds were being spoiled by increase in recent years of *Spartina townsendii* at the expense of *Zostera marina*. Since they graze so much on land, it is doubtful whether this opinion is of value.

A hybrid Wigeon/European-Green-winged Teal, shot at Hayling Island during December 1961, was shown at a meeting of the British Ornithologists' Club on 20 March 1962 (*Bull. B.O.C.* 82.61) and fully described and illustrated in *Bull. B.O.C.* 82.9.165.

A drake ringed in Holland on 15 March 1958 and a duck on 14 October 1960 were shot on 17 October 1960 and 19 February 1961 at Christchurch and Southampton respectively (*B.B.* 56.527).

See Appendix I for details of various localities.

[**51. American Wigeon.** *Anas americana**: A drake at Titchfield Haven on 22 December 1963 was probably an escape (*B.B.* 57.265).]

52. Pintail. *Anas acuta*: K & M call it: 'a winter visitor to the coast of the county and Isle of Wight, but not in any great numbers'. Today it is a regular winter visitor in rather modest numbers to the coast and to the Avon valley between Ringwood and Fordingbridge. Scattered records occur each year from the rest of the mainland. Occasional birds are seen in the summer months.

Until recently there were only a handful of records from the Island, but in the last few years Newtown has been one of the main Pintail haunts in the county. This is just one example from the records of recent years that suggest the species is becoming more common both on the mainland and the Island.

Winter counts decline in late March, but April birds are no longer unusual as apparently they were until quite recently. A few records have then occurred from

May to August with September records a little more frequent and the main winter counts from October onwards. At the time of writing, a count of 30 at the most favoured waters would be considered a normal winter peak and a count of 50 would be thought quite high, but 110 were counted in the Avon locality in January 1961 and 84 in Langstone Harbour in December 1969 (*H.* 1969). The new importance of Newtown (referred to above) may be judged by the following peak counts: winter 1967/8, 42; winter 1968/9, 62; winter 1970/1, 126 — this last count on 5/6 December (*H.* 1970).

In March and April, a few birds have been recorded flying east past St. Catherine's Point and the mainland coast.

One ringed in Friesland (Holland) on 13 August 1955 was shot at Farlington on 20 February 1956 (*B.B.* 51.60). A juvenile ringed at Hamilton Inlet (Labrador) on 7 September 1951 was recovered at Christchurch on the 25th of the same month (*B.B.* 45.461). An immature drake ringed at Wick on 22 February 1966 was killed at Ringwood on 15 January 1968 (*H.* 1968).

53. Shoveler. *Spatula clypeata*: K & M called it: 'A winter visitor in small numbers, occasionally remaining to nest.' Numbers of winter visitors have increased since then but breeding, more often suspected than proved, is still at best sporadic.

Most of the winter records from the mainland occur in the southern half of the county, the coastal stretch, the Avon above Ringwood and the group of waters to the east of Winchester being the most favoured places. It is still scarce in the north of the county, viz. — Fleet Pond and Yateley G.P., with maxima of six and seven respectively, were the only northern waters with records in 1970; six at Fleet Pond on 13/14 December were the only northern records for 1969; one at Stratfield Saye on 14 January was the only 1968 record from the north.

As with most surface feeding ducks, most of the Island records occur on the north coast where Brading has been the most favoured water recently with yearly maxima of 23 on 15 February 1970 (*H.* 1970) and 56 on 12 January 1969 (*H.* 1969). The Island maximum is 60 at Newtown on 14 January 1962 (Mrs. Seabroke).

As for numbers on the mainland, in recent years the most favoured waters would count a maximum between 20 and 40 as normal but very much larger numbers have been recorded on occasions. 230 on the Avon above Ringwood in early 1961 (*H.* 22. Part 2) is the highest post-war count for any water, though 224 at Titchfield Haven on 12 February 1961 was almost as large (*H.* 22. Part 2), and any count of over 100 would be unusual. Drakes seem to outnumber ducks. At present, a typical annual peak population for the whole county would be 3/400 (JHT).

The only proved cases of breeding on the mainland since the 1939/45 war were in 1952, 1958, and each of the years from 1966 to 1969 when the species bred at Needs Oar. From the Island, the first breeding record appears to be at Brading in 1937 when 11 ducklings were hatched (*B.B.* 31.354). Since then, the species has bred in the same area in 1966, 1967 and 1969, with two pairs in the last named year (*H.* 1966, 1967 and 1969).

54. Red-crested Pochard. *Netta rufina*: One in K & M on 20 January 1820. Subsequent records possibly concern 'escapes', viz. — a drake at Dogmersfield on 5/13 April 1965 (*H.* 1965); a drake at Wherwell on 14 August 1968 and two at Farlington Marshes on 14 December 1968 (*H.* 1968); in 1971, a drake on Farnborough G.P. from 13 January to 4 February, probably the same bird on Ash Vale G.P. on 25 April, another drake at Hayling Island on 2/3 November and probably the same bird at Sinah G.P. (Hayling) on 20 November (*H.* 1971).

55.   Scaup. *Aythya marila*: K & M describe this species as common on the coast in winter. Since Scaup figured quite frequently in the 'bags' of Col. Hawker between 1802 and 1853, it also appeared to be common at that time. Today it is far from common and such has been the case at least as far back as World War II, so the species has clearly experienced a marked decline in the county at some stage between 1900 and 1940. Numbers occurring can be judged by the following which are total counts of individuals seen each year from the mainland and Island, making every possible allowance for duplicate records: 1965, 6; 1966, 30; 1967, 16; 1968, 5. The totals are typical for the post-war period.

The majority of records are of single birds or *very* small parties, larger flocks or a greater number of sightings usually being the result of very hard weather. Larger numbers have been: 38 in Dibden Bay during a cold spell in February 1954; between 30 and 40 off Hengistbury in a very cold spell between 5 and 19 February 1956; 29 off Black Point and 46 flying east off Hurst on 26 January and 9 February 1963 respectively in the very severe weather of that period. One of the features of cold-spell records is the speed with which the birds arrive, the first appearing almost with the onset of cold as though they have not come from very far. Cold weather birds often stay until the thaw whereas birds in normal weather typically stay very briefly.

Nearly all records are from the coast and most are between November and February. March and October records are less frequent, April birds unusual, whilst the first post-war May records were in 1962. In the last few decades at least, there have been no June, August or September sightings whilst one drake in Christchurch Harbour from 11 to 23 July 1964 (*H.* 23. Part 2) and one at Fawley on 28 July 1971 (*H.* 1971) are possibly the only records ever for that month in Hampshire. A few reports have come from inland waters such as Avington, Alresford, Awbridge Danes, Blashford and Frensham Great Pond.

In *B.o.H.* EC lists six Island records but recent years have seen more frequent reports including 12 off Brook on 13 February 1966 (*I.o.W.* 6. Part 1).

56.   Tufted Duck. *Aythya fuligula*: K & M say: 'A common winter visitor to our inland waters and coasts, now nesting in a few localities'. This would apply fairly well to the bird's status today though salt water records are infrequent except when a cold spell has frozen inland waters, and breeding has become more widespread. This increase in breeding reports was also noted by K & M who recorded the first known case for the county in 1890.

In recent years, breeding has been reported mainly from the upper Itchen waters, the Test valley and a few lakes in the extreme north of the county, but during this period there is only one record of nesting on the Island; a pair at Bembridge in 1970. Although breeding records have become more frequent, they could not be described as common, and 21/2 pairs in 1966 (*H.* 1966), 21 pairs in 1970 (*H.* 1970) and 26 pairs in 1971 (*H.* 1971) are the largest numbers reported in post-war years, though coverage of the county was by no means complete.

As for winter numbers, EC in *B.o.H.* said that 'reports are usually of 10 birds or less', but this is a little misleading for at the time of writing every recent year has produced several waters where the annual maxima exceed 20, and counts of 40, 50 or 60 are by no means rare. Even larger counts have been made but those in excess of 100 are likely to be the result of an influx in cold spells. 428 at Redbridge in very severe weather on 18 February 1963 (*H.* 23. Part 1) is easily the largest post-war gathering with 300 at Titchfield Haven in the same cold spell on 3 February (*H.* 23. Part 1) the next highest.

On the Island, Bembridge with a winter peak of 30/40 has been the main locality in recent years.

EC in *B.o.H.* gives K & M as recording the species in the county for the first time in 1811 with a quote to the effect that it was rare at that time. However, Hawker included 27 in his 'bag' from 1802 to 1853 and it seems probable that the lack of early records is due to writers not mentioning the species rather than the species' absence.

57. Pochard. *Aythya ferina*: EC in *B.o.H.* and past Hampshire Bird Reports (*H.* 22. Part 2 and 22. Part 3) state erroneously that the first breeding records for the county were in 1950, 1961 and 1962. K & M admitted only probable breeding but *The Handbook of British Birds* (1939) states that the species breeds 'very locally but regularly' in Hampshire. Therefore, the records from 1950, 1961 and 1962 are only the first *post-war* occurrences. Since then, a handful of pairs have nested each year, the most being 19 in 1966 and 1971, the vast majority of these breeding records coming from the Test valley south of Stockbridge. The wildfowl collection at Leckford is just above Stockbridge and escaped Pochard have reared full-winged young outside the confines of the pens in the past, and the present breeding population is probably descended from these birds.

Winter records are much more frequent from inland waters than from the coast, salt-water records being infrequent other than in very cold weather when fresh water is frozen over. By far the largest number ever recorded was 400 — mainly drakes — at Titchfield Haven on 10 October 1948 (Suffern), previously rejected by JHT in *Wildfowl in Hampshire* but now accepted with apologies in the light of further evidence. Normal winter counts often reach 30/50 but larger counts do occur, anything over 100 being considered high. Apart from the above record of 400, the highest post-war gatherings have been 300 plus at Blashford on 27 December 1961 (*H.* 22 Part 2), 274 at Sowley Pond on 29 November 1969 (*H.* 1969), and 257 in very severe cold at Redbridge on 18 February 1963 (*H.* 23. Part 1). November to February usually sees numbers at their highest. Dispersal begins in March and returns usually start in October, and apart from breeding birds, Pochard are uncommon from May to September inclusive.

Pochard

Up to 1962, they were not often reported from the Island, but from that year onwards Bembridge has been a regular haunt with a typical annual peak around 70/80 though 200 were on the sea there on 5 January 1965 and 163 were recorded on 16 February 1964 (*I.o.W.* 5. Part 10 and 1963/64).

An adult female ringed near Reposaari (Finland) on 15 June 1964 was shot at Bembridge on 31 January 1966 (*B.B.* 62.16).

58. Ferruginous Duck. *Aythya nyroca*: K & M admit very few occurrences, none of them thoroughly authenticated. Kelso in his book *Notes on Some Common and Rare British Birds* (1912) writes that 'it has been obtained' from Hayling Island, a locality not included in K & M, and Shaw in his *List of Birds of Haslemere and District* (January 1921) says that there was one at Frensham on 8 October 1920 but is not concerned to state whether it was ever at the Hampshire end of Frensham Great Pond. However, Brice, Le Brocq and others saw a drake there on the Hampshire side on 11 January 1961 (*H.* 22. Part 2).

The latest record is the first for the Island, a drake on a pool in Brading Marsh from 14 December 1964 to 15 January 1965 (*I.o.W.* 5 Part 5 and *B.B.* 58. 358).

60. Goldeneye. *Bucephala clangula*: A regular winter visitor in rather modest numbers mostly from November to March. The last birds have usually been seen in late March or early April and the first returns in October. September birds are very unusual but have occurred, viz. — 12 at Stanpit on 13 September 1937 (Barfoot in *H.* 14.99). In the post-war years, there were no records for May to August inclusive until a drake was seen in full plumage off St. Catherine's Point on 30 July 1955 (Bowers and Rees). In recent years however, there have been a few summer records, viz. — a duck at Bembridge on 21 July 1968 (*H.* 1968); one at Beaulieu in late June/early July 1968 (*H.* 1968); a duck at Christchurch from 25 May to 2 June 1969 (*H.*1969); one injured by wildfowlers at Hill Head on 6/7 June 1970 (*H.*1970); one pricked duck at Langstone Harbour through the summer of 1970 (*H.* 1970).

Nearly all are on or very near the coast and for at least the past fifteen years, two (possibly three) localities have been the only waters to hold regular winter gatherings. The two localities are Langstone Harbour and Southampton Water (especially the area off Dibden Bay before it was reclaimed), where winter maxima of 70/80 and 30/50 respectively would not be unusual. The last few years have also produced regular gatherings in Portsmouth Harbour, possibly overlooked in previous years. Apart from these localities, most years produce a rather thin scattering of records from the rest of the mainland coast and even fewer from the Island.

Numbers could possibly be increasing for the post-war maximum has been exceeded in each of the three years 1968/9/70. 100 at Langstone Harbour in very cold weather on 7 February 1956 *was* the maximum but this was exceeded by counts of 103 in Portsmouth Harbour on 21 December 1968, 120 at the same locality in December 1969 and 153 in Langstone Harbour on 3 January 1970 (*H.* 1968, 1969, 1970).

In Hampshire, it is clearly a bird of the large harbours and estuaries and most of the birds on the remaining coast are seen in creeks and sheltered waters with very few on the exposed sea. Fewer than 10 per cent of the birds recorded are adult drakes.

Away from the coast, almost every year produces a very small number of sightings from waters well inland.

61. Long-tailed Duck. *Clangula hyemalis*: K & M record only three instances. On 19 November 1934 an immature drake was shot near Shedfield (six miles from the coast) — (*B.B.* 28.241) and then two at Stanpit on 20 and 25 December 1938 (*H.*

14.256) were passed without comment by Jourdain who was then the editor. The remaining records up to the winter of 1953/4 are all from Langstone Harbour where in 1952 there was a female on 26 October and 1/2 November, and a pair on 28 December; again, in 1953 a pair on two dates in January, two pairs in summer plumage on 5 April, an immature drake and a female on many occasions between 7 November and 23 December, and up to three birds in the winter of 1953/4. Since then however, every year has produced records but the annual total of birds has usually been less than a dozen and always less than 30, so it is still an uncommon winter visitor. To what extent the increase in the number recorded recently reflects a true change in status or just the much better observer coverage is not clear, but some other parts of Britain report a similar increase in winter records.

Most of the birds are seen from November to February but March birds have been quite usual. The number of April records is much increased by birds seen moving past St. Catherine's Point, while one at Hurst on 13 May 1961 is the latest date (*H.* 22. Part 3). There are no reports for June, July and August, and September birds are rather rare. The first returns may well be in October.

The birds are mostly seen from the mainland coast, and apart from the St. Catherine's Point records, very few have been reported from the Island. There have also been several reports from inland waters, as far north as Frensham, and single birds were seen on the gravel pits around Blashford in each of the four years from 1967 to 1970 (*H.* for those years).

62. Velvet Scoter. *Melanitta fusca*: K & M say: 'an occasional winter visitor to the coast.' Records up to 1956 pointed to a similar status, but from then onwards better observer coverage has shown the species to be a regular but *very* scarce winter visitor and an annual spring migrant in small numbers. In this recent period, the annual total of winter birds has typically been below 30 and several years have produced fewer than 10, whilst on migration it has been recorded mostly off St. Catherine's Point where the birds are seen flying east. A small number doubtless pass there every spring, sometimes with Common Scoter flocks but often separately, the most in any spring being 48 in 1965 when 33 flew east on 29 April alone. Coverage at St. Catherine's has been quite good, though not of course complete, so these numbers give a good indication of the population involved.

Velvet Scoter

Up to 1956, records were sparse. In January 1933 an oiled drake was picked up on the beach at Christchurch; in December 1933 there were two drakes off Southbourne, two at Christchurch and a party of 15 off Christchurch; in January 1954, 15 were at Mudeford (all but the first of these records by Rooke; the last two records probably refer to the same party). From 18 November to 1 December 1937, between two and 10 were seen on various dates (*H.* 14.99). On 26 September 1942, about 12 were in flight off Sea Pie Point (*H.* 15.317); a drake and two females were off Hurst on 7 January 1950; a drake was found dead at Keyhaven on 5 April 1951; a female and immature were off Lepe on 17 February 1952 and a drake was found oiled and dead at Calshot on 10 February 1954.

The only inland record is that of two on Heath Pond, Petersfield, on 18 January 1961 (Miss White), one of which stayed until 16 April (*H.* 22. Part 2).

The first record from the Island was in 1954, a duck in poor condition (later died) at Freshwater Bay during a spell of cold weather (Hopkinson). The second record was two drakes at Newtown in a westerly gale on 30 December 1955 and another drake was at Newtown on 5 July 1957 (Mrs. Seabroke). Apart from the annual spring passage of St. Catherine's, the species is still very scarce on the Island coast, the years 1959/68 inclusive producing a total of four birds.

Nearly all the winter records are between November and February. April sees most of the spring passage, though May records have occurred lately with May 17th as the latest date. There have been no June records and the above drake at Newtown has been the only July bird. A party of six near Christchurch is the sole August record and very few have been seen in September or October.

63.   Surf Scoter. *Melanitta perspicillata* *: Kelso (1912) writes: 'I have been informed from a reliable source that one of these birds was killed off Hayling Island a few years ago.' This record cannot be accepted as anything other than 'possible'.

A drake, possibly accompanied by a duck, flew fairly close in off St. Catherine's Point on 18 April 1963 (Bryant and Taverner). The record was accepted by *British Birds* Rarities Committee.

64.   Common Scoter. *Melanitta nigra*: K & M say: 'An abundant visitor during the winter.' This is certainly not true today. In the post-war years Bournemouth Bay has been the only locality to hold a *regular wintering* flock (a typical year's peak there being around 300) but even this gathering has not been seen from 1967 onwards. Elsewhere on the coast, occasional flocks may occur in the winter months but they do not stay in one place, and in most parts of the Solent coast a regular visitor may well go through a whole winter without seeing a single bird.

Today the species is seen most frequently in spring when from March to early May flocks are seen flying east. Some move through the Solent but most pass St. Catherine's Point where they are the main feature of the sea passage. The largest numbers usually pass in south-east winds and if the wind is from the north or west, the watcher will probably see very few. The largest daily totals at St. Catherine's have been 6,910 flying east on 5 April 1966, 3,060 moving in the same direction on 4 April 1966 (*H.* 1966) and 3,000 flying east on 7 April 1969 (*H.* 1969). The birds pass in flocks of up to 300 at such times and in spring, flocks that are presumably resting migrants may be seen more frequently from the mainland coast, viz. — 1,000 plus in three flocks on 8th March 1958 off Boscombe Pier and Southbourne (JHT), and 300 off the Needles on 17 April 1952 (N.F.O.C.) were probably such birds.

In June, Scoters are not unusual and small flocks have occasionally been recorded at this time. The first return migrants are seen passing in July or August but passage is much smaller than the spring numbers recorded above.

Inland, a female was at Winnall on 4 April 1957 (Taverner), a drake on Petersfield Lake in early April 1958, one on Frensham Great Pond on 15 November 1967 (*H.* 1967), a female at Badshot Lea on 22 March 1969 (*H.* 1969) and a female at Fleet Pond on 15 September 1971 (*H.* 1971).

67. **Eider.** *Somateria mollissima*: K & M say: 'A rare winter visitor to the coast.'

From 3 to 5 March 1929, four off Hengistbury Head (*B.B.* 22.327); 10 March 1946, a drake on the lake at Paultons Park, Ower (four miles from the nearest salt water) with many other species of duck (R. E. Williams); two at the mouth of the River Meon, March 1947, during very hard weather; an immature drake off Pennington on 28 December 1949 and 11 January 1950 (probably the same bird) — (E.C.); an immature drake in Langstone Harbour on 18 December 1953 which was found dead 27 December 1953; a female 20 yards off the Hayling Yacht Club on 16 January 1954 (Pilkington).

From the Island during this period, one of a party of five immature drakes was shot in Bembridge Harbour on 28 November 1925 (*I.o.W.* 1.6.401), an immature drake was on the sea at St. Catherine's Point on 25 April 1937 (Hollom) and another immature drake was inshore at Gurnard on 11 January 1954 (Curber in *I.o.W.* 4.9.337).

Since then the species has undergone a dramatic extension of its winter range in England (for a full survey, see Taverner in *B.B.* for August 1959, August 1963 and December 1967) so that today it is a regular winter visitor to the coast in small to moderate numbers with very occasional records in summer. The largest gatherings have been a flock at Hill Head which reached 130 in early 1969 (*H.* 1969) and a flock at Hurst which reached 71 on 2 February 1963 (*H.* 23. Part 1). Otherwise, several localities have had counts in the 20s and 30s and a few moderate numbers have been seen flying past several points, such as in 1969 when 70 flew west past Calshot on 7 January, 48 flew east past Needs Oar on 9 February and 40 moved west at Hengistbury on 6 November (*H.* 1969).

A female at Titchfield Haven on 5/6 July 1958 was the first *ever* county record for that month. Similarly, the first June birds were in 1962 when three were at Barton on 6th and a pair were at Gilkicker throughout the month (*H.* 22. Part 3). 1962 also produced our first August Eiders with birds at Black Point, Gilkicker and Hurst. Subsequently there have been a few more summer records.

During this spread, very few adult males have been seen, nearly all the birds being females or immatures.

69. **Red-breasted Merganser.** *Mergus serrator:* K & M say: 'A winter visitor more plentiful than Goosander but usually visiting the coast and not so often found on fresh water.' If the word *so* was removed from the above, the statement would describe the species' status today. It is regular in rather modest numbers round the mainland and north Island coast from mid-October to late May, most of the April and May records being birds on passage. In post-war years, there have been two records for June (on 15th in Langstone Harbour in 1968 — *H.* 1968 — and on 7th at Pennington in 1971 — *H.* 1971), five July occurrences and two reports for August.

Certain localities are especially favoured, Langstone Harbour and Osborne Bay being two of the most-used areas. The annual maxima there may well reach 50 and 40 respectively. The highest counts have been 90 at E. Hayling in December 1971 (*H.* 1971), 70 at Langstone Harbour on 5 December 1970 (*H.* 1970) and 63 at Osborne Bay late in 1957 (Adams). Chichester Harbour, Portsmouth Harbour, Hill Head, Pennington and Newtown are the other places where the main gatherings are found, an annual peak exceeding 30 being quite normal at any of these.

Inland birds are very scarce. One was at Winnall on 28 December 1956 and 6 February 1957 (Taverner). One was at Alresford Pond on 7/8 November 1962 (Doble and Jackson). Five were seen inland in 1966 (*H.* 1966) and two were on Alresford Pond on 15 December 1968 (*H.* 1968). At Blashford G.P. in 1971, three were present on 26 March and two on 18 December (*H.* 1971).

During their stay, birds are seen flying south out of Langstone and Chichester harbours every day at dusk, the birds apparently vacating the harbour waters to roost on the sea. For example, 71 were seen flying out of Chichester harbour on 31 December 1959.

Numbers do not seem to be much affected by cold weather, though counts of up to 55 at Needs Oar in early March 1963, immediately following the very severe period, were most unusual.

In April and May, birds are seen moving eastwards past St. Catherine's Point, and along the Solent, the total *seen* each year always being fewer than 100 at either area, apart from 1971 when 135 flew east past St. Catherine's and 105 flew east at Hurst (*H.* 1971).

70. Goosander. *Mergus merganser:* An uncommon annual visitor from November (once in September, once in October) to April, though it is only in the last few years that April records have been other than rare. In May, one flying east off Hengistbury on 4 May 1963 (C.H.O.S.G. 1963) and two flying east off Gilkicker on 1 May 1965 (*H.* 1966. p.44). Records have been from all over the mainland so that inland birds are much more frequent than those of Merganser, but reports from the Island are still rather scarce.

Most reports concern four birds or less though there have been gatherings of six or seven on a few occasions. By far the largest gathering was on the Avon near Fordingbridge in severe cold from 7 January to 10 March 1963. Beginning with 33, numbers rose to at least 100 on 26 February, declining to 41 on 7 March and 25 on 10 March 1963 (Ash). It is typical for numbers to be higher in a cold spell, but apart from these exceptional counts, the only other double-figured records are 13 redheads at Frensham Great Pond (? Hampshire or Surrey) on 13 March 1920 (Shaw), 13 redheads again at Frensham on 29 December 1968 (*H.* 1968) and a flock at Sowley Pond which reached 10 on 1 March 1970 (*H.* 1970).

The total number reported in several recent years has not reached double figures and if any year sees more than 20 Goosanders in Hampshire it can be counted a good year for the species.

Single birds flew past St. Catherine's Point on 29 April 1965 (*H.* 1965) and 18 April 1968 (*H.* 1968).

71. Smew. *Mergus albellus*: The 'irregular winter visitor' of K & M describes it well, but whereas they add 'to the coast' subsequent records show that it is nearly as often met with inland e.g. at Winnall, Blashford, Leckford, Hurn, Stockbridge, Alresford etc.

Of the *regular* ducks recorded in Hampshire, this is the rarest. A few years since 1945 have produced no records at all (e.g. 1965 and 1966 when observer coverage was very good) and a typical year's total of birds seen would be fewer than 10. Cold weather brings the largest totals, the cold in early 1956 and the winter of 1962/3 being excellent examples of this (*H.* 1956 and *H.* 23. Part 1). Most reports are of single birds and although small groups have been seen in normal winters, larger gatherings are nearly always seen in severe cold spells. The most remarkable assembly was at Titchfield Haven in 1956 when over 30, including nine adult drakes, flew in just before the end of a prolonged cold spell in February (Bowers and Dennis), whilst the early part of 1963 produced counts of 10 at Redbridge and Titchfield Haven, seven at Needs Oar and five in Christchurch Harbour (*H.* 23. Part 1).

December to February are the months in which most have been seen. March and November birds are unusual. There have only been four records for the months from April to October inclusive, viz. — a drake, probably 'pricked' in Christchurch Harbour from 30 March to 27 May (*Wildfowl in Hampshire*), one at Alresford on 10 April 1963 (*H.* 22. Part 1), a redhead at Christcburch Harbour from 1 to 16 July 1963 (*H.* 22. Part 1) and a drake off Hengistbury on 27 August 1964 (*H.* 23. Part 2).

There are since 20 February 1955 about half a dozen reports from the Island where it is still very scarce. The *I.o.W. Bird Reports* give only one bird from 1958 to 1968 inclusive.

[**72.　Hooded Merganser.** *Mergus cucullatus:* K & M include one shot 1854 and one other possible. But B.O.U. Check List admits none for *England* in the nineteenth century.]

73.　Shelduck. *Tadorna tadorna*: This species has greatly increased since K & M. It is now very common along the coast in winter where increasing numbers remain to breed, and the species has also bred inland in the New Forest (about 12 pairs there in 1959) and as far north as Winchester (*H.* 1970 e.g.).

In winter and spring counts of hundreds in Langstone Harbour would have been noteworthy up to 1954 but since then thousands have been recorded regularly with maxima increasing from 3,000 on 4 March 1956 to 4,000 on 27 February 1965 (*H.* 1965) and in February 1968 (*H.* 1968). Similarly, *B.B.* thought it worth while

Shelduck

publishing that 40 together were seen off the Island in the spring of 1910 (*B.B.* 4.182), an occurrence that would call for no comment today when Newtown — the main island locality — has a regular winter gathering that has reached 600 on 10 January 1968 (*H.* 1968). Counts such as 1,500 in Chichester Harbour on 10 February 1969, 1,200 in Portsmouth Harbour on 21 December 1968, 540 in the Hurst area on 28 December 1969 and 367 around Calshot on 8 February 1970 would all have been outstanding twenty years ago, indicating how the species has increased.

Very few adults are seen in August or September except for 'caretaker' birds left with 'birds of the year' whilst their parents have flown to moulting grounds. The first return from this moult (60 birds) was as early as 1 October in 1955, but not until 3 November in 1956 (160 birds) and 9 November in 1957 (150 birds).

In the past few years, two to three dozen pairs have been recorded breeding each season. Needs Oar (12 pairs in 1968) probably has the densest breeding population and some nests at that locality have been found in open reeds, not in burrows. On the Island, there was a breeding colony of at least 12 pairs at Newtown in 1923 and at least 100 were reared there in 1955, this being the chief contender to Needs Oar for the main nesting area. The position of the species at Newtown, at least as far as the winter flocks are concerned, has been much enhanced by the breaking of the sea-wall in 1954, since when the gatherings have steadily increased. The first young are seen in the second or third week of June.

Of three ducklings of the same brood ringed in the county on 6 July 1912, one was recovered in August 1913 in Schleswig-Holstein (*B.B.* 9.255), another was shot on 18 August 1917 at the mouth of the R. Weser, Germany (*B.B.* 13.244), and the third was reported in February 1913 at Saltash (*B.B.* 13.244). In the reverse direction a bird ringed in the Weser estuary on 9 August 1959 was found dead at Emsworth in February 1962 (*B.B.* 56.528). A juvenile ringed on 20 July 1962 in Denmark was shot near Southampton on 5 January 1963, an adult ringed on 9 September 1964 on the Weser estuary was found dead at Farlington Marshes about 3 August 1965 and a nestling ringed on 8 July 1959 in Zeeland (Holland) was found dead at Cowes on 11 February 1963 (all *B.B.* 60.70).

74.   Ruddy Shelduck. *Casarca ferruginea*: K & M calling it 'A rare accidental visitor' accept three (two of them shot) in 1892 as probably genuine wild birds. Occurrences of this species are always suspect as being possible escapes.

Subsequently there have been five (possibly six) reports, all since 1940. A female watched feeding at Stanpit on 6 August 1940 'seemed quite tame' (*H.* 16.80). One at Chilbolton on the Test in October 1945 was described as 'probably an escape' (*H.* 16.301). One (sex uncertain) was in Langstone Harbour on 20 April 1952 (Billett and Tubbs). One at Newtown Marsh from 20 to 27 November 1966 was the first accepted record for the Island (*B.B.* 61.362). A probable escape was around Ringwood on 2 June and 3 August 1971 (*H.* 1971).

In 1968, one at Newtown from 12 to 23 April was put in square brackets in the Island report (*I.o.W.* 6. Part 3). Around this time, a hybrid bird that was 95 per cent Ruddy Shelduck was seen on the mainland coast at several points, remaining for a week or so. JHT saw it at Needs Oar Point, just opposite Newtown, on 30 March.

Mandarin. *Aix galericulata*:* Has already bred in a feral state in several counties and Hampshire can be counted amongst these, for there was a period in the 1950s when escapes from the collection at Leckford nested in the surrounding villages. Since hollow trees are the species nesting site, this section of the Test is ideal, but several females came to grief by descending chimneys, evidently mistaking the entrance for a hole in a tree.

It is difficult to trace its occurrences since few observers regard the species as anything other than an 'escape' and so do not record sightings but it is clear that individuals are seen from time to time. An adult male frequented a marshy field at Brown Candover with *ca.* 70 Mallard in the autumn and winter of 1955; it could fly strongly. In 1956 it apparently mated with a semi-tame Mallard of the flock (Taverner and Pierce). Two males and one female were shot near Lymington in 1957. A male was seen on Sowley Pond twice in December 1960, once in March and twice in December 1961. The prospects are that it will establish itself generally as resident just as the introduced Canada Goose has done, although as it breeds in holes in trees it will have to compete for sites with, for example, Jackdaws.

75. Grey Lag Goose. *Anser anser*: K & M say: 'A scarce winter visitor', having heard of it only three times in all and never since 1888. The trouble today is to separate truly wild birds from feral birds such as the free-flying young raised at Stratfield Saye since the early 1960s. In 1970, the local flock there numbered 21 (*H.* 1970) and 29 in 1971 (*H.* 1971).

The first since K & M was at Needs Oar on 21 March 1936, remaining for about three weeks (*W.* 1949 and *H.* 13.276). Then an immature male was shot near Ringwood on 11 February 1947 and another was flying there with the White-fronts on 9 March (Rooke in *H.* 17.190). From 1952 onwards, the instances have been too many to record, though some years have produced none at all and no year has had more than ten possibly wild individuals. They have occurred on the coast and inland and the fact that so many have been seen in the winter months suggests that some are genuine wild birds.

From the Island, eight were at Newtown on 15 December 1955 (Mrs. Seabroke), six flew out to sea past St. Catherine's Point on 26 October 1963 in a south-east direction (*H.* 23. Part 1) and one flew east there on 13 April 1971 (*H.* 1971).

76. White-fronted Goose. *Anser albifrons*: K & M call it 'the commonest of the grey geese which visit the coasts of the mainland and Isle of Wight in winter. They stray frequently inland.' They gave the earliest recorded date as 1827 but Dr. Suffern has kindly drawn attention to a much earlier record, as follows:

John Walcott in his *Synopsis of British Birds* (London 1789) says: 'December 1788, I received a pair from Edward Hillman Esq. of Cobley near Ringwood; near to which place they were shot.' Dr. Suffern adds: 'This is the earliest record that I can find of this species in Hampshire and it is not long after the species was first recognised in Britain. Willughby (1678) did not know it but Pennant (1768) did.'

Today it is a visitor in considerable numbers, nearly all to the Avon valley between Ringwood and Fordingbridge, usually not arriving in any numbers before late December and staying until the third week in March. Occasionally the first numbers arrive in November, as in 1947 when 600/800 were present before the end of the month. The regular annual appearance of this flock dates only from about 1940; they were never previously numerous (the Earl of Normanton *per* Rooke). In February 1947 the estimated number there was over 2,000 (Rooke), but this is far more than usual and was no doubt due to the very hard weather at that time. Numbers reach their maximum in January or February, and over the years the gathering has steadily built up as the following figures of annual maxima show: 1943, 150; 1950, 100 'fewer than usual'; 1951, 100; 1952, 600/650; 1953, 700/800; 1962, 1,200; 1966, 1,200; 1967, 1,150; 1968, 1,100; 1969, 1,550; 1970, 1,550. The birds stay in their feeding grounds in the valley all night and do not flight to the coast as do most geese (Orr in *H.* 23. Part 1). This increase in numbers over recent years is probably due in part to the fact that the area is wardened by the Hampshire Naturalists' Trust.

From the rest of the mainland, flocks are seen moving at migration time and the odd group may settle for a short while on coastal fields. These however do not stay and are no doubt birds moving to or from wintering grounds elsewhere. The only time flocks are likely to stay in these coastal areas is in severe cold when such areas are probably not affected so much as the Avon valley.

The only records from the Island until 1963 were of two adults and an immature at Newtown from about 4 to 22 January 1951, seven there on 6 and 9 January 1958, two there on 10 February 1960, four there on 24 December 1961 and 12 on 2 January 1962 (Mrs. Seabroke); eight flew over Yarmouth to the mainland on 17 March 1956 (*I.o.W.* 5.1.23). In the severe cold of early 1963, flocks appeared at several localities such as Bembridge (126), Brook (77), Chale (75), Newtown (57) and the Medina (47) — (*I.o.W.* 63). Each subsequent year has produced records of small flocks that did not stay long at any locality.

Late records were one flying west at Gilkicker on 18 April 1966, one in Langstone Harbour on 15 May 1966 (*H.* 1966) and one at Needs Oar from 30 March 1969 to 13 April 1969 (*H.* 1969). These birds may well have been injured.

A possible hybrid Lesser White-front/White-front occurred among a party of 14 White-fronts at Hayling Island (Shackleton); a detailed description appeared in *B.B.* 44.229.

White-fronted Goose

78. Bean Goose. *Anser a. arvensis*: Up to 1960 the only mention since the very few in K & M is that 'it is at times obtained at Hayling' (Kelso), which must refer to before 1912 and is the same statement he often makes about other species without giving any evidence whatever. But on 8/9 March 1960, Le Brocq saw five on Farlington Marshes of which he gave a full description (*H.* 22). Then up to 10 were at Farlington Marshes and the nearby Portsmouth airfield from 20 January to 17 March 1963 in very hard weather (*H.* 23. Part 1). In 1964, eight flew into Chichester Harbour on 1 February followed by one at Newtown on 23 February which is the only record from the Island (*H.* 23. Part 2). Finally, a flock of 17 flew south-east over Black Point on 2 March 1969 (*H.* 1969), and one was at Ibsley on 10 January 1971 (*H.* 1971).

78. Pink-footed Goose. *Anser arvensis brachyrhynchus*: K & M say: 'An occasional winter visitor'. Today, a very scarce winter visitor, the following having been reported since K & M. *From the mainland*: One was killed by impact with a car at Warneford in 1923 (*W.* 1931). One at Stanpit on 13 October 1937 (Miss Popham in *H.* 14.98), and one was found dead there on 28 January 1940 (*H.* 15.81). In the winter of 1939/40 there were more grey geese than ever at Portchester, principally this species (Stares, who was a wildfowler, in *H.* 15.81). On 19 January 1946, a flock of 24 flew over Meon towards Shedfield (Portal, *per* Miss Barraud). One at Titchfield Haven on 13 February 1966 (*H.* 1966). Two flew north-east at Gilkicker on 10 January 1968 and four were in the Tournerbury area on 22 December 1968 (*H.* 1968). Kelso again says it was sometimes obtained at Hayling.

From the Island, one was at Newtown from 24 to 31 January 1963, four flew from Brading Marsh over Sandown rubbish tip towards Culver Cliff on 9 January 1964 and one was shot at Brading on 15 January 1964 (*I.o.W.* 1963/4).

80. Brent Goose. *Branta bernicla*: K & M say: 'A common winter visitor to the coasts of the county and Isle of Wight.'

Occasionally from September, but mostly from the second half of November until mid-March though some stay until April; there are records of four at Keyhaven as late as 25 May 1947 and a quite remarkable report of one and possibly five others over the Solent on 23 June 1947 (Day). Rarely inland (20 on 9 January 1941 on the Avon ten to twelve miles from Christchurch Harbour – *B.B.* 34. 223).

Large numbers are mainly reported from Langstone and Chichester Harbours, the only places suitable for supporting a considerable winter population. Regular counting at Langstone Harbour since 1952/3 has shown a most marked increase and today the flock that winters regularly in the two harbours is one of the largest in Britain and by far the largest on the whole south coast. The winter maxima since 1952/3 have increased from 70 to 3,050 in December 1970. Maxima for the years 1965/70 were: 1,000; 1,240; 2,400; 2,300; 2,500; 3,050 (all these counts were in Langstone Harbour in January or February except for the last count which was December, so the numbers are minimum ones for the whole population since they do not include Chichester Harbour birds, and up to 1,500 were counted there). However, a count of the two harbours in January, February and March 1971 gave totals of 6,965, 7,374 and 5,750.

The arrival of the first birds has become earlier over this same period. In 1952/3 the first party of 25 did not appear until 4 January, whereas in 1957/8 the first arrived on 6 November and in 1970 the earliest date was 10 October. Maximum numbers are usually reached between early January and the middle of February. Numbers are maintained at peak level for anything up to two months in the Langstone/Chichester area and the tendency has been for that level to be maintained for a longer period as the increase has continued, and for departure to be delayed later. Thus on 30 March 1958 there were still 500 in Langstone Harbour, 300 there on 7 April and 350 on the 12th, whilst 850 were still there in April 1971.

Tubbs, writing in *The Field* of 27 November 1958, says of this population:

'In Langstone Harbour feeding habits pass through a distinct pattern with the progress of the winter. While numbers are building up to the winter maximum all the Brent feed in a single gaggle along the creek and channel edges in the centre of the tidal marshes. Once the peak level has been reached – and presumably as they begin to exhaust the original feeding ground – they start to split into smaller gaggles and scatter widely about the harbour. At the same time there is a distinct tendency to feed up on the open mud-flats rather than along the creek edges and in the shallows, apart from periods of spring tides when the small remaining beds of zostera are exposed. Competent analysis of droppings, incidentally, has shown that the staple diet is the alga, *enteromorpha*. By the latter half of February the Brent are very scattered, gaggles often feeding on the saltings close to the shore. As numbers begin to drop with the advent of spring, however, scattering becomes less evident and towards the end all the Brent are once again concentrated together. Brent in Langstone and Chichester Harbours do not flight out to sea at dusk and return at dawn. Numerous writers have alluded to this habit at one time or another but here, on the south coast at least, there has been no evidence over the past six winters to support it. In the weeks before their departure in spring the Brent becomes extremely restless and excited, large gaggles constantly skidding about all over the harbours and indulging in high aerial evolutions. A gaggle will sometimes lift off the mud and sweep backwards and forwards, rising higher and higher, calling until barely visible, finally coming down again in a series of long glides and a final whiffle on to the mud . . . There can be no doubt that the Brent Goose is re-establishing itself quite firmly as a wintering bird on the south coast. In the winter of 1957/8 there were 1,000 Brent in Langstone and Chichester Harbours and — if I stuck my neck out — I should add another 150 for the remainder of the south coast. This is encouraging but gives no cause for complacency. To begin with, Langstone Harbour is very close to Portsmouth and schemes for its development are constantly being advanced. As already pointed out, there are very few places in the south capable of maintaining a substantial number of Brent Geese'.

A new departure for the Langstone Harbour Brent occurred in the winter of 1969/70 when birds started feeding *on* Farlington Marshes. Up to 20 were there in December and 100 on 10 January 1970.

Elsewhere on the mainland coast, sightings are very spasmodic, the most likely area being between Hurst and the Lymington River. In some years, a group has wintered there with as many as 284 recorded on 20 January 1970. Eling Salt Marsh used to be another favoured haunt, 70/100 being there from mid-January to early March 1944; at times they came quite close to the railway and to one of the busiest roads in southern England, as recorded in *A Short History of Nursling* by O. G. S. Crawford (1948).

On the Island, Newtown appears to be the most favoured spot in recent years with as many as 86 early in 1967 (*I.o.W.* 6. Part 2). A few pass eastwards off St. Catherine's Point in spring but records from the remainder of the Island are very erratic.

The dark-breasted form is far the commoner (*Branta b. bernicla*) but there are a number of records of the pale-breasted race (*Branta bernicla hrota*), e.g. in Christchurch Harbour on 14 November 1936, two (Miss Popham in *H.* 13.219), at Keyhaven, two parties of eight and 12 on 3 March 1929 (Jourdain in *B.* 21.58), 11 on 9 March 1955, seven on 11 November 1956 and 10 on 10 February 1957, all in Langstone Harbour (P.G.)

At Langstone Harbour, counts are made of first winter birds which gives some indication of breeding success e.g. in December 1969, 62 per cent of the flock were first-winter whilst the figures for December 1970 and January/February 1970 were 32 per cent and 44 per cent respectively.

81. Barnacle Goose. *Branta leucopsis*: To the very few records in K & M can be added one of three tired birds that stayed a day at Mottisfont in January 1895 (Meinertzhagen). Since then, probable wild birds have been: three on the Pennington salterns in hard weather on 17 December 1946 (Day in *H.* 17.191); six on Eling Marsh on 16/17 November 1961 (*H.* 22. Part 2); one at Titchfield Haven on 1 December 1962 (Suffern *in litt*).

Birds thought more likely to be feral than wild were: one at Redbridge between 21 February and 6 March 1963 (*H.* 23. Part 1); one at Alresford on 17 November 1963 that stayed for some 10 days (*W.* 1963); one at Ibsley on 4 January 1964; one at Blashford around 23 January 1966; two at Keyhaven on 3 September 1968 which allowed a close approach (*H.* 1968); four to five in Dibden Bay from 10 to 23 November 1968 (*H.* 1968); one on the Avon with the White-front flock from 29 December 1968 to 1 March 1969 (*H.* 1968 and 1969) and another there in January/February 1971 (*H.* 1971).

Birds known to be 'escapes' have been: one bird on one date in October, November and December 1949 at three points on the coast, at all times rather or very tame, probably originated from 10 full-winged birds that were lost in the winter of 1949/50 out of the late Major Pam's collection at Broxbourne, Herts; one at Fleet Pond from 22 to 28 October 1950 was also possibly one of these; a bird seen at various points in the north of the county from 1964 to 1971 had almost certainly escaped from Hartley Wintney though more than one individual could have been involved (*H.* 1964 to 1971).

82.   Canada Goose. *Branta canadensis*: K & M square-bracketed it saying: 'Another introduced species which frequently occurs in an apparently wild state but can only be considered as escaped from captivity or spring from semi-wild parents'. Most of the records down to 1955 come from Heath Lake, Petersfield, where there was a resident pair from 1936 to 1946, the gander of which used to drive off visiting Canada Geese. These visitors first came in any numbers in 1941 (nine dates between 13 February and 9 May with a maximum of nine, and on 19 December 1941, 16 to 20); on 17 December 1942 there were 22, on 2 October 1945, 28, 'more than usual', and on 3 March 1947, 32; in March, June and July 1949 there were again from three to nine (Miss White). On Fleet Pond one was seen on 4 May 1905 (Munn), and between 1 October and 31 December 1950 the species was always present, with a maximum of 44 on 4 November (Boswall and Crewe); there were 30 on 29 January 1955 (Cundall) and three pairs bred there in 1956 and 1957. On 3 April 1952 there were 21 on the lake at Elvetham, where they bred successfully in 1954 and 1955 and probably in most recent years. In this early period, by far the largest number reported was 'about 150 near Ringwood on 1 January 1939, most of which were Canadas with a few White-fronts' (Ponchaud, who was a well-known local taxidermist).

Within the last fifteen years the species has increased its numbers considerably, partly due to successful breeding and partly due to releases such as the group of about 50 liberated at Needs Oar in 1964 and which have grown into a regular flock at that locality. They are now likely to be seen in any part of the mainland, sometimes in large numbers, though some areas are favoured with regular records whereas others are used *only* occasionally. The following list of well-used localities with post-war maxima give some idea of the species' present status: Aldershot Camp sewage farm, 89; Ash Vale gravel pit, 69; Bramshill, 161; Dogmersfield (Tundry), 300 plus; Elvetham Lake, 220; Farnborough North gravel pit, 63; Fleet Pond, 200; Needs Oar, 110; Heath Pond, 68; Stratfield Saye, 520; Yateley gravel pit, 170.

EC in *B.o.H.* listed only one record from the Island, 10 flying off Gurnard on 3 August 1959 (*I.o.W.* 5.4. 150). Two in Brading Marsh on 31 March 1961 was the next occurrence (*I.o.W.* 5. Part 6) and then three flew past Newtown on 29 April 1962 (*I.o.W.* 5. Part 7). 1963 and 1964 produced a number of sightings and the species has been recorded in each subsequent year with as many as 56 at Newtown on 12 December 1970.

Breeding occurs in several mainland localities where flocks are found. The greatest concentrations have been about 20 pairs in less than a square mile of the Needs Oar area in 1971, 13 pairs there in 1970, and eight pairs at Yateley gravel pit in 1970 and 1966. The concentration at Needs Oar in 1971 proved too much of a threat to the grazing and the farmer destroyed most of the clutches.

Two ringed as fully grown birds at Needs Oar on 27 June 1964 were shot on 31 March 1965 in the Pas de Calais and on 21 September 1964 in the Somme department. The only previous French recoveries of British-ringed Canada Geese were reported during the cold weather of 1963 (B.B. 59.458).

83. Red-breasted Goose. *Branta ruficollis* *: The first record for Hampshire was of one in the Avon valley at Blashford with the White-front flock from 18 January to 19 February 1967. It may have been the wild bird from Slimbridge which left there for a while (B.B. 61. 338 and H. 1967). Another was seen in the same locality from 11 to 19 January 1969 (H. 1969). Both were accepted by *British Birds* Rarities Committee.

84. Mute Swan. *Cygnus olor*: The census organised throughout England and Wales in the 1955 breeding season by Dr. Bruce Campbell for the British Trust for Ornithology gave, for the mainland, 63 nests and 171 non-breeders, and for the Island, 17 nests. This was out of a total for England of 2,505 nesting pairs and 8,014 non-breeding birds. Details from the mainland: 19 nests on lakes or ponds, 30 on rivers, five on gravel pits and five on canals, these spread all over the county (*Bird Study*. 7.4).

The largest herds may be seen in Christchurch Harbour where the pattern in the main is of numbers beginning to rise in May, reaching a peak around mid July and falling to about 30 in October. High winter numbers there are exceptional though 150 were present in December 1970. The year's peak in recent years has exceeded 300 and 490 were counted on 10 September 1958. Southampton Water is another place where numbers have been seen in summer. Munn reported them there in 1917 'for some years past', whilst in more recent times, the head of the estuary at Redbridge has been the most favoured spot and summer herds there and at the mouth of the Itchen have exceeded 100. Finally, data from Langstone Harbour also suggests summer maxima. At all these places, the herds are composed almost entirely of adult birds (or, at least, white birds), but judging from bill colour and development, JHT suspects that most of them are too young to breed and they gather in these coastal localities during the breeding season where they will not infringe on the territories of breeding pairs. However, in *B.B.* 26.38, after 250 had been seen in Christchurch Harbour in April 1934, there appeared the following: 'Owing to the disappearance of *zostera* at Abbotsbury great numbers deserted the swannery and stayed at Poole, Christchurch and Southampton Water all summer without attempting to breed'.

Other localities only have numbers of consequence in the winter months and these are not only coastal but include inland waters where flocks in the breeding season would interfere with territories. Sturt Pond is such a place, holding up to 90 birds in winter, whilst the Avon valley around Ibsley has had counts such as 180 which occurred on 11 November 1955.

On the Island, the largest herd we can trace is 110 on 20 March 1955. On 10 September 1957, two approached St. Catherine's Point from the west and alighted on the sea five to seven miles out.

An adult ringed on 5 September 1956 at Durleigh (Somerset) was recovered near Christchurch on about 17 April 1958; one ringed at Christchurch in July 1962 was recovered at Winchester on 31 March 1963 (W. 1963); one ringed as fully grown at Emsworth on 15 August 1963 was controlled there on 27 October 1963 and found dead in Schleswig-Holstein on 15 May 1964; a first-summer bird ringed at Bedford on 27 June 1964 was retrapped at Southampton on 6 April 1968; one ringed 5 August 1969 at Radipole (Dorset) controlled in Christchurch Harbour on 8 September 1971 and 16 September 1971.

Readers interested in mentions of this species in Hampshire as an article of food at royal banquets in the thirteenth century are referred to N. F. Ticehurst's learned account 'The Early History of the Mute Swan in England' (*B.B.* 17.174 et seq.).

85. Whooper Swan. *Cygnus cygnus*: A rather scarce winter visitor that would seem to be less common now than when K & M wrote. Even today, when observer coverage is so good, a year may pass without any being seen (e.g. 1967) and if more than two dozen appear in a year, it would be a good one for the species. Hard weather usually brings higher counts.

Records are few between K & M and the post-war years but some of them are interesting. In 1934 a bird stayed all summer at Warren Flats near Needs Oar (Murray in *B*.). Each winter from 1936/7 to 1939/40 from two to six birds stayed all winter at Beaulieu, two becoming so tame that they were assumed to be the same two birds each time; they almost fed out of the hand and were quite undisturbed by passing traffic. They were last seen on 11 April 1940 (*B.B.* 30.31 and 32). On 12 March 1939 a pair were watched courting there (Hollom).

The hard weather of 1946/7 produced the greatest number of observations for many years but a far greater influx occurred in the long cold spell of February 1956. This period brought 32 flying E. low along the seawall at Titchfield Haven on the 4th, whooping loudly and continuously; on the 13th, 18 flew E. to W. over Langstone Harbour (Dennis *et al.*); 17 were at Fullerton on the Test and 20 flew down the Itchen at Swaythling. The estimated number of individuals in this period was around 83 (JHT).

Whooper Swan

Whoopers are likely to occur both on the coast and at inland waters, nearly all records being from November to February with very few staying to March. In normal weather the birds are mostly seen on one day only, not staying at one locality, but some individuals or small groups may stay for some weeks.

All the above has referred to the mainland. There were no reports from the Island until the cold of February 1956 when there were three in Brading Harbour on the 4th, all fresh water being frozen (Stafford). One was at Newtown on 8 and 10 December 1958 (*I.o.W. 5.3.111*). One was at Sandown from 24 to 28 January and again on 4 February 1963. Four flew E. over Porchfield on 8 November 1966 and seven were at Newtown the following day (*I.o.W.* 6. Part 1). Two were at Brading Marsh on 17 November and seven were there on 14 December 1968 (*I.o.W.* 6. Part 3). This number of records after the first sighting in 1956 suggests either that the birds previously escaped notice or that the species is becoming a more frequent visitor to our waters.

86. Bewick's Swan. *Cygnus bewickii*: Reported on only five occasions since K & M until the long cold spell of February 1956, namely: 26 at Christchurch on 25 December 1938, all gone next day (*B.B.* 32. 190); an adult at Hurn with six Whoopers on 5 April 1947 (*H.* 17.190); a dead bird at Hengistbury Head on 22 December 1952 of which the head and foot were brought to EC for identification by the finder, Henson, and although the yellow on the bill had turned rather orange after death (? through action of salt water), there was no doubt about the identification; 22 flew over Langstone Harbour, calling occasionally, on 20 March 1954 (EC *et al.*); three adults stayed at Witton Pond near Burley through the last three weeks of February 1955, during part of which time the water was almost entirely frozen over (Miss Popham and EC). The paucity of records from K & M to 1956 must be partly due to thin observer coverage of the county.

In February and March 1956 many more than usual were recorded, the number of individuals recorded being between 105 and 165 (JHT). Birds were at Titchfield Haven from 22 February (14) to 24 March (six), the peak being on 18 March when 27 were seen to go, leaving seven behind. Only two or three were immature. Langstone Harbour too had its quota: 14, of which 10 were adult, arrived from the E. on 11 February; 20 flew over from E. to W. on the 18th, and 14 on the 21st; there were 28 there, of which four were immature, on the 25th and these later left to the W. On 18th March, 12 flew from W. to E. in the evening over Portsmouth (PG). From 7 to 9 March there were 21 (about 10 immature) on Long Pond, Burley; they had gone by the 12th (Miss Popham). Smaller numbers were seen inland on the Avon and the Test.

Subsequently the species has been recorded every year (except 1959) and in the last few years a total of around 40/50 would be typical, making it more numerous than the Whooper. However, this total is largely due to a herd that has taken to wintering on the Avon around Ibsley. Over recent winters, this herd's numbers have reached the following maxima: 28 (19 adults) winter 1965/6; about 30, 1966/7; 21 (all adults), 1967/8; 32, 1968/9; 17, 1969/70. The largest gathering yet recorded in the county during this century, however, was 46 in Langstone Harbour on 21 December 1963.

K & M make no mention of any record from the Island but Stafford has kindly drawn attention to the following extract from 'Birds' by R. H. Fox in *A Guide to the Natural History of the Isle of Wight* edited by F. Morey, Newport, 1909, page 156: '*Cygnus bewickii* (Bewick's Swan): Occasionally obtained in winter: I know of two stuffed specimens, both obtained near Bembridge between 1870 and 1880'. Three at Brading on 17 February 1964 appear to be the first Island record since the above but there have been subsequent records for 1966, 1967 and 1970 including a herd of eight (falling to six) that stayed at Bembrdige from 26 November 1966 to 9 January 1967.

Most birds are seen from November to February with occasional early and late birds in October and March. One at Ibsley on 28 May 1965 was a very late date (Ash — H. 23. Part 3).

Apart from the Ibsley herd, the species is most likely to be seen in the coastal area though there have been records from as far inland as the very north of the county.

87. Egyptian Vulture. *Neophron percnopterus* *: One at Bishop's Dyke from 16 to 18 June 1968 was the first record for Hampshire (Green and Nalder — H. 1968 and 1969). One observer recorded it as immature but apparently this was an error. This was accepted by *British Birds* Rarities Committee though there is always the possibility of the bird being an escape.

An adult at Farlington Marshes, 31 October/1 November 1969, was later caught in Sussex and allegedly showed signs of having clipped primaries denoting previous captivity.

88. Griffon Vulture. *Gyps fulvus*: One soaring around Southampton a few years previous to 1889, mentioned in Howard Saunders *Manual of British Birds* as being seen by an observer 'who must have seen thousands of Griffons but will not allow his name to be mentioned' was square-bracketed by K & M but apparently accepted unreservedly in *The Handbook* and the B.O.U. Check-List, 1952. EC omitted this from *B.o.H.* by reason of K & M's square brackets, being unaware of the other two publications. Rees brought this to EC's attention *in Litt* (H. 23. Part 1, addendum).

[**89. Golden Eagle.** *Aquila chrysaëtos*: K & M mention four possible occurrences between 1828 and 1885 but regard all the records as doubtful, either through insufficient evidence or because the tameness of the birds strongly suggested escapes from captivity. Similarly, one at St. Helens (I.o.W.) on 11 March 1968 was almost certainly an escape (*I.o.W.* 6. Part 3).]

[**90. Spotted Eagle.** *Aquila clanga:* See under White-tailed Eagle (97).]

91. Buzzard. *Buteo buteo*: In 1905 K & M seemed uncertain as to whether this species was nesting regularly in the county at all. It seems probable that in the eighteenth century it must have been fairly widely distributed. Gilbert White describes them as 'soaring round' at Selborne. The somewhat unreliable Wise stated that several nests were taken yearly around the middle of the nineteenth century. That there was a very great decline in numbers during the last century seems certain. It is likely, however, that one or two pairs may have continued to breed in the New Forest. Certainly a pair bred there in 1915 and H. F. Witherby stated at that time that he had seen them in the Forest for several years and at all times of the year (*B.B.* 10.272). Records between the two World Wars were few and often vague, e.g. in 1935 New Forest 'numbers well maintained' (*H.*), but it seems probable that the species was increasing. Watson, a reliable and cautious observer, estimated that about 10 pairs were breeding in the New Forest in 1940 and by the early 1950s this figure had probably been doubled. About this time, too, there was an obvious spread into other areas. Miss Barraud (*in litt.*) watched a pair at Droxford on 6 October 1948 and subsequently found a nest in an oak with rabbit fur and feathers, suggesting breeding. In 1950 breeding was at least attempted in the north of the county, and 1951 produced the only nesting record for the Isle of Wight.

The advent of myxomatosis in 1953 appeared to have only a temporary effect on this species. In 1955 Ash reported that they were only about half as common as in previous years, though in the New Forest numbers were maintained. But in 1956 fewer were reported both in the Forest and outside and there was only one actual record of a successful brood. Three nests found in the Forest in April of that year by Day had fresh greenery on them but had been abandoned by May. Subsequently numbers have increased and it is estimated that over 25 pairs probably bred in the Forest area in 1958, 34 pairs in 1959, 28 pairs in 1960 and 35 in 1961, although very few of these last were known to have reared more than one chick (Tubbs *et al.*). More detailed Forest records for 1971, 1970 and 1968 are as follows:

	1971	1970	1968
Number of pairs present	36	36	33
Number of pairs proved breeding	22	18	19
Number of young reared	27	23	19/20

In recent years, outside the Forest, pairs have been breeding with some regularity in the Damerham area, in the Winchester/Hursley area, in the Test valley, on the chalk in the north of the county and perhaps in one northeast locality. Unfortunately persecution continues in spite of the law, and where the species is very thin on the ground this is probably the factor which prevents it from becoming established. In 1946 a bird was shot at Ramsdell, near Basingstoke, and in 1950 another at Crux Easton, near Andover. Between August and December 1955, seven were present in the Micheldever area, of which four were killed. However, perhaps an even greater threat today is the use of chlorinated hydrocarbons. Eggs that failed to hatch in 1963 were taken from Forest nests and were found to contain such chemicals (*H.* 23. Part 1).

For a very full account of the species' status in the British Isles the reader is referred to N. W. Moore's report published in *B.B.* 50.

It has been suggested (*H.* 21. Part 3) that there is evidence of passage in the county, as outside the Forest records tend to show a concentration in September and October. One flew S. out to sea at Hengistbury on 1 October 1966 (C.H.O.S.G.), another did likewise on 20 September 1969 and three flew S. out to sea together at St. Catherine's Point on the same day (*H.* 1969). The suggestion is made that this passage may be of birds from the Forest and from a brood of three nestlings ringed there in 1957, one was recovered dead at Bosham (Sussex) on 4 April 1958 and another near Poole (Dorset) on 9 February 1960. Another nestling ringed by Wright in June 1962 was recovered on 28 September 1962 in the Aisne Department (France), the first British-ringed Buzzard to be recovered abroad. Another nestling from the same area was recovered at Hornsea (Yorkshire) on 17 September 1962 (Spencer, personal communication). It may be noted that most records from the Isle of Wight occur in the winter months and if 30 pairs breed with even fair success in the Forest, mere pressure of numbers might reasonably be expected to force birds to range more widely (P. E. Brown).

Two flew in from the S. at The Needles on 3 January 1960 and flew off to the E.

92. Rough-legged Buzzard. *Buteo lagopus*: Until recently a very rare visitor outside the breeding season. In addition to the 10 records given in K & M, the late Captain Bacon (*in litt.*) reported that his keeper shot one at Burghclere in 1892, adding that 'it had been taking a heavy toll of rabbits'. A cock was trapped in the Isle of Wight on 11 March 1907, and another was trapped near Stockbridge in January 1916. Phillips (*B.B.* 21.203) reported one on the Hants/Berks border on 18 December 1927, and added that the species was a regular winter visitor. This seems unlikely, but it is well-known that a bird (presumably the same one) will often haunt the same spot for some weeks during a series of winters. One was seen on the western outskirts of the New Forest on 9 December 1937 (*B.B.* 31.275) and a cock was trapped near Andover in 1940 (Payn in *H.*). in 1945 one was seen at Stockbridge and then another appeared at Rockford on 7 April 1962 (Orr).

Either the species has genuinely become a more frequent visitor, or recent years have been abnormal, or better observer coverage has revealed its true status, but it can no longer be called very rare because seven of the nine years from 1964 to 1972 inclusive have produced records. During this period 11 birds were sighted, all between October and April and spread all over the county. They include one in Rowborough Valley from 18 to 19 February 1967, which was the first Island record for 60 years (*I.o.W.* 6. Part 2) and one which stayed at Longwood Warren (near Winchester) from 10 December 1966 to 26 February 1967 (*H.* 1967 and 1968).

Several others have been reported in this period but rejected by the county Records Committee on grounds of insufficient evidence but they may well have been genuine records. Identification of this species is far from easy because some examples of *buteo* are pale and have white tail feathers and if such a bird should hover, as *buteo* occasionally does, an observer unfamiliar with *lagopus* could convince himself that he had seen one. For differences between the two species, readers are advised to consult *B.B.* 64. 249—263.

A falconer near Fordingbridge reared and released a brood of four *lagopus* around the late 1950s. They had been sent to him from Norway as Goshawks! (*per* Ash).

93. Sparrowhawk. *Accipiter nisus*: Generally though rather thinly distributed throughout the county and the Isle of Wight, its density as a breeding species being

Sparrowhawk

highest in the New Forest. There is evidence to suggest a great decline at least in the north since K & M, who call it 'still a fairly common resident', but from the mid 1960s there has been a substantial recovery in the species' fortunes. By 1966, Ewart Jones considered it as common as in pre-war days in some areas whilst the results of the B.T.O. *Atlas* survey and a wealth of sightings sent in each year point to a reasonable-size and growing population. The early decline was no doubt due in part to game-keepers and such persecution still exists today; the young of no fewer than five pairs were destroyed in Micheldever Wood in 1963 (*W.* 1963). More recently the species has had to contend with chlorinated hydrocarbons and an unhatched egg taken from the Forest in 1963 was found to contain such chemicals (see also under Buzzard — *H.* 23. Part 1).

In the New Forest, the species may well have escaped the decline experienced in the rest of the county owing to the absence of game-keepers. For the years 1960/70 inclusive, between 13 and 24 pairs are known to have bred there each year, the highest figure being in 1961, the lowest in 1966 and 1970. In 1968, 17 young flew from 15 nests and in 1970 at least 22 young flew from 13 nests (*H.* 1968 and 1970).

There is evidence of spring passage from the coast, e.g. a cock flew in off the sea at St. Catherine's Point on 30 March 1968 and a very tired female arrived at Hengistbury from the SW on 21 April 1968 (*H.* 1968). There is also evidence of autumn passage. Thus a nestling ringed in Aust Agder (South Norway) in June 1952 was shot at Ringwood on 17 September in the same year. In 1955 at St. Catherine's Point, there were four birds in the bushes on 26 August, two on 10 September and one on 11, whilst no birds had been present on four dates between 13 and 25 August (Rees). In 1957, at the same place, a cock flew in from the SE on 2 September, and again at St. Catherine's, one flew south out to sea and was watched out of sight at 07.40 hrs on 8 September 1958. Other similar records have occurred at mainland coastal localities.

On a game preserve of some 4,000 acres in West Hampshire the annual totals of this species killed rose from 45 plus in 1949 to 64 in 1952, and dropped from 58 in 1953 to seven in 1956, rising again to 18 in 1959. Of 64 examined after death, females outnumbered males by two to one (Ash, in *B.B.* 53).

94. Goshawk. *Accipiter gentilis*: K & M found insufficient evidence to include this species in their list for the county, but it is interesting to note that Munn, in his diaries, records one shot at Highclere by Marshall in 1886 and considers the record should be accepted, and Meinertzhagen in his diaries records that an adult female was trapped undamaged on the Lockerley estate in October 1896 and sent to the Vaynol Park collection. In *B.B.* 4. 182, Kelsall also records a pair in the Isle of Wight in 1896, one of which was shot and found to be wearing jesses.

The first record for this century was one soaring over Sloden Inclosure in the New Forest alongside a Buzzard in June 1938 (Lack *in litt*). Ash then recorded one near Fordingbridge on 8 September 1953, and another was seen at the same locality on 8 February 1957. One was seen on Farlington Marshes on 7 July and 24 October 1953, and (*H.* 19.82) on three dates in August 1954. Wooldridge withdrew his record of one near Beaulieu on 27 September 1959 which appeared in *B.o.H.* having become familiar with the species and so changed his identification. One was seen at Pilot Hill on 3 September 1958 (*H.* 22. Part 2 — p.32). This species has bred or attempted to breed on a number of occasions in the 1950s in an adjacent county. Unfortunately, the species is imported in some numbers by falconers, who not infrequently lose them, so that one can seldom rule out the possibility of a bird being an 'escape'.

A first-summer bird was seen at Wroxall (I.o.W.) on the 1 April 1963 and a bird answering the same description took a Blackbird at Wootton on 14 April (*I.o.W.* 1963/4). In the Hengistbury area an immature female was seen between 25 and 30 August 1970, an adult male was present from 15 to 20 September 1970 (*H.* 1970), a female wearing jesses was seen on 14 April 1971 and a male on 30/31 August 1971 (*H.*1971).

95. Kite. *Milvus milvus*: Once bred widely in the county and possibly also in the Island, though there appears to be no evidence available. K & M accept the last breeding record as 1864, when three eggs are said to have been taken from a nest in a fir tree near Stockbridge. There appears to be no reliable record in the county between January 1890 (one near Alresford) and 1956, when a bird was present at Old Winchester Hill on 15/17 August and was watched by Ian Presst and others (*H.*), apart from a comment by 'Fish-Hawk' (*B.T.O. Bulletin* No.22, March 1967) that the only British Kite he had ever seen was observed from a train between Ringwood and Bournemouth in 1935.

Recently, Ewart Jones saw one between Preshaw and Dur Wood on 23 August 1970 (*H.* 1970), one flew SW over Lyndhurst on 21 October 1971, and one flew over Emsworth on 26 November 1971 (*H.* 1971).

97. White-tailed Eagle. *Haliaetus albicilla*: A very rare vagrant, almost invariably during the winter months. K & M gave a number of records, including one seen in July 1885 by Meade-Waldo, a reliable observer. The record of a Spotted Eagle *(Aguila clanga)* included by K & M should be deleted, as this was an immature Sea-eagle shot near Somerley on 28 December 1861. Mackworth-Praed examined this specimen and there can be no doubt about the original error. Occurrences since K & M are very few: one at Highclere, 18 December 1927 (*B.B.* 24. 231); one in the Island, from the end of January to mid-March 1932 (*B.B.* 25. 338); an immature at Somerley Park, Ringwood, on 6 January 1947 (EC).

K & M accept that this species once bred in the Island (Culver Cliffs) until about 1780. The only evidence appears to be based on the Rev. Richard Warner's *History of the Isle of Wight*, published in 1795. Warner wrote: 'The last eagle known to build in Culver Cliff (according to the information I could obtain) came there in 1780. An adventurous countryman, who had frequently descended the rock for the eggs of its other winged tenants, having watched the eagle from the nest, paid a visit to it also. He found this fabrication to be of considerable size, and formed of sticks and rushes laid alternately; containing one solitary young bird. This he took, but, not knowing how to manage it, the eaglet soon died.' Can one really feel certain that this record does not refer to a cliff-nesting buzzard? The species never bred, apparently, on the cliffs of the West of England nor in Wales. The *Handbook* only accepts breeding in the Isle of Wight as 'probable'. I feel that, in admitting that the species *possibly* bred, one is stretching the evidence just about as far as is reasonable (P. E. Brown).

98. Honey Buzzard. *Pernis apivorus*: In 1905 K & M wrote: 'This species is perhaps the most interesting of our Hampshire birds, on account of its having been found, in former years, more commonly in this county than in any other part of England; but, having gained notoriety from being known as a regular summer visitor to the New Forest, it was much sought after there by collectors and has been by now nearly exterminated.' K & M, however, provide very little evidence to show that the species nested with any regularity after about 1870. Nesting took place annually from 1928 to 1932 in the New Forest (*B.B.* 26. 278) and again, successfully, in 1934 (*B.B.* 29. 124). A pair probably bred in 1936 or 1937 in Milkham Inclosure, but it is said that the adults were killed in August. Very possibly, it was only the lack of coverage by observers in the 30s and 40s that prevented more records from coming to light.

In 1949 a pair were present and may have nested near Ashmansworth, in the extreme north (*B.B.* 43. 189). Over the past two decades, breeding has again taken place in the county. Perhaps the day will come when our approach to nature is sufficiently civilised to allow the details to be published. If details were printed at the moment, the egg-collectors would once again drive the species from our county. Indeed, at least one clutch has been lost in recent years.

Records outside the breeding season or away from areas where nesting is known to have occurred are very few. Recent ones include one flying due N. at Tidpit Down (near Martin) on the evening of 10 May 1951 (Ash *in litt.*), one at Needs Oar on 3 October 1959 (*H.* 21. Part 3), and one flying S. out to sea at St. Catherine's Point on 17 September 1966 (*I.o.W.* 6. Part 1), the last record being rejected by the mainland Records Committee but accepted by the Island recorder.

99.   Marsh Harrier. *Circus aeruginosus*: K & M describe this species as a rare winter visitor, formerly resident. There is little satisfactory evidence of breeding in either of the eighteenth or nineteenth centuries but EC in *B.o.H.* (1963) states that nesting has occurred within the last ten years in a locality which cannot be disclosed. Today it is a very scarce visitor to the mainland coast and a rare visitor inland and on the Island. During the years 1960/1970 inclusive, 39 were reported and since nine of these were in 1960, the other years averaged three sightings each. None were reported on the Island during this period and an analysis of the records shows monthly totals to be: January, four; February, six; March, nil; April, seven; May, six; June, two; July, one; August, two; September, six; October, three; November, one; December, one. The small peak in April/May (one third of the records) and six in September suggest that passage birds account for many of the sightings.

The last Island records appear to be a female at Newtown on the 17 September 1958, one at Shorwell on 31 January 1971, and a female that came in off the sea at St. Catherine's Point on 21 April 1971 (*H.* 1971).

100. Hen Harrier. *Circus cyaneus*: K & M suggest that this species once bred in the county, but there is practically no evidence to substantiate this and it is well to bear in mind that, until after the eighteenth century, this species was not separated from *C. pygargus* and there has probably often been confusion between the two since then. The *Handbook* admits one record of breeding in the present century. It is a regular winter visitor to the county in small numbers, most records coming from the New Forest and the coastal stretch of the mainland. Reports from the Island are far less regular and several recent years have produced no sightings from there.

The first sighting is usually in October and the last birds are typically in March or April. Recent records between these dates have been a male at Farlington Marshes on 6 May 1956, one at Winnall on 15 June 1962 that had been released at Alton two days earlier (*H.* 22. Part 3) and a pair at Rocken End (I.o.W.) on 10 September 1969 (*H.* 1969).

Areas away from the coast and Forest that at times have had fairly regular visits are round Damerham and Micheldever, though much of the chalk is suitable as winter quarters and since this area is not well covered, birds could easily escape notice. The chalkland records are probably confined to those birds that happen to select an area where someone is watching regularly. This lack of coverage could well account for the paucity of records in some parts of the north.

Most of the sightings are of *ringtails*. For notes on prey taken, see Ash in *B.B.* 53.

102. Montagu's Harrier. *Circus pygargus*: K & M say: 'A regular summer visitor to certain districts of the mainland; less common in the Isle of Wight.' Kelso (1912) states that it nested on Hayling Island for several years and was afforded protection; he saw one there on 18 May 1906. During the past 20 years, from one to four pairs have usually bred or attempted to breed each season, mostly in the New Forest and the Fordingbridge area but at other localities on a few occasions. Several of these nests have failed due to egg-collectors, destruction of nest by farming machinery, bird-watchers disturbing birds so that unguarded eggs are taken by predators, or one of the adults disappearing (presumed shot). It is one of those species that is facing an almost impossible task in attempting to nest in modern Hampshire. On occasion, the young have been well-grown before disaster overtook them.

Although scarce, it occurs fairly widely outside the known breeding areas, including the Island. The earliest known date is 16 April 1958 when a female flew E. at St. Catherine's Point (Dennis *et al.*); the latest date is one at Micheldever on 2 November 1960 (*H.* 22. Part 1).

A young bird ringed in the New Forest in August 1949 was shot at Champagne-les-Marais, Vendée (France) on 22 September in the same year, and the remains of another were found in the Scilly Isles in May of its first year.

Their food on a 4,000 acre W. Hampshire game preserve (1949/59) was very varied, but only one record involved a game-bird (Ash in *B.B.* 53. 295).

Montagu's Harrier

103. Osprey. *Pandion haliaetus*: K & M described this species as a scarce but regular passage migrant and then proceeded to give details which cast considerable doubt upon the regularity. Certainly there appear to be comparatively few records between 1905 and 1940. One was reported in the Avon Valley in 1922. A more reliable record is of one which remained over two days in August 1929 at Laverstoke Park, Whitchurch, and which was seen fishing in the Test (Portal and Jourdain) (*B.B.* 22. 54). One stayed several days on the Test at Mottisfont in October 1936 and took mainly trout (Meinertzhagen). An immature male was reported at Christchurch on 18 September 1939 (*H.*) which is a likely date but, unless the bird was shot, the sexing throws doubt upon its validity. The number and the reliability of the records improved during and after the Second World War: a hen was found shot at the River Meon, early November 1941 (Portal in *H.*). There is a less substantial record of a bird at Hengistbury, 9 March 1942 (*H.*), but Rooke watched a bird on the River Avon on 2 May 1942 and again, fishing at the same place and probably the same bird, on 31 May. In that same year a bird was present at Portsmouth from 13 September until 28 November (a very late date). This bird roosted on a signal post in a railway-siding and was eventually found dead, the corpse partly eaten by rats. On 18 September 1948, R. E. Williams watched an Osprey at the mouth of the River Hamble (*B.B.* 42. 400).

During the years 1950/71 inclusive, there have been around 80 occurrences, the coastal stretch of the mainland producing rather more records than inland areas with the Island reporting fewest of all. During the last 10 years of the above period, about 80 per cent of the records were from August to October and over half of this 80 per cent were in September. For the whole period, there is a slight peak for May/June indicating spring passage and one was seen coming in off the sea from the south at St. Catherine's Point on 29 March 1970. Two very late records were: on 5 December 1953, Adams recorded a 'probable' at Newtown but as a bird was seen by Mrs. Rogers on 7 December on the mainland opposite to Newtown, it seems reasonable to accept this very late record; one at Alresford Pond from 3/6 December 1967 was only the third December record for Britain (*H.* 1967).There are no records for January or February.

Two interesting records are of three together (one immature) at the mouth of the Beaulieu River in autumn 1967, and again three together at the same place (one immature) on 28 September 1969. Could these have been family groups (perhaps even the same pair) on migration (*H.* 1967 and 1969)?

An Osprey which frequented the Fordingbridge area from 5 to 15 June 1953 was shot and turned out to be an adult male weighing 3¾ lb. It was seen, while hovering over the river, to drop on, catch, and eat a Swallow (*per* Ash).

104. Hobby. *Falco subbuteo*: Probably more pairs of Hobbies breed in Hampshire than in any other county in Britain, yet there appear to be only two nesting records for the Isle of Wight, where the species is not even recorded very often. The two records were: a nest near Shanklin from which one egg was taken in 1947 (*per* Mrs. Bannerman) and a nest found by Major Christie near Calbourne, date unknown (*Zoologists' Record*, February 1964 reviewing *B.o.H.*). Breeding records from the mainland suggest that the number of pairs fluctuates considerably from one year to another but no comprehensive census has been made outside the New Forest so these fluctuations may be misleading. In the New Forest, where the species is most strongly represented, at least 10 pairs, and possibly double that number, attempt to breed in most years. Reports suggest that from five to 10 pairs (possibly more) nest on the chalk and greensand areas in the remainder of the county, but in the east it appears to be scarce.

The first arrivals are likely to be seen in late April, though the earliest date is

31 March 1961 when one was seen in the New Forest (*H.* 22. Part 2). The last are likely to be in the first half of October, the latest being on 5 November 1963 when one was seen over Portsmouth docks (*H.* 23. Part 1). In spring, birds have been seen coming in off the sea from the S. e.g.: one at Hengistbury on 28 May 1969, another there on 28 April 1968, and birds at St. Catherine's Point on 17 April 1966 and 9 April 1959. In autumn, birds have been seen to fly south out to sea, viz. — at St. Catherine's Point, on 4 and 5 October 1967 and at Hengistbury on 11 October 1959 (*H.* for those years).

Under 'Food', the *Handbook* says: 'Turtle Dove pursued'; Meinertzhagen reports that one was taken once at Mottisfont and P. E. Brown has also seen one taken.

Hobby

105. Peregrine. *Falco peregrinus*: As a breeding species since K & M, almost wholly confined to the Isle of Wight, although there have been mainland records such as the nest on the ground at the base of a small Scots Pine recorded in 1928 by Ashford and Jourdain (*B.B.* 22. 190/191). On the Island it has probably fluctuated between one and four pairs with probably none in some years. In 1905, K & M said it had been reduced to one pair but from 1926 to 1928 at least four pairs bred or attempted to breed and this was undoubtedly the period when the status of the species was strongest. Since the end of the Second World War it seems unlikely that more than a single pair have bred in any one season (except possibly two pairs in 1953 and 1955), and probably none at all since 1956. The cliffs at Main Bench were always a favourite site.

They were persecuted during the war because of their attacks on Carrier Pigeons and their subsequent failure to recoup losses and further decline in the last two decades can be ascribed largely to the enormous increase in the general use of toxic chemicals in agriculture and horticulture in the fifties. If their natural prey takes sub-lethal doses these would build up in the Peregrines until they caused death, sterility or inability to lay eggs with sufficiently strong shells to prevent breakage.

The species is now a scarce visitor, most of the records coming between October and April. The decline can be judged from the following figures taken *only from the mainland*: in 1959, the species was recorded on 28 dates from widespread localities; from 1962 onwards, no year has produced more than nine birds and some (1970) as few as three. Nearly all these mainland records in recent times have been from the New Forest or the coastal strip and the vast majority of birds have not stayed, only being seen on one date.

106. Greenland Falcon. *Falco rusticolus candicans**: No mention of any of the races of *F. rusticolus* in K & M. Meinertzhagen, however, records that there was one at Mottisfont on 18 January 1896 which 'descended on to a large white Aylesbury duck, carried it 20 yards and ate almost the whole of it'.

107. Merlin. *Falco columbarius*: This species occurs regularly on the mainland and the Island outside the breeding-season, most often between September and April. May and August records are rather exceptional and in the period 1950—1971, there has been one report each for June and July, viz.— one at Brownwich on 10 June 1961 (*H.* 22. Part 2) and one at Hengistbury on 26 July 1970 (*H.* 1970). Most birds are seen in the coastal strip, whilst the New Forest has also had regular records. Fewer are reported from the remaining inland areas though this may be due to lack of coverage because they were seen regularly around Damerham when that area was well watched.

Some observers believe the species has decreased in recent years. Ash found a considerable decline in numbers between 1949 and 1959 on a game preserve in the west of the county, but he was unable to assign a cause. It is harmless to game as 'its food appears to consist entirely of small birds taken in flight' (*B.B.* 53). Billett, too, finds it scarcer now and no longer a winter resident on Farlington Marshes. There is some evidence of recovery however, because the number of sightings has increased since the trough of 1963 and 1965. Today, 30 or 40 sightings a year would be typical, though some of these must be of the same individual seen on more than one occasion.

K & M accepted it as a breeding species, but the grounds for their decision seem unacceptable. In the *New Forest* (1862), by John Wise, it was reported that in three successive years Merlins nested in holes in trees in the Forest. A main point of identification was apparently the eggs, which — it was alleged — were smaller than those of a Kestrel. But as large Merlin eggs are bigger than small Kestrel eggs, this evidence is far from convincing. Wise did say that a male was shot at one nest in 1862 by Farren and K & M also refer to a clutch of three taken on 28 May 1887 in Doles Wood, north of Andover, and that four young were hatched from a repeat clutch. However, the *Handbook* ignores these records so the species has not yet been proved to breed with us.

Birds have been seen to fly southwards out to sea from Hengistbury and St. Catherine's Point, e.g. at St. Catherine's on 25 September 1960 (*H.* 22. Part 1), and also at Hengistbury on 11 December 1966 (*H.* 1966) and on 4 August 1968 (*H.* 1968).

108. Red-footed Falcon. *Falco vespertinus*: K & M mention four, all shot, between 1854 and 1882. The next occurrence is of a party of five (adult male, immature male, adult female, two immature females) at Bishop's Dyke in the New Forest on 16 May 1959, the first record of a party of Red-footed Falcons for Great Britain or Ireland. One or more were seen in the area until 6 June when the adult male was the last sighting. There was a marked influx into other counties in that spring and it is known to have extended to southern Sweden (*B.B.* 53. 417).

An immature male flew NW at Farlington Marshes on 29 May 1960 (*H.* 22. Part 1). In 1964 one was at Verely Hill on 17 May, an immature male was at Nursling gravel pits from 30 May to 9 June (joined by a second bird on the last date), a male was at Ashley Walk (New Forest) on 31 May and one was at Milford on 2 October (*H.* 23. Part 2). An immature male was at Rhinefield Walk (New Forest) on 7 June 1965 and a male was at Bishop's Dyke on 9 May 1970 (*H.* 1965 and 1970). All these were accepted by *British Birds* Rarities Committee.

109. Lesser Kestrel. *Falco naumanni*: K & M give two records for the Isle of Wight; a male shot in November 1895, and a female picked up dead in April 1903. Both were accepted by H. F. Witherby. None since.

110. Kestrel. *Falco tinnunculus*: Widely distributed throughout the county and the Island; taken overall, our least uncommon bird of prey. In some places recently it has been outnumbered by other raptors; in parts of the north it was certainly scarcer than the much less conspicuous Sparrowhawk until the mid 1950s (P. E. Brown), whilst a New Forest census in 1961 showed 14 pairs, i.e. fewer than Buzzard, Sparrowhawk or Hobby (*H.* 22. Part 2). Furthermore, numbers declined quite seriously in the years preceding *B.o.H.* (1963) but since then it has staged a marked recovery and is once again present in strength as a breeding species. Toxic chemicals have been blamed for the decline though game-keepers like the one at Hinton Admiral whose 'larder' held 25 corpses have not helped (Miss Popham). As a breeding species it is by no means confined to country areas for six pairs nested in the city of Portsmouth and its suburbs in 1970 (*H.* 1970).

Apart from ringing returns, several observations support K & M's note of spring and autumn migration. Moreau saw 14 migrating together near Lymington on 11 September 1922 (*B.B.* 16. 191). There are several records of birds arriving from the south off the sea in spring at St. Catherine's Point and Hengistbury whilst in autumn at those same two localities, birds have been seen to arrive off the sea, leave out to sea, or simply fly past (*H.* 1959/70).

A young bird ringed at Everley (Wilts.) on 21 July 1957 was recovered at Wootton (I.o.W.) on 30 December 1957. Of four birds ringed as nestlings (three by EC at Sway) two were recovered less than three months later and two in the following winter, 42 miles NNW, 65 miles NNE, 23 miles NE and 48 miles E. respectively (*B.B.* 43. 317 and 46. 302). An adult male ringed at Sway on 29 December 1952 was found freshly killed on a railway line two miles away on 25 March 1955 and a full-grown female ringed at Sway on 1 December 1957 was killed at Marcilly-en-Gault, SW of Orleans (France) on 27 February 1959 (*B.B.* 53. 476). An adult male ringed at Damerham on 24 March 1953 was released at Goodwood (Sussex) and recovered where ringed four days later (Ash). A young bird ringed on 21 June 1950 at Wooburn (Bucks.) was recovered at Basingstoke on 10 July 1951 (*B.B.* 45. 276). Two others travelled by October in their first year from Cambridgeshire to Hampshire (*B.B.* 20. 247 and 51. 185). A nestling ringed at Winchester on 14 June 1961 was recovered at Moncontour (France) on 24 September 1961 (*H.* 22. Part 3).

113. Black Grouse. *Lyrurus tetrix*: The indigenous stock which K & M said had never quite died out in the New Forest is no more. Several were seen near Picket Post (near Ringwood) in 1908, but they were getting very scarce then. A few were said still to remain in 1918/19 (Munn in *H.* 1920) though Cadman in a B.B.C. broadcast on 5 August 1962 said that they had died out in about 1909. An unsuccessful attempt to introduce them was made in the thirties and six were reported at Gorley and Somerley in October/November 1934 (*H.*).

In *The New Forest* (Tubbs, 1968, p.201) it is stated that 'local stories are told of black game surviving in the extreme north of the Forest until well after the 1939/45 war. At all events the species has now become extinct in the Forest for a number of years'. These local stories have not been put into print, but in *The Shooting Times* of 17 October 1963, Knowlton refers to several Greyhens in thick snow and frost at Foxhills Sewage Farm (Lyndhurst) in February 1954, 'birds with small heads perched incongruously on very plump bodies terminating in wedge-shaped tails'.

We are indebted to Stafford for the following extract from *A Royalist's Notebook*: the Commonplace Book of Sir John Oglander. Transcribed and edited by Francis Bamford. London, 1936.

Page 12. 'There were many heath-cocks and hens heretofore in our Island (Wight), especially in Borthwood Forest. In Anno Domini 1585 there were some and, as I take it, were destroyed about them. Old Forder of Newchurch was punished by Sr. Edward Horsey for killing of them with his gun.'

115. Red-legged Partridge. *Alectoris rufa*: K & M described it as resident and common in many parts of the mainland but very rare in the Isle of Wight. Apparently it gained its first real foothold in the county due to releases at Beaulieu and near Bournemouth around the 1860s and 70s (K & M). Meinertzhagen says that its nests were destroyed on the Mottisfont estate down to 1893 but that thereafter, when driving of Partridges began, it was common and about one bird in 12 was a Red-leg.

Today it is widely spread over the mainland but generally much less common than the Partridge. It is particularly widespread in the chalk to the north of Winchester and random counts in 1971 gave a ratio of 1:3 between Red-legs and Partridges, and in the same year a covey of over 50 was seen in this area. At Micheldever in 1953, between five and 20 pairs were estimated on a 1,000 acre estate (Jenkins) with an estimated ratio to Partridge of 1:7 in 1956. It is also well distributed along parts of the mainland coast, especially around the Gins (where birds are released) and Sowley, and counts of 30 and 50 respectively have been made there in recent years.

In other areas it seems less common. It has recently been reported as becoming scarce in the east of the mainland (*H.* 23. Part 3) and in a 1966 survey, only 12 pairs were located on 15,120 acres of New Forest heath and bog (*H.* 1966). In the early 1960s, the ratio with Partridges in the north of the county was estimated to be 1:50 (P. E. Brown) which suggests Red-legs are much less numerous there than round Winchester.

In some places it is quite uncommon. One at Chute and two at Netheravon near Andover in April 1951 were seen by Boys who commented: 'never seen before in this part of the county, this sudden influx most interesting'.

For the Isle of Wight, Commander Minchin (an authority on Island Partridges) has made the following statement: 'Red-legs in the Isle of Wight are almost certainly not native birds, nor have they flown from the mainland. They are hand-reared. Several attempts have been made in recent years to rear and/or introduce them. These attempts have always had very limited success; the reason for this is obscure.

Birds released have lived for a season or two, then disappeared. So far as I know, none have been observed to breed in the Island [written in the late 1950s].

The last release of birds was in July or August 1953 and 28 were put out near Bowcombe in the centre of the Island. These birds were reared and released by Mr. F. Cram, Ladylands, Shorwell. Another lot were reared and released between the wars but I am not sure of the year or number. They too disappeared'.

Two pairs nested on the Island in 1957 for the first time following recent introduction, and one pair in 1958 (Cram and Stafford).

The Isle of Wight reports still list individual sightings and so the species must still be scarce. Some reports carry no records at all.

116. Partridge. *Perdix perdix*: K & M described it as universally distributed in all districts of the county, including the Isle of Wight. Today it breeds freely in all suitable localities, being especially numerous in some area such as the chalklands around Winchester. From this area, two-hour drives in April 1971 would regularly reveal 60 or 70 just by stopping the car at frequent intervals and counting the birds in the roadside fields. It seemed that any field in the area was likely to hold pairs (JHT). On a 1,000 acre estate near Micheldever, further evidence of numbers in this chalk downland were counts of over 100 pairs in 1953 and 60—70 pairs in 1956, the estate being one where the species is well looked after (Jenkins). It is also common on the Island.

In 1965 it was reported to have become very scarce in some places (*H.* 23. Part 3) and the following year saw a further decline in the Silchester/Bramley area, whilst Boys said it had become very scarce around Sopley (*H.* 1966). This decline was not confined to Hampshire but was reported from various parts of Britain, though on the Winchester downs it continued to be numerous. As yet it is too early to say whether the decline is temporary or of a more serious nature.

117. Quail. *Coturnix coturnix*: K & M call it 'a rather scarce summer visitor to all districts' on the mainland and 'rare' on the Island. EC in *B.o.H.* says it had 'increased as a breeding species since K & M' but there is little evidence today to support that view. Indeed, in the *Atlas* survey, the species was only proved to breed in three mainland 10-kilometer squares with birds heard in seven others. The position at the time of writing suggests the species has further declined since K & M and is now a *very* scarce resident. The comment in *B.o.H.* was probably based on temporary increases in isolated areas, viz. — in 1953 it was really not at all uncommon on an estate in the west of the county being heard or seen from 26 May until 15 September, and again on 7 November; birds in other areas were thought to be related to increased barley crops on downland (Currie). Such records have not continued, and in some recent years, only one or two birds per annum have been reported. Further evidence of the decline comes from Mottisfont where on 3,000 acres there was always a single pair breeding between 1887 and 1901, with three pairs in 1893, but the keepers say that no Quail had been heard or seen since 1912 (Meinerthagen, writing in 1950).

It is occasionally recorded in winter, sometimes flushed by beaters at shoots, but most of these birds are from October to the year's end and one shot on 1 February 1939 at Wick near Christchurch (Jourdain in *H.* 14. 381) and one flushed on 5 March 1950 at Hill Head (Suffern) are unusual.

The one place where reports are a little more frequent than K & M is the Island where it is now *very scarce* rather than *rare*. Eight were shot between 1922 and 1954, including two in December, and the species was seen with young about 1947 or 1948 (Mrs. Bannerman). Six or more were killed at St. Catherine's Light in April/May from

1905 to 1908 but despite very full coverage in recent years, one caught at the Light on 10 May 1958 is the only spring record. Amongst other recent Wight records were birds at four different localities in 1970 (*H.* 1970).

Passage on the coast is suggested by records such as 1/3 at Hengistbury from 4 to 10 April 1966 and birds at St. Catherine's Point on 21 September 1963 (*H.* 23. Part 1) and 10 October 1970 (*H.* 1970).

In the spring of 1906 they were introduced from Italy on the estate at Heroncourt but they disappeared (Munn).

Quail

118. Pheasant. *Phasianus colchicus*: Munn writes (1906): 'The true-bred *P.colchicus* is, of course, now very rarely met with in the county, the commonest pheasants being hybrids between this and the Chinese (*torquatus*), Japanese (*versicolor*), Bohemian, and lately, the Mongolian varieties.'

EC asked Dr. Ash, who is exceptionally well-qualified to know the status of this species in the county, to give his opinion. This he kindly did as follows:

'I should summarise as follows: widely and commonly distributed throughout the county except in the built-up areas; least numerous in the New Forest and in an area to south-west of Ringwood. Feral birds are in variable numbers in all these areas, but practically everywhere high numbers are due to the release of hand- and brooder-reared birds. Locally there are many very high concentrations. A very few hand-reared birds were released in the New Forest in recent years but there is evidence that they did not survive for long. The following figures gleaned from 17 estates covering 40,340 acres well distributed in Hampshire give some indication of Pheasant numbers:—

Season	No. of Pheasants	
	Shot*	Released
1956–1957	13,079	14,791
1957–1958	15,104	12,901
1958–1959	13,995	17,445

Total	42,178	45,137
Average	14,059	15,046

*Including 'wild' birds

A common resident in the Island.'

119. Crane. *Megalornis grus*: One in K & M, shot in 1852. One found walking about a field at Keyhaven (date?) was found to be an escape (Watson).

An adult which had been seen flying about the mouth of the Beaulieu River since at least 5 November 1959 was found dead there on the 29th (*B.B.* 53. 417). Two at Eastleigh on 2 June 1961 (*H.* 22. Part 2) were accepted by *B.B.* and published (55. 571) erroneously as one only.

An unprecedented influx took place from 30 October to 3 November 1963, during which time at least 118 and possibly 187 birds were seen. Various reports concerned flocks of between 17 and 30, but 50 were reported off Milford on 1 November and a few lone individuals were seen as well. They were reported from the mainland and Island coasts, and inland at Bishop's Dyke and Chandlers Ford. It is impossible to say how many were really present because several reports may have concerned the same flock (*H.* 23. Part 1).

One was at Shalfleet (I.o.W.) on 22 October 1967 (*H.* 1967).

[**Demoiselle Crane.** *Anthropoides virgo* *: 23/25 October and 9 November 1927 near Beaulieu, one with three, and on 9 November two, Spoonbills — 'may have been an escaped bird' (Paddon in *B.B.* 21. 182).]

120. Water Rail. *Rallus aquaticus*: K & M say: 'Resident in suitable localities throughout the county and in some places not uncommon'.

The elusive nature of this species makes its present status uncertain. Some certainly breed, and in the *Atlas* survey, birds were recorded as present or in territory in almost half of the mainland 10-kilometer squares so that it *may* be a widespread resident in the county. Some reports confirm this view so that EC in *B.o.H.* states: 'said to breed in some numbers on the Rivers Test, Meon and Wallington', whilst in the same book, a report by Ash says that in 1952 several were resident between Alderholt Mill and Damerham along Ashford Water on the Hants/Dorset boundary. Ash also said that several bred between Damerham and Martin, and that it was plentiful at Fordingbridge, although latterly it has become very rare in those areas in summer, possibly due to increased grazing of waterside rough meadows. Furthermore, the proven cases of breeding have been very widespread. However, the nests found in the last 20 years have been very few in number, so there is a possibility that it is only a scarce resident. A detailed survey is needed.

A clutch of 10 was destroyed at Great Salterns Lake within three miles of the centre of Portsmouth on 31 May 1952.

What is known for certain is that the species is a widespread and not uncommon bird from August to April. Most reports are of single birds or small numbers but some localities seem to be especially favoured. Christchurch Harbour has held the highest counts in recent years, numbers reaching 50 on occasions (e.g. December 1966 — *H.* 1966/67/68), but Titchfield Haven has been a well-used area (e.g. 17 on 16 January 1961 — *H.* 22. Part 2) and Browndown held 40 on 13 November 1960 (Heath *et al.*).

Most of these winter birds are probably immigrants as opposed to Hampshire stock. Migration is suggested by records at St. Catherine's Point. 10 were killed there between 1905 and 1910 (one in May, four in October, five in November), four were seen in March and many on 1 April 1911, and birds were recorded in the area in March/April 1962, September 1962, March/April 1968 and October 1968 (*H.* 1968 and 22. Part 3).

Other than these St. Catherine's records, the Island position is much as the mainland. Nicholl said that it bred at Osborne in the years 1906 to 1916 and others say that it is still an all the year round resident and that it breeds. More are recorded in winter and there were 12 round flood-water at Yarmouth in December 1952 (Adams).

Fluctuations are reported from time to time. Some are local, such as the reported decrease round Winchester since 1927 owing to illegal trapping in watercress beds. Others are more general, hard weather seeming to be a major factor, and the species apparently suffered heavily from the winter of 1962/3, though it seems to have recovered subsequently.

Water Rail

121. Spotted Crake. *Porzana porzana*: K & M call it 'a very local resident'. Since then it has apparently become less numerous for though it is now recorded annually, it is *very* scarce and reports are almost wholly in autumn and winter.

An analysis of records from 1959 to 1970 shows birds reported every year from the mainland, sometimes with only one per year (1965) and probably never more than six. All birds save four were in the period August/January with August/October having about 60 per cent of the total. The four exceptions were one at Stanpit on 30 July 1968 (only just outside the above period) and three in March, two of these being found dead at Farlington Marshes (*H.* 23. Parts 2 & 3). None were seen in February, April, May or June, the absence in February being a little surprising for January produced at least eight in this period. All records were from the coast except for one at Braemore on 30 January 1967, and one found dead at Mottisfont on 22 August 1966 which was sent to the Cumberland House Museum, Southsea (Forster). Most reports were of single birds but some were of twos and threes with five at Redbridge in severe cold on 5 January 1963 (*H.* 23. Part 1). None were reported from the Island. This picture of 1959/70 seems typical of the position today.

There has been no proven breeding since K & M. In 1913 it was described as a scarce resident in the parish of Milford, 'being met with in this part of Hampshire in almost every month of the year but no record of a nest being found in the parish' (*B.o.M.*). The report most suggestive of breeding was of one present for some weeks on the heaths of East Dorset and West Hampshire, when the peculiar clicking note was frequently heard, but it is not known whether it bred (Jourdain in *B.* 22. 55).

The only Island records since K & M are one caught at Carisbrooke on 27 November 1906 and kept alive for two months (Wadham *per* Munn), one found dead between Sandown and Alverstone in October 1951 and another found dead on 26 April 1954 at Whitely Bank (Mrs. Seabroke).

One found 'dodging the traffic' in London Road, Portsmouth, on 15 October 1954 was kept alive for four days by Inspector Hindle of the R.S.P.C.A., and released on Bedhampton Marshes. It was wrongly reported as a Quail in the *Portsmouth Evening News* of that date.

123. Baillon's Crake. *Porzana pusilla*: Since the four specimens 'procured' (latest, July 1886) and mentioned by K & M there has been only one and that on the Island. On 4 January 1943 one was brought in at Chale (near St. Catherine's Point) uninjured but in very poor condition; it was carefully identified and on release flew off normally (*I.o.W.* 1943, p.391).

124. Little Crake. *Porzana parva*: K & M admit four, 1866, 1885 and two undated. The only subsequent records are of a male at Farlington Marshes from 14 to 20 September 1959 (*B.B.* 53. 417), and a female in the Stanpit area from 21 to 27 March 1970 (*H.* 1970).

125. Corncrake. *Crex crex*: K & M call it 'a common summer visitor to all parts of the county including the Isle of Wight'. Today, breeding records are rare and it has been reduced to a *very* scarce visitor, mainly on passage.

This decline seems to have started at the turn of the century. K & M were not aware of a general deterioration in numbers but they did note a scarcity throughout the county in 1904, the year before their book was published, so this may have been the start of the slump. By 1913/14, H. G. Alexander's report on the Land-rail enquiry (*B.B.* 8. 83) said that not only were there very few in the county, but to the east and west of the New Forest 'the decrease has reached vanishing point' and that 'it seems to have begun at least 20 years ago'. In 1907 it 'was neither seen nor heard' in Hampshire (*Bull. B.O.C.* 22 and *B.B.* 2. 248). In 1911 it is mentioned among a 'list of rarer birds to be found' near Winchester (*W.* 1915) and, while saying that several were heard in the summer of 1910 in the Laverstoke district, Munn adds that 'it was becoming very scarce'.

Since the 1930s, every example seems to have been thought worth recording. There are definite records of regular spring and autumn (particularly autumn) passage at Damerham in the 1950s (Ash) and of breeding in 1938, 1948, 1957 and 1959. An analysis of records from 1959 to 1970 showed only 25 birds from the mainland with none in three years and only single birds in five others. All the reports were from March to November with about half of them in August/September. On the Island, only three were reported during this period apart from 'more than for many years past' at Combley Farm, Havenstreet, when corn was being cut in August and September 1966 (*I.o.W.* 6. Part 1). If this survey is compared with the similar analysis for Spotted Crake, it will be seen that the present species is the more scarce of the two. Apart from the 1959 Damerham breeding, a pair nested at Hook/Brownwich in the same year, the latest proven cases (*H.* 21. Part 3). None were reported in the *Atlas* survey.

Perhaps the decline on the Island was a little later. Thirty were killed at Rowlands in mid-September 1905 and Munn, quoting Morey's *Guide to the Natural History of the Isle of Wight*, says it had decreased as a breeding species there but was found abundantly in autumn. In 1923 it was thought to be steadily decreasing and there were no records until 1930 when one was at Bembridge. In September 1938 a farmer found 13 when cutting barley near Newtown and in 1952 and 1953 a few turned up in autumn at Brook.

There are three records since K & M of presumably wintering birds. One was near Christchurch on 4 February 1935 and had been there for a week (*B.B.* 28. 314). One was near Bedhampton on 11 February 1951 (*B.B.* 45. 38) and the third was near Basingstoke in mid-December 1951 (Simond in *The Field* of 19 January 1952 and 2 February 1952).

Birds were at St. Catherine's Light in April 1906 (killed), 5 May 1908 (killed) and the night of 31 August/1 September 1956 (one caught, one seen).

One was amid traffic in Emsworth High Street on 9 November 1967 (*H.* 1967).

126. Moorhen. *Gallinula chloropus*: An abundant resident on the mainland and the Island wherever there is fresh or brackish water, but Meinertzhagen says that a breeding population of between 31 to 44 pairs through the nineties on the Mottisfont estate was reduced to 15 pairs in 1945. There have been temporary declines at times, such as in the severe winter of 1962/3, but generally the species seems to thrive. There are three records of breeding in winter, the latest example being at Brading in 1965 (*I.o.W.* 5. Part 10).

Counts of 30 to 50 in quite small areas are fairly common in winter, and in recent years Farlington Marshes, the Gins area, Brading/Bembrdige, Winchester sewage farm and Badshot Lea have had populations exceeding 100 (*H.*), whilst a careful count at Farlington Marshes on 13 December 1967 revealed 268 birds. These populations are spread over the areas concerned but Hollom saw 120/150 *together* in cold weather at Thorley Marsh (I.o.W.) on 9 March 1947. Another unusual count was of 40 at sea off Hill Head in very cold weather on 8 February 1956 (Brice).

Ringing has shown that some of these winter birds are immigrants from the continent, e.g. one adult ringed Amsterdam 18 May 1932 shot at Ringwood 26 December 1933 (*B.B.* 28.141); immature ringed Denmark 27 August 1961 trapped at Stockbridge 29 October 1961 (*B.B.* 56.530); one ringed Holland 5 December 1962 killed at Alresford 6 January 1963 (*B.B.* 60.72); immature ringed Holland 6 September 1965 killed near Ringwood 9 December 1965 (*B.B.* 60.72). Birds ringed in Hampshire in winter have often been recovered abroad, e.g. one ringed Stanpit 27 November 1962 recovered Denmark 20 April 1963 (*B.B.* 57 Supplement — the second British-ringed Moorhen to be recovered in Denmark); one ringed Winchester 25 January 1965 recovered Holland 20 April 1965 (*W.* 1965); adult ringed Fordingbridge 15 February 1969 recovered Belgium 22 April 1969 (*B.B.* 64.160).

Other birds ringed in Hampshire have shown local movement or movement to other counties such as Wiltshire and Hertfordshire.

Two were killed at St. Catherine's Light on 22 February and 24 October 1957, almost certainly migrating birds.

127. Coot. *Fulica atra*: Munn thought that by 1918/19 it had increased since K & M and found it very plentiful. Today it breeds all over the county in reasonable numbers though not quite as widespread and certainly not as abundant as the Moorhen which is less demanding in its breeding habitat. It is persecuted in places and Meinertzhagen reports a breeding population of 28/32 on the Mottisfont estate in the nineties reduced to about six pairs through the activities of the water-keeper. It breeds rather sparingly on the Island, though regularly in places.

Flocks of two to three hundred are common in winter in many harbours, on many lakes and on the River Avon above Ringwood. Christchurch Harbour is likely to hold the highest numbers, 1,062 being counted there in February 1971 (*H.* 1971) and a cold weather concentration reaching 1,000 on 29 December 1961 (*H.* 22. Part 2). Eling (317 on 15 February 1970) and Titchfield Haven (over 300 in some winters but Suffern says 'nothing like as numerous' as 30 or 40 years ago) are two other much-used coastal areas, whilst 800/1,000 by Hayling Island toll-bridge on 2 February 1952 (Mrs. Highway) ranks amongst the highest-ever counts. On the Island, Bembridge seems to hold the largest gatherings and numbers there have steadily increased in recent years (Adams) reaching 402 on 18 January 1970. Yateley gravel pits, Alresford Pond, Avington, Northington and Fleet Pond are examples of inland waters holding winter concentrations, but some favourite waters such as Sowley Pond have been much less used recently because of disturbance by fishermen.

Winter flocks begin to build up in September and disperse about the end of March.

One ringed as a juvenile at Abberton (Essex) on 24 November 1962 recovered at Milford-on-Sea *ca.* 25 January 1963 (*B.B.* 57. Supplement). One ringed at Westeinderplassen (Holland) on 9 June 1968 killed in Christchurch Harbour on 16 January 1971 (*H.* 1971).

128/129. Bustard spp. *Otis*: E. J. M. Buxton has kindly drawn attention to an old record not known to K & M:

'In October 1633, there happened to come onto our Island (Wight) six birds called bustards, never seen or known here before. They settled at Shalcombe at Mr. Jordan's who, wondering at the novelty, stalked with a horse unto them and killed one of them with a gun, never having seen such a bird before. He sent him unto me for a great rarity'.

A Royalist's Notebook (Sir John Oglander). Edited by E. F. Bamford, 1936, p.96.

128. Great Bustard. *Otis tarda*: An adult female was shot at St. Mary Bourne near Whitchurch on 12 January 1910. The weather was most unsettled with gales, snow, hail and rain from the SW, W. and NW (*B.B.* 4. 190).

K & M calling it 'A rare accidental visitor formerly resident' give a few instances in the eighteenth and nineteenth centuries, the last being on 2 January 1891 (shot), recorded in *The Field* of 10 January.

129. Little Bustard. *Otis tetrax*: One of the Eastern form was shot at Stockbridge on 14 December 1935 (*B.B.* 29. 252).

Early in January 1944 one appeared at Avington and later one was reported at Bighton and Chawton Park near Alton, perhaps the same bird (*H.* 16, and noticed without comment in the review of that number in *B.B.* 40. 31).

Both the bustards are described as rare accidental visitors in K & M.

131. Oystercatcher. *Haematopus ostralegus*: It was first reported to have bred for a few years prior to 1922 on the northern shore of the Island and a c/4 was found there on 13 May 1922 (Poole in *I.o.W.* 1. 143). In 1923, it was said of the same area that a pair or so lay but are generally robbed (*I.o.W.* 4. 179). The first mainland breeding record was in 1934 (*W.* 1949. 12), discovered by Heycock, *not* 1938 as stated by Jourdain in *B.* 1937/8. Today it has consolidated this foothold and breeds regularly in modest numbers. In the area of the Newtown reserve, eight pairs nested in 1971 (Mrs. Seabroke). On the mainland, Needs Oar and Pennington hold the largest concentrations (11 pairs and seven pairs respectively in 1970), whilst the Lymington saltings are probably a regular site. Langstone and Christchurch Harbours have also had recent records. 14 pairs nesting in the very limited area at Needs Oar in 1971 represents the largest mainland concentration to date, three of the nests being in fields a little away from the shore (JHT, *H.* 1971). 15 pairs at Newtown in 1953 is the most for the Island.

Outside the breeding season it is also increasing and nearly always to be seen along the coast with Langstone Harbour easily the main locality. The increase has been noted at several points (Christchurch Harbour and Calshot, for instance), but it is reflected by the following peaks from Langstone: March 1962, 250; October 1962, 382; January 1963, 400; September 1963, 415; October 1964, 470; December 1966, 500; December 1967, 583; February 1968, 600; February 1970, 730; October 1971, 905. Portsmouth Harbour, with 600 in September 1971, probably shares some of its birds with Langstone. Otherwise, the Titchfield Haven area, Dibden Bay, Calshot, Needs Oar, Pennington and Christchurch Harbour are the main areas where gatherings of 100 plus are likely to be found (especially at high tide), anything in excess of 300 being considered *very* high at the time of writing. Calshot has tended to have its peaks in September, indicating passage, and Christchurch Harbour has also experienced autumn peaks (for full details of autumn migration at Christchurch, see the paper by Rogers and Webber in *H.* 1970). On the Island, Newtown with 40/50 seems the main place with only low counts from elsewhere.

Birds have been seen in the beams of St. Catherine's Light in spring, late summer and early autumn.

There are occasional records of birds inland as far north as Basingstoke.

A nestling ringed at Blakeney (Norfolk) on 27 July 1953 was found at Netley on 30 January 1957 (*Norfolk Bird Report* 1968). A young bird ringed near Beaulieu on 20 June 1949 was recovered at Bricqueville, Manche (France) on 8 August 1952 (*B.B.* 46. 302).

133. Lapwing. *Vanellus vanellus*: Widespread as a breeding species on the mainland and Island. It nests freely in the coastal fields, has come to terms with arable farming on the chalk better than some species, and a 1966 survey of 15,120 acres of New Forest heath and bog (half that type of vegetation in the Forest) revealed 95 pairs

(*H.* 1966). Several observers from 1912 onwards reported a decrease in breeding birds and the opposite opinion has been expressed in more recent years but no quantitative data exist to make a positive statement on such trends. Cold weather can cause temporary declines; the New Forest population was reduced to less than a tenth by the winter of 1917 (Longstaff in *Ibis*, October 1926).

Large flocks occur in autumn, winter and spring; 1,000 or more are not uncommon and even 4,500 at Timsbury on 19 February 1966 (*H.* 1966), 3/4,000 at Blashford on 26 January 1967 (*H.* 1967) and counts of 3,000 plus from Emsworth on 19 December 1945 (*H.* 16. 303) and the Gins in 1968 and 1972 (*H.*). These large concentrations are mainly coastal but they also occur inland at places such as Eastleigh Airport, Middle Wallop airfield, Chilbolton and the Avon above Ringwood. On the Island, Newtown has held up to 2,000.

Cold weather movements are often observed, their direction depending on the weather that caused them. Large numbers are sometimes involved, e.g. 29,000 flew S. over the south east of the county in the last eight days of 1961 (*H.* 22. Part 2) and 7,500 flew S. at Hengistbury on 8 January 1967 (*H.* 1967).

Adults in a flock of up to 40 are occasionally seen in early June in the same area as breeding birds (Champion and Rees).

Nine birds ringed in the county as young between 1927 and 1963 have been recovered in various parts of France, Spain and Portugal in winter. Also, one ringed at Damerham on 17 January 1959 was killed at Oviedo (Spain) on 29 December 1963 (*H.* 23. Part 2).

One ringed in Lancashire on 6 July 1952 as a young bird was recovered a year later at Basingstoke (*B.B.* 45. 380).

Lapwing

134. Ringed Plover. *Charadrius hiaticula*: Munn, writing of 1918/19, considered that it had already increased considerably both on the mainland coast and in the Island since K & M (1905). K & M thought it was increasing, but since they describe it as 'a common resident' on the mainland coast (less so on the Island), it would seem that the increase has come to a halt. Today it breeds in modest numbers on the mainland coast (30/47 known pairs each season in the years 1966/71) and smaller numbers in the Island (11 pairs in 1966). No *complete* survey has been carried out, so allowing for pairs missed, the total number of breeding pairs may exceed 60, nearly all along the Solent coast. Newtown (eight pairs 1966) has been the main Island locality (*I.o.W.* 6. Part 1). Needs Oar (up to 15 pairs), the Hurst/Lymington stretch (up to 18 pairs) and perhaps Calshot (up to 9 pairs) are the mainland's chief areas but most suitable spots from Stanpit to Hayling Island have produced records in the past twenty years. Occasionally it breeds well away from the coast, viz. — Hatchet Pond, 1936/8 (Venning), leaving in 1939 probably because of work on Beaulieu aerodrome; Janesmoor in 1965, and on the disused Stoney Cross aerodrome in the same year (Webber *in litt.*); Stoney Cross again in 1967 (*H.* 1967). There have been very few breeding records from Langstone Harbour.

Outside of the breeding season, gatherings of up to a few hundred are likely to occur at many localities on the mainland coast, peaks in August/September and to a lesser extent May indicating passage (e.g. *H.* 1969 and 1970. For full details of autumn migration at Christchurch, see the paper by Rogers and Webber in *H.* 1970). Winter flocks are somewhat erratic, numbers fluctuating much from year to year with some localities being used regularly and others intermittently. Langstone Harbour usually holds the highest counts but whilst numbers reached 1,000 there in December 1956 (*H.* 19), no more than 100 were reported in December 1970 (*H.* 1970). Needs Oar (the main nesting area) is an example of an area where winter counts are usually very low — often less than 10 — but where high counts occur on isolated dates, e.g. 300 on 20 October 1965 (*H.* 23. Part 3) and 250 in a high-tide roost on 13 October 1962 (*H.* 22. Part 3). A particularly large gathering built up at Emsworth in 1945 to 2,300 on 22 November and 3,600 on 19 December (P. E. Brown in *H.* 16. 30). On the Island, flocks are also erratic, 1,000 at Newtown in the last few months of 1957 being unusually large, but mainland numbers were low at that time and perhaps this is the answer to the erratic winter flocks, that they move about a great deal.

Occasionally birds are recorded well inland, always singletons or very small parties and mainly at times of spring and autumn passage.

Apart from the higher counts at migration times already mentioned, there is other evidence of movements. Large numbers are sometimes heard in spring at night moving past St. Catherine's Light, mostly from mid April to early May (e.g. 1963, 1965 and 1966 — see *H.* for those years). To a lesser extent, nocturnal movements have been heard there in autumn (*H.* 1966). Daylight movements have been seen as well, birds moving east along the coast in April, or flying off inland such as seven which flew NNE from Farlington Marshes over the Portsdown Hills at 07.10 hrs. on 6 May 1953.

The leg of a nestling ringed in Denmark in 1932 was found at Hengistbury in January 1941 (*B.B.* 38). Another nestling ringed in Denmark on 4 June 1936 was recovered in the county on 23 September 1936 (*B.B.* 33. 71). A bird ringed in the Frisian Islands on 25 June 1954 and recovered there in the summers of 1958 and 1961 was found dead at Hurst on 29 January 1963 (*B.B.* 57. Supplement). A nestling ringed at Ottenby (Sweden) on 20 May 1961 was found dead at Yarmouth on 26 January 1963 (*I.o.W.* 1963/4).

135. Little Ringed Plover. *Charadrius dubius*: A new breeding species since K & M, but still very uncommon. Their last record was in 1879, and its next recorded appearance was in 1951 when two were identified by Fleet Pond (Boswall) on 4

June, and one at Milford on 26 July (Tyson). In the following year a pair hatched two out of a c/4 in a disused gravel pit near Sway, between Brockenhurst and Lymington (A. and N. Pearce-Smith and EC), but it is not known whether the young reached the free-flying stage. Other suitable gravel-pits at Ibsley and Stoney Cross were under observation that year but no birds were seen. One bird was, however, seen at Needs Oar on 12 July (Kinsey). On 6 April 1953 a pair were back at the same gravel-pit near Sway; a scrape was found but no eggs and between 12 and 15 May the site became flooded due to heavy rain and the adults were not seen again (EC). The site is now much less suitable.

One was at Farlington Marshes on 8 May, 4 and 14 August 1954 (*H.* 19. 83) and in April 1958 (P.G.). A pair were present at one site on the west shore of Southampton Water in the breeding seasons of 1955, 1956 and 1957; display flights were seen but no nest or young were found despite a careful watch (Palmer *et al.*). In 1957 a pair nested unsuccessfully in another locality (Goodhart) whilst in 1958 a pair nested successfully at a new site. 1959 saw yet another unsuccessful nest at yet another site (*H.* 21. Part 3) and then in 1962 a pair raised two young at a gravel pit in the south (*H.* 22. Part 3). Three pairs were present in 1963; coition was seen and scrapes were found but nesting was not proved (*H.* 23. Part 1). All these breeding attempts since the Sway ones were in the coastal stretch, centred around Southampton Water. All subsequent breeding has been in the far north of the county, viz. — 1965, three pairs bred, two of them successfully (*H.* 23. Part 3); 1966, two pairs (*H.* 1966); 1967, two pairs possibly bred (*H.* 1967); 1968, one pair bred successfully (*H.* 1968); 1970 breeding probable but not proved (*H.* 1970). It has almost become a regular breeding bird on the mainland therefore, though in the smallest numbers as yet.

As a passage bird, an analysis of records from 1959 to 1970 show it to be of annual occurrence in increasing numbers. From one bird in the autumn of 1959 and two or three birds in 1960, numbers increased to at least nine in the spring and 10 plus in the autumn of 1969 (*H.* 1969) and to at least 23 in the autumn of 1970 including six at Fleet Pond on 9 August and five flying west at Christchurch Harbour on 22 August (*H.* 1970). All the spring birds have been in April or May, about two thirds of these being in April. The autumn movement has mainly been in July and August (especially August) with a few in September and the last on 4 October. They have been from the coast and from inland gravel pits, sewage farms and lakes.

There have been no records from the Island.

136. Kentish Plover. *Charadrius alexandrinus*: The last record in K & M was in 1874. The first record *ever* from the Island was one killed at St. Catherine's Light on 9 October 1910 (*B.B.* 6. 324). One in May 1910 (*B.B.* 5. 208), one in September 1930 (*B.* 22. 54) and one in April 1934 (*B.B.* 28. 54) were the only records up to 1948. From 1948 to 1970 there have been 22 birds, most years having at least one but 1959 being the best with six individuals. They have all been from the coastal area and all save two between April and October, the monthly totals being: April, four; May, one; June, one; July, four; August, three; September, six; October, one. The exceptions were two at Black Point on 23 December 1959 (Yorke-Norris in *H.* 21. Part 3).

137. Killdeer Plover. *Charadrius v. vociferus*: K & M give one, in 1859, 'the first ever procured in England'. None since.

139. Grey Plover. *Charadrius squatarola*: A common winter visitor and passage bird to the mainland coast; much less numerous on the Island. Some are present through the summer.

Langstone Harbour usually holds the largest winter numbers with as many as 400 in January 1968 (*H.* 1968) and over 300 in several recent years. Hayling, Calshot/Fawley, Needs Oar and the Pennington area are the other main wintering places, but any count of over 200 would be very high and the annual maxima from each one is very likely to be below 100. Needs Oar acts as a high tide winter roost for a considerable stretch of nearby shore. On the Island, Newtown seems to be the only place of consequence for the species with a peak of around 30/50 each year. West of Hurst the species is very scarce. In Christchurch Harbour for instance, the annual maxima for 1970 and 1969 were three and four respectively (*H.* 1969 and 1970).

Some years show peaks in March and September/October, indicating passage, e.g. at Langstone Harbour, peaks of 450 on 16 March 1969 (*H.* 1969), 300 on 7 September 1963 (*H.* 23. Part 1) and 400 on 22 October 1960 (*H.* 22. Part 1); at Needs Oar, a peak of 200 on 1 March 1964 (*H.* 23. Part 2). Movement is also *seen* on the coast, e.g. 76 moving east at St. Catherine's Point on 20 April 1969 (*H.* 1969); from Langstone in 1956, 15 flew NW over Portsdown Hills on 18 April, 25 flew NNE over the same hills on 13 May and three flew NW on 26 May, also over Portsdown.

Numbers in June and July vary considerably. In 1970, there were less than 20 reported from the whole county in this period and 1969 produced very few. In other years counts are much higher, Langstone again being the only place likely to hold other than odd birds. At that locality, 350 were seen on 1 July 1961 (*H.* 22. Part 2) whilst in 1968, 65 and 127 respectively were the highest June and July counts (*H.* 1968).

In K & M there is a surprising statement that Meade-Waldo had seen large numbers at Hatchet Pond (four miles from the coast); the only subsequent inland records are one unsubstantiated by any details whatever of 50 passing over Ringwood on 26 April 1947 (*H.* 17. 194) and a bird at Fleet Pond on 22/23 May and 12 June 1970 (*H.* 1970). The *Handbook* describes the species as a rare vagrant inland.

A male was killed at St. Catherine's Light on 5 November 1907 (*I.o.W.* 1922).

A nationwide estuaries count in mid-December 1971 showed Hampshire holding about 25 per cent of this species' total.

140. Golden Plover. *Charadrius apricarius*: A common winter visitor that is very occasionally seen in summer. Most of the records are from October to March/April. Within this period, flocks occur mostly in the coastal fields, on the chalk hills and in the wider river valleys such as the Avon. The Gins area, Pennington and Brownwich are regular coastal sites: Danebury and Winnall Down are typical chalkland haunts. It is less numerous on the Island but at Newtown it is described as a regular passage migrant.

These mainland winter flocks frequently reach the 2/300s and may occasionally reach 600. Even higher counts have been about 1,000 coming from the E., north of Andover, on 8 December 1941 (*H.* 15. 192), 1,000 at Bisterne on 27 March 1962 (*H.* 22. Part 3), 1,000 plus flying over Thornhill in cold weather on 27 December 1965 (*H.* 23. Part 3) and 750 at the Gins on 20 December 1970 (*H.* 1970). 400 at Atherfield on 27 February 1955 and 350 at Newtown on 13 December 1970 (*H.* 1970) were large counts for the Island.

May and July records are scarce and since K & M there appear to be only four birds in June, one over Langstone Harbour on 11 June 1955 (Champion *et al.*), two at Pennington on 15 June 1966 and one at Farlington Marshes on 29 June 1966 (*H.* 1966). Several years have had the first returning birds in August and September, and in 1954, E. L. Jones saw 150 on 19 September.

Summer plumage birds in spring have included both *C. a. apricarius* (southern race) and *C. a. altifrons* (northern race). At the Gins in 1963, 1964 and 1968, only *altifrons* was seen. Of the 1,000 at Bisterne in 1962, many were in summer plumage and showed the characteristics of *altfifrons* (Ash and Mills). Round Andover, birds are usually *apricarius* but occasionally there are a few *altifrons* (E. L. Jones). Some of a flock of 23 near Martin on 31 March 1952 were *apricarius* (Ash).

At St. Catherine's Light, singletons were killed on 3 April 1908 and 10 February 1910 and there have been several records of birds heard there at night, mainly in March (e.g. in 1962 – *H.* 22. Part 3 – and 1969 – *H.* 1969).

The breeding trill was heard amongst a party of 16 at East Hayling on 15 April 1956 (K. Brown and Henty).

142. Dotterel. *Charadrius morinellus*: K & M called it a rare visitor on both migrations and said that it had decreased considerably in late years. To their records can be added: 'four on high ground S. of Dunbridge 17 May 1895'; regular spring visitors to Farley Mount in the nineties (Meinertzhagen). Munn, in his notes for a second edition, said that it still visited Bransbury Common (near Andover) on spring migration and that a pair were seen there in the spring of 1920. The only other completely authenticated mainland records are of six on 6 May 1934 near Gorley – Fordingbridge area – (*B.B.* 28. 175), three in winter plumage on Farlington Marshes on 26 September 1955 (Billett), one at Hengistbury on 31 August and 2 September 1960 (*H.* 22. Part 1), one at Keyhaven on 27/29 August 1969 (*H.* 1969) and one at Needs Oar on 24 August 1971 (*H.* 1971).

Two records from the Island. One was killed by telegraph wires near Brook in 1922 and was set up by Jeffrey, a Newport taxidermist (*I.o.W.* 1.4.204). Around 1954, a tired and tame bird was on Freshwater golf course.

143. Turnstone. *Arenaria interpres*: Widespread along the mainland coast in winter and on passage, though rather scarce on the sandy beaches west of Hurst. Island numbers smaller than those of the mainland. Usually scarce through June and July.

From August to May, birds are spread out all along suitable stretches of the mainland coast, gathering together at various spots in high-tide roosts. Such congregations may exceed 100 (e.g. at Pennington, Needs Oar, Calshot, Warsash, Dibden Bay and Langstone Harbour) in winter or on passage. 400 plus at Langstone Harbour on 4 March 1957, a sudden peak from 36 on the previous day (P.G.), represents the largest count, whilst at Hamble, 236 flighting from a high-tide roost on 4 September 1956 (Dennis) and 231 doing likewise on 17 September 1957 (Truckle) are also high counts. All three records were at times when passage would be expected, as were 282 at Calshot in August 1971.

Spring passage is from March to mid-May. Apart from peak counts at that time, parties have been seen leaving Langstone Harbour to the N. or NW over Portsdown Hills (e.g. 254 seen to leave on fine evenings in May 1964 between 15 and 20 – *H.* 23. Part 2), birds are seen moving E. along the coast (e.g. 119 passed Hurst between 19 April and 3 May 1969 – *H.* 1969) and birds have been heard at night over St. Catherine's Light (e.g. the nights of 19/20 and 20/21 May 1961 – *H.* 22. Part 2).

June and July records are usually very few but on 7 June 1953 and 24 June 1956 there were as many as 40 in Langstone Harbour and such records occur occasionally. Birds are seen in summer plumage. August/October sees the return passage when some areas may have their annual maximum counts.

The only inland records are of a party calling over Fordingbridge at 23.25 hours B.S.T. on 28 August 1953 (Ash) and two at Winnall on 13 May 1962 (*H.* 22. Part 3).

Numbers from the Island are smaller. Parties of 25 to 40 occur along the north coast with 50 plus over Quarr on 24/25 April 1968 (*H.* 1968).

62

144. Short-billed Dowitcher. *Limnodromus griseus*: K & M record one (under its old name of Red-breasted Snipe) in September 1872, and one in October 1902: both shot. Both these specimens were identified by Nisbet as the Short-billed species after examination of their skins in the City Museums and Art Gallery, Leicester. He identified the 1902 bird as of the race *L.g. hendersoni* from its bill, tarsus and wing measurements. The Short-billed and Long-billed species, much less the three races of the former, had not been separated when K & M wrote.

There has been one possible since — on 5 September 1943 at Stanpit Marsh (Miss Popham in *B.B.* 38. 18), but this sight-record was rejected as 'not convincing' by I. C. T. Nisbet in an article in *B.B.* 54. 343 et seq. reviewing the occurrences of the species in Great Britain.

Dowitcher spp. *Limnodromus griseus or scalopaceus*: One at the Gins 5 October/2 November 1963 called like a quiet Greenshank and so was probably Short-billed (*H.* 23. Part 1). Two at Stanpit 23/27 September 1968 (*H.* 1968). One at Pennington 13/14 September 1970 (*H.* 1970). All accepted by *British Birds* Rarities Committee.

145. Snipe. *Capella gallinago:* K & M say: 'A local resident on the mainland largely reinforced in winter'. They added that it was not known to nest on the Island. This status would apply equally today except that single pairs have nested at Brading around 1919 (*I.o.W.* 1. Part 4. 179), 1967 (*I.o.W.* 6. Part 2) and 1968 (*I.o.W.* 6. Part 3).

Breeding numbers have fluctuated. In 1918/19, Munn noted that it was increasing its breeding range and was constantly found nesting in new localities. As late as 1949, far more were said to nest at Alresford than did 20 years before (Shelley). On the other hand, a marked decrease as a breeding species was noted round Burghclere, Kingsclere and Baughurst (P. E. Brown) and at Titchfield Haven (Suffern) in the 15 years before *B.o.H.* (1963) and numbers were much reduced by the cold winter of 1962/3. In a survey of 15,120 acres of New Forest heath and bog in 1966 (half the area covered by such vegetation in the Forest), 16 pairs were located. In the first four years of the *Atlas* survey, although birds in territory were found in most 10-kilometer squares, breeding was proved in only seven.

Winter gatherings build up from October onwards. The largest of these in recent years have been: Christchurch Harbour during February 1970, 500; November 1961, 450; Titchfield Haven in November 1961, 400; Brading on 18 February 1968, 400 (*H.* for those years). Otherwise, concentrations between 100 and 350 are recorded from several localities every winter, mostly from the coastal area but also from inland localities such as the Avon valley, Stratfield Saye, Ash Vale gravel pits and Winnall. On 19 December 1954, 170 flushed at Titchfield Haven in wisps of up to 48 and 30 flew out to sea, unusual behaviour for Snipe flushed there, but EC saw 97 behave in a similar way at Keyhaven on 3 March 1959.

The main spring departure is in April. 40 birds in various sized flocks rose from Stanpit in the late afternoon of 29 March 1958 and made off very high to the NE.

Since Newtown Marsh was flooded in 1954 it now hardly ever occurs there, although formerly it was numerous outside the breeding season (Mrs. Seabroke).

One ringed at Stanpit on 1 January 1964 was killed by a cat at Vyshniy Volochok (about half way between Leningrad and Moscow) on 1 May 1964 (C.H.O.S.G.). Two ringed at Stanpit on 2 December 1961 and 25 November 1962 were killed in France within two months of ringing at Le Verdon and Brignogan respectively (C.H.O.S.G.). Another ringed in Christchurch Harbour in 1964 was found dead at Berville sur Mer (France) on 22 September 1967 and one ringed at the same place on 1 January 1964 was shot in Guernsey on 1 December 1964

(C.H.O.S.G.).

One ringed on 24 August 1960 in Finland was shot in January 1962 at Stockbridge.

146. Great Snipe. *Capella media*: A rare visitor. One shot and another seen the same day at Mottisfont in late September 1897 (Meinertzhagen) (not recorded in K & M). One shot in September 1905 near Newtown Stacey (Munn in *H.* 9. 1); another shot near Fordingbridge on 3 September 1934 (*B.B.* 28. 244); and one is said to have been watched for three minutes at 20 feet on 19 October 1949 at Kingsley Pond, near Alton, by Chard of the Alton N.H.S. This is recorded as it stands (*H.* 17. 340) and without any description so is not worth much. There is another curious record in *H.* 14. 257 to the effect that one was seen on 26 December 1938 near Dockens Water (New Forest) 'as in 1937', but there is no record of one in the *H.F.C.* report covering 1937. Yet, though Jourdain was then the editor of *H.F.C.*, these two records are passed without comment; he was, however, a sick man at the time and probably overlooked them.

147. Jack Snipe. *Lymnocryptes minimus*: K & M say: 'A winter visitor to all parts', adding that it was 'not abundant'. This fits the species today. It is to be found on the mainland coast, inland and on the Island in widespread localities from September to April. It has been reported five times in the first week of May, once on 23 June 1957 at Titchfield Haven (Dennis *et al.*) and once from 8 August/September 1960 at Dibden Bay (*H.* 22. Part 1).

Numbers at any locality are always small. The highest counts in recent years have been 22 at Ash Vale gravel pit on 4 November 1966 and 18 February 1967 (*H.* 1966 and 1967), 17 at Farlington Marshes in January 1967 (*H.* 1967) and 16 at Christchurch Harbour in March 1970 (*H.* 1970).

148. Woodcock. *Scolopax rusticola*: Breeds in all parts of the county where suitable habitats exist but it is only thinly distributed, except in the New Forest and one or two other localities where it is reasonably concentrated. It is equally widespread in winter. 1943 and 1947 were good years; also November/December 1956 and 1958 in West Hampshire. 1961 was a very good breeding season in the New Forest (*H.* 22. Part 2).

The status of this species is exhaustively discussed in *The Woodcock in the British Isles* by W. B. Alexander in *Ibis*, volumes 87 to 89 and reprinted as a booklet. This enquiry was carried out in 1934/5 on behalf of The British Trust for Ornithology and the following information in so far as it relates to the years between K & M (1905) and 1935 is condensed from that (p.19 in the booklet).

'Not known to breed Hayling Island and absent or very scarce in summer on chalk areas such as Winchester, Selborne, Alton and Middle Wallop. At least 12 pairs bred in Harewood Forest and many on the Sussex border between Haslemere and Petersfield. Estimated minimum of 100 pairs in New Forest and at least 12 pairs breeding on a 10,000 acre adjoining estate.'

In 1960, 40 roding birds were located in the west of the county and 11 within a mile radius in the Chandlers Ford/Hursley area (*H.* 22. Part 1). The *Atlas* survey showed breeding proved or suspected in most 10-kilometer squares with more in the southern half of the mainland than in the north.

K & M say that the species was resident in the Island also but they give no breeding record after 1834; they give the extent of the breeding range on the mainland but not a word about that in the Island. In 1935 it was not known to breed there (W. B. Alexander) and EC in *B.o.H.* raised doubts about *regular* breeding on the

64

Isle of Wight. However, eggs or young were seen in 1930, 1952, 1953, 1956, 1958, 1960, 1961 and 1962 (*per* Mrs. Seabroke) and 12 roding males were found in West Wight in 1958, and then in 1963 the breeding population in Parkhurst and Brighstone Forests was said to be 'about normal' (*I.o.W.* 1963/4) so perhaps the species is present in greater strength than reports suggest.

Single birds have been seen at St. Catherine's Point in March, April and November and at Hengistbury in March.

A young bird ringed in Eastern Bohemia on 16 May 1938 was recovered at Winchester on 26 October 1943 (*H.* 16. 296). One ringed near Stockholm on 15 June 1952 was shot at Basingstoke on 12 October 1952 (*B.B.* 49. 445).

150. Curlew. *Numenius arquata*: Winter flocks may be between 1,000 and 2,000 at favoured coastal areas such as Langstone Harbour and the Gins, and gatherings of a few hundred may be seen at several localities east of Hurst. West of Hurst it is not at all common and the annual maximum in Christchurch Harbour may not reach double figures (e.g. eight in 1969 — *H.* 1969). The coastal gatherings begin to disperse through March and heavy spring passage from March to early May is indicated by high counts at this time, by numbers *seen* moving east along the coast, and by birds *heard* at night (e.g. over Portsmouth in 1960 — *H.* 22. Part 1). Inland in winter the species is very scarce or rare except for the lower Test valley where birds are seen regularly flying up and down river in the Romsey/Timsbury area with as many as 68 at Romsey in January 1971 (Thelwell).

There has been a considerable increase as a breeding species since K & M, in whose day it only very occasionally bred. This increase seems to have been going on since the early thirties and now quite a few pairs breed both in bogs and open heaths in the New Forest. About 44 pairs were found there in 1960 (Tubbs *et al.*) and 29 pairs were located in 15,120 acres of New Forest heath and bog in 1966, about half the area covered by that type of habitat (*H.* 1966). They return to their Forest grounds from early March. It does not breed at the moment outside of the New Forest and its immediate surrounds of connected heath (*Atlas* survey).

Through May/June, counts are low on much of the coast though a few hundred may be in Langstone Harbour. Numbers build up from mid June and peak numbers (up to 2,000 at Tournerbury on 16 September and 2,858 at East Hayling on 22 August 1962 — *H.* 22. Part 3) in July/September indicate passage.

They apparently did not breed in the Island in K & M's time, nor do they now. Otherwise the pattern is like that of the mainland only numbers are smaller, 1,000 seen by Hollom on 24 May 1946 at Newtown being the maximum.

Some have been seen to cross from the mainland to feed on the ebbing tide at Yarmouth and Newtown and return to the mainland at dusk. In 1962, 1963 and 1964, up to 400/500 were seen to arrive regularly in winter around 10.00 hrs. G.M.T. at Needs Oar from the direction of Newtown regardless of the state of tide (JHT).

A juvenile ringed in S. Sweden on 26 May 1935 was picked up nearly dead and very emaciated at Beaulieu on 6 August 1937 (*B.B.* 33. 72). A nestling ringed in Holland on 12 May 1957 was shot in Bournemouth on 25 November 1957 (*B.B.* 54. 501).

151. Whimbrel. *Numenius phaeopus*: K & M quote Wise (New Forest) saying that they have been met with in the depth of winter. A few still very occasionally overwinter in Langstone Harbour and elsewhere.

It is really just a bird of passage, numbers usually being greater in spring than in autumn and most reports are from the coastal area. Further inland, birds are occasionally heard at night or seen by day as they pass over (e.g. parties heard flying up-river over Fordingbridge at night in May — Ash), but it is rare to find them on the ground in those parts.

The first arrive in March or April and the main spring passage is in April/May. The largest flocks are nearly always in Langstone Harbour where up to *ca.* 200 were seen in late April 1958 and 150 in early May (P.G.). A count of over 100 elsewhere would be unusual. Otherwise, small to moderate numbers are seen moving east along the coast or past St. Catherine's Point, although a vast easterly movement went on all night at St. Catherine's on 30 April/1 May 1965 (*H.* 23. Part 3). Spring movements from Farlington Marshes leave between NW and E, the northerly ones over the Portsdown Hills.

June records are infrequent. Autumn passage is mainly from July/September with a few late individuals occurring in October or even November. Langstone Harbour is again likely to hold the largest number, the highest counts there being a rather exceptional 300 on 27 July 1963 (*H.* 23. Part 1) and 200 on 1 August 1960 (*H.* 22. Part 1). On 21 August 1956 a party of 37 left Langstone Harbour at 13.00 hrs. G.M.T. to the S. gaining a considerable height. On 21 July 1952 two flew over Hurst at 16.00 hrs. G.M.T. at about 500 feet calling loudly and going straight out to sea in a SSW direction (EC).

Island numbers are much smaller apart from St. Catherine's movements.

154. Black-tailed Godwit. *Limosa limosa:* The status has altered entirely since K & M where it is called 'an occasional visitor to our coast on the spring and autumn migration' and 'is not included in the Island lists'. Now it may be seen on the mainland coast in every month of the year, sometimes in large flocks. As early as 1910 Troubridge classed it as a *regular* autumn migrant, and from 1930 to 1947 Hampshire was one of the five southern counties from Kent to Devon which together provided two-thirds of the total numbers in the United Kingdom (*B.B.* 39. 192). Yet Suffern had never seen it in the Hill Head (Fareham) area between 1920 and 1945, after which he often saw it, sometimes in numbers. It was unknown on the Island until 1938 (*B.B.* 49. 261) but it is now seen regularly though in smaller numbers than those of the mainland.

The pattern is rather erratic, differing from year to year and also from place to place within any one year, but the following features can be seen.

1. Nearly all records are coastal. Since the two in K & M there have only been eight inland records involving 14 birds in March, April, May, August and September, although birds seen leaving inland from Langstone Harbour in spring must mean migrants pass overland.

2. Numbers west of Hurst are low. In Christchurch Harbour during 1968, only seen on 14 dates with a maximum of six. 1967 at the same locality produced birds on only 10 dates with a maximum of eight.

3. Very few localities hold large gatherings but *they* are used regularly. On the mainland, Langstone Harbour usually produces the highest count, Hayling Island, Portsmouth Harbour, Titchfield Haven, Dibden Bay (until reclamation), the Gins and Pennington being the other main areas. Newtown is the only Island site used by numbers, the maximum being 270 on 26 December 1965 (*I.o.W.* 5. Part 10).

4. Winter numbers at these favoured mainland sites commonly exceed 100 and the yearly peak for a locality may be at this time, e.g. 650 at Langstone Harbour on 17 December 1960, 550 at the Gins on 10 December 1960 (*H.* 22. Part 1) and 600 at Titchfield Haven on 11 November 1962 (*H.* 22. Part 3).

5. Peak counts may occur in March/April, e.g. 750 at Langstone Harbour on 28 March 1959 (H. 21. Part 3) and on 19 April 1965 (H. 23. Part 3). These must be passage birds and small easterly movements are seen along the coast. At Langstone Harbour birds are seen to leave to the N. or NW over Portsdown Hills in the evenings, e.g. 494 on 22 April 1962 (H. 22. Part 3), 180 on 29 April 1967 (H. 1967) and 182 on 27 April 1969 (H. 1969).

6. June numbers are usually low and counts at favoured localities are often in single figures.

7. August/September often sees annual maxima for some localities, much more so than March/April. Langstone Harbour had such peaks in September 1964, August and September 1967, September 1968 and August 1969, these counts all being between 600 and 650. Similarly, there were 700 at Tournerbury on 15 September 1963 (H. 23. Part 1) and 500 at East Hayling on 14 August 1967 (H. 1967).

The largest counts are of 1,500 in company with 1,000 Curlew and 2,500 Redshank near Tournerbury Ring on 19 October 1952, the result of a high spring tide, and 900 at the same place on 29/30 August 1953 (both Shackleton — B.B. 48. 281).

There is no evidence yet of breeding but an immature picked up dead by EC at Keyhaven on 22 October 1945 and sent to the late B. W. Tucker proved to be of such small measurements that he was of the opinion that it could *only just* have crossed the Channel.

Measurements of a bird found dead at Thorness Bay in February 1957 were sent to K. Williamson who replied that it was almost certainly a male of the Iceland race *islandica* which is thought to winter chiefly in Ireland. The question is discussed in B.B. 50. 524—526. Another, which was seen to die at Farlington Marshes on 30 August 1957, was also of this race as proved by the length of its bill (78—79mm.) against 83—89mm. of the male *limosa*; (the female's bill is longer) (Renyard *in litt.*).

155. Bar-tailed Godwit. *Limosa lapponica:* K & M say: 'A regular spring and autumn visitor to all our coasts, very rarely seen inland'.

Today, as a winter visitor, it is only numerous in the harbours around Portsmouth. In Langstone Harbour, numbers from October to March are commonly between 100 and 300 with as many as 700 plus in January 1966 (H. 1966). Less frequent counts on E. Hayling suggest that numbers there and in the Hampshire part of Chichester Harbour are also high for 690 were counted on 22 December 1968 (H. 1968) and around 1,000 on 6 November 1971 (H. 1971). Elsewhere on the coast in winter numbers are low and the species is almost entirely absent from some places. Ashlett, Calshot and Hurst are used quite regularly and numbers around 50 are likely to be found at those localities. At Needs Oar however, the species is seen very infrequently, only being recorded on three dates in both 1969 and 1967 in regular weekly visits, and numbers are very low in Christchurch Harbour.

Large numbers occur on spring passage, moving eastwards through the Solent or past St. Catherine's Point. At St. Catherine's for instance, 1,188 flew east on 18/19 April 1969 by day (H. 1969), a vast easterly movement continued all night on 30 April/1 May 1965 (H. 23. Part 3) and 1,055 flew east in one and a half hours on the afternoon of 27 April 1960 (Simmonds, Walker *et al.*). One of the largest Solent movements was on 28 April 1962 when 1,307 passed Needs Oar between 06.00/09.25 hrs. B.S.T. (JHT) and observers reckoned some 7,650 moved through in the course of the whole day. The peak movement is usually in the last two weeks of April and perhaps the first days of May. At such times numbers may be high in places where it is not numerous in winter; for example, 200 plus were in Christchurch

Harbour on 8 May 1935 (Smith in *H.* 13. 221).

Numbers in June and July are lower, Langstone Harbour again being the only area where numbers of any consequence are likely to be found, and counts have been as high as 300 on 4 June 1966 and over 100 have been there in July. Autumn passage is usually small compared with that of spring.

On the Island (other than birds on migration) records of small numbers are quite widespread on the northern shore, many of the sightings concerning odd birds or single-figured counts.

It has not been recorded inland since K & M.

156. Green Sandpiper. *Tringa ochropus*: Recorded in all months. Wintering birds from November to February are reported every year from several inland, coastal and Island localities. At these times, ponds and watercress beds in the upper Itchen valley are particularly favoured with eight at Alresford on 17 February 1963 (*H.* 23. Part 1) and seven there on 9 February 1964 (*H.* 23. Part 2). Spring migration is very small, perhaps around a score of birds occurring from March to early May. Few are seen through the rest of May and most of June and there is no suspicion of breeding. K & M thought it might but courtship display seen by Bundy near Tichborne, where two remained until 19 June 1952, is the most that has happened.

The largest numbers occur on autumn passage which is from late June or early July to October, August nearly always seeing the peak movement. Dibden Bay has been the most favoured locality in recent years, the annual peaks there from 1963 to 1970 being 22, 23, 22, 23, 10, 24, 15 and 22. Inland, 15 at Alresford on 23 August 1953 (Jenkins) and 15 at Kingston Common on 18 July 1958 (Mrs. Maddox) are the highest.

Six flew over Hurst to SW on 14 August 1968 (*H.* 1968).

157. Wood Sandpiper. *Tringa glareola*: From the late thirties onwards it has been much more often reported than when K & M wrote. They called it a rare occasional visitor but in the last 20 years or so it has been observed with increasing frequency and small numbers are now reported every year.

Wood Sandpiper

There is a *very* small spring migration from April to early June (mostly in May) when typically less than half a dozen are seen. Most are from July to September (occasionally into October), the bulk of these being in August and nearly all from the mainland coast. In the last 20 years there have only been 15 inland records, an exceptional count being 11 at Woolmer on 12 and 16 August 1970 (*H.* 1970), and there were only about half a dozen Island records from K & M to 1962, since when the species has been seen there almost annually. On the mainland coast, counts may occasionally reach double figures, e.g. 10 plus at Farlington Marshes on 13 August 1954 (*H.* 19. 85), 11 at Dibden Bay on 9 September 1965 (*H.* 23. Part 3), 12 in the Pennington area on 24 August 1966 (*H.* 1966) and 11 in Christchurch Harbour on 21 August 1970 (*H.* 1970).

159. Common Sandpiper. *Tringa hypoleucos*: Recorded in all months. A few birds winter every year, and then perhaps up to 50 birds are seen on spring passage from March to May. Occasional reports occur of birds staying through summer (e.g. at Newton in 1959 and some subsequent years — *I.o.W.*), but although K & M accepted that it occasionally nested in the county, there is no evidence of that since. In fact the only statement to that effect is that of Munn himself in his notes for a second edition, where he says that 'no doubt it breeds at Brading Harbour on the reclaimed land where Morey found it in May and June'.

The largest numbers occur on return passage from late June to October, the bulk passing through in July/August. Counts of 20 to 40 are then reported regularly from favoured coastal localities with as many as 50 at Stanpit on 15 August 1959 (*H.* 21. Part 3), at Dibden Bay on 20 July 1960 (*H.* 22. Part 1), and at Pennington on 15 August 1969 (*H.* 1969). Together with Farlington Marshes, those localities are usually the ones with the largest numbers.

At all times, the mainland coast is the area producing the bulk of the records, inland areas and the Island having the same pattern with smaller numbers. Eight at Winchester sewage farm on 14 August 1963 (*H.* 23. Part 1) and seven at Fleet Pond on 21 August 1970 (*H.* 1970) are the most from inland localities in recent years.

It is one of the few waders that occur regularly on the south coast of the Island, apart from those flying past that area. There were at least 19 at St. Catherine's Point on 17 May 1964 (*H.* 23. Part 2) and a flock of 25 on the shore there on 9 September 1956 flew S. out to sea and were watched out of sight (Marr *et al.*).

One ringed at Farlington Marshes on 2 September 1962 was recovered at Salvaterra de Magos (Portugal) six days later (*H.* 22. Part 3).

For a detailed account of migration at Christchurch Harbour, see *H.* 1970, p.42.

161. Redshank. *Tringa totanus*: Meinertzhagen never saw it at Mottisfont in the nineties: the first breeding date there was 1907. The increase noted in K & M appears to have been going on ever since, although two observers express the opinion that as a breeding species it has decreased in the New Forest in the last 30 years (Branford) and at Titchfield Haven during the same period (Suffern). Still, 34 pairs bred in the SE part of the Forest in 1960 (*H.* 22), 66 pairs over the whole of the Forest in 1961, and 45 pairs in 15,120 acres of Forest heath and bog in 1966 (that is half the area covered by such vegetation — *H.* for those years). It breeds freely on the Island, all along the mainland coast and in the water-meadows of the river valleys throughout the county, including the Upper Itchen, the Test as far as Whitchurch, the Anton, the Bourne Valley and, sparingly, by the Loddon between Basing and Sherfield. Examples of breeding numbers are: Gins, 20 pairs, 1969; Pennington, 20 pairs, 1969;

Langstone Harbour, 28 pairs, 1968; Bembridge, 15 pairs, 1966. In 1953 at least three pairs nested on rye grass/clover leys at Micheldever half a mile from the nearest water (Jenkins). Munn states that they leave the river valleys in July after the young are reared for the coast and tidal estuaries, but birds are seen on at least some of the inland breeding grounds all through the winter. At times they frequent cress-beds even as far inland as Andover. The first birds return to their breeding grounds inland from February/mid-March which is about the time that the coastal flocks break up, and the first returns to the coast are in mid-June.

Gatherings at Langstone Harbour, Hayling Island and Portsmouth Harbour quite often exceed 1,000 between July and February. The highest estimates have been 3,500 at Langstone on 31 July 1961 (*H.* 22. Part 2), 3,100 there on 28 July 1962 (*H.* 22. Part 3) and 3,000 there on 13 November 1966, 4 August 1953 and 11 October 1953 (P.G.). 2,500 on 19 October 1952 (Shackleton) and 2,000 plus on 22 December 1968 (*H.* 1968) have been the highest counts from Hayling Island and 1,472 in December 1969 the most from Portsmouth Harbour (*H.* 1969). The four figure counts in July and August indicate the size of the passage at that time.

From the rest of the mainland coast, gatherings of up to 300 are common at favoured spots such as Pennington, Needs Oar and Warsash, counts even exceeding 500 at times, but 1,000 at Warsash on 22 August 1961 (*H.* 22. 2) was very high for anywhere other than the three main localities in the east. Island gatherings at a few places on the northern shore may also reach a few hundred.

The species was very badly hit by the cold weather of 1962/3. About 50 dead were found at Needs Oar and about 30 at Hurst, and following this, 1963 breeding numbers were very low, e.g. seven pairs in the Forest, seven at Gins, four at Pennington and one at Stratfield Saye (*H.* 23. Part 1).

Examples of passage in spring and autumn: many heard at St. Catherine's Light on the night of 19/20 May 1961 (*H.* 22. Part 2); 42 leaving Langstone Harbour to WNW on the evening of 11 April 1966 (*H.* 1966); a flock of 22 left Hurst out to sea to the west, calling loudly, on 15 August 1967 (*H.* 1967).

There are several ringing returns, amongst which may be noted: birds ringed as young in Northumberland, Lincolnshire and Kent have been recovered in Hampshire in winter; pulli ringed at Farlington Marshes on 2 July 1960 and 25 May 1961 were retrapped there on 12 April 1968 and 20 September 1967 respectively; one ringed in Denmark on 2 May 1960 was shot at Hayling Island on 24 January 1963.

161. Iceland Redshank. *Tringa t.robusta**: An adult female picked up dead at Beaulieu on 12 January 1936 was considered by H. F. Witherby to belong to this race (*B.B.* 29. 325) but the *Handbook*, by putting a query after 'Hants', would appear not fully to accept this record. The remains of a bird found at Hurst on 7 April 1956 had a wing measurement of 167mm, which would indicate that it was of the Iceland race (Billett). In November 1971, members of the Wash Wader Ringing Group caught 19 Redshank on Hayling Island and from the measurements and weights reported that 'few if any' were of the Icelandic race (*in litt.*).

162. Spotted Redshank. *Tringa erythropus* : Much more often reported today than when K & M wrote. Since the Gins has been covered regularly, it has shown itself to be easily the main locality in the county for this species, indeed one of the most-used in Britain. Monthly maxima at the Gins have been: (— = datum not available)

1960	6	4	10	23	1	3	18	18	42	55	30	16
1961	17	29	10	22	1	0	10	·27	40	40	6	20
1962	15	17	10	12	7	1	20	20	70	50	20	22

1963	3	0	–	7	2	12	14	40	50	55	21	2
1964	6	6	6	9	0	2	–	61	40	22	7	7
1965	4	5	4	11	2	7	–	–	51	15	2	2
1966	5	6	4	5	2	7	24	43	36	25	8	7
1967	5	12	5	3	4	19	37	32	52	22	15	5
1968	4	6	9	6	2	2	16	35	35	31	25	2
1969	6	6	12	3	0	1	13	33	24	21	10	11
1970	8	6	12	7	0	12	–	23	–	35	15	25
1971	6	11	7	6	5	1	–	70	65	60	50	–

The county pattern can be seen from this, i.e. some wintering birds, a very small passage in March/April with very few or none in late May and early June. From late June to October, return passage brings the greatest numbers. The mainland coast follows this pattern but numbers are much smaller, counts usually being in single figures and winter birds rather scarce. High counts elsewhere have been: 55 arriving at Hayling Island from Thorney Island on 24 August 1967 and 50 likewise on 6 September 1967 (Bundy); 28 at Farlington Marshes in October 1965 (P.G.); 27 at Tanners Lane on 1 October 1969 (*H.* 1969); 17 at Dibden Bay on 20 August 1964 (*H.* 23. Part 2).

From 1964 there has been a handful of inland records, e.g. from Woolmer and the sewage farms at Aldershot Camp, Basingstoke and Winchester.

It is a new species to the Island since K & M, the first having been seen by Adams at Yarmouth on 17 September 1951 flying NW towards Pennington and calling. Since then records have become more frequent and Spotted Redshanks have occurred annually in small numbers since 1961 (*I.o.W.* for those years).

One ringed in Holland on 7 April 1960 found dead on Hayling on 6 January 1963 (*B.B.* 60. 74), the first British recovery of a foreign-ringed Spotted Redshank.

164. Lesser Yellowlegs. *Tringa flavipes**: The first was watched at close quarters between Keyhaven and Pennington by Sharland on 28 September and 2 October 1953. Subsequent records have been:

One, Keyhaven, 29 August 1954 (Kinsey).

One, Farlington Marshes, 20/28 September 1954 (P.G. *et al.*), was photographed by Des Forges and Paulson. All the above three recorded in *B.B.* 48. 364.

One, Farlington Marshes, 19/21 July 1962 (P.G. *et al.* – accepted by *British Birds* Rarities Committee).

One, Farlington Marshes, 29 June/1 September 1963 (*B.B.* 57. 268. – also accepted by Rarities Committee).

Kelso remarks that the Yellowshank (species not stated) has been obtained at Hayling; this would refer to 1912 or earlier and is of no value as it stands nor is it included in the *Handbook* list of the times either species has been seen or obtained.

165. Greenshank. *Tringa nebularia*: For the past 10 (perhaps 20) years at least, a few have wintered annually, especially at Pennington, Needs Oar, Newtown and Langstone Harbour. These are usually small numbers or single birds, the most being at Newtown where there were 14 on 29 November 1970 and 15 on 12 December 1970 (*H.* 1970).

Spring passage is small, around 30 birds a year being reported, nearly all from the coast but occasionally inland, e.g. several flying N. over Basingstoke on the night of 9/10 April 1961 (*H.* 22. Part 2) and one at Fleet Pond on 27/28 April 1968 (*H.* 1968). Few are then reported in late May and the first half of June, but one stayed through the summer of 1953 at Newtown (Curber).

Numbers are greatest on autumn passage from July (even late June) to October, the peak usually being in August/September. Langstone Harbour is the main locality, with a typical peak between 50 and 80 but higher counts have been made, the highest being 106 on 18 August 1962 (*H.* 22. Part 3) and 100 in September 1966 (*H.* 1966). Elsewhere at favoured localities on the mainland coast and at Newtown, the peaks may well reach 20/40 for any one place, 55 at The Gins on 24 September 1961 (*H.* 22. Part 2) being the most away from Langstone. 30 at Langstone Harbour on 12 November 1966 was unusually late for such a number (*H.* 1966). Inland records on this passage have occurred in most recent years, mainly from ponds and sewage farms such as those at Avington, Aldershot, Avon village, Basingstoke and Longparish. Numbers inland are very small but six were at Winnall on 29 August 1963 (*H.* 23. Part 1).

Nine out of a party of 22 plus at Pennington on 23 September 1956 left SW over Hurst till out of sight, the whole party apparently excited and calling continuously (Kinsey). It has been heard at night at St. Catherine's Light.

One ringed at Farlington Marshes on 21 July 1967 killed Baie de Somme (France) on 8 August 1969. An adult ringed at Farlington Marshes on 17 September 1967 was killed at Bures, Troarn (France) on 15 August 1968 (*B.B.* 64. 163). These were the fourth and fifth British-ringed Greenshanks to be recovered in France.

168. Terek Sandpiper. *Tringa terek* *: One probable on 16 May 1925 was seen by Penrose in Christchurch Harbour and his full description was published as a 'probable' (*B.B.* 19. 53). The first definite record was one seen at Pennington by Hobby, Williams and Wiseman on 25 May 1963, which appeared again at the same place on 31 May (*B.B.* 57. 269). It was accepted by *British Birds.*

169. Knot. *Calidris canutus*: K & M say 'a winter visitor to all our coasts, not uncommon on the shores of the mainland during autumn and winter.' We do not get the enormous packs that occur on other coasts; in fact over recent years, the only sites to be used *regularly* in *winter* are: Langstone Harbour, the maximum being 850 plus on 5 January 1964 (*H.* 23. Part 2) but the typical winter peak is around 3/400; E. Hayling, where the highest count was 700 on 22 December 1968 (*H.* 1968); Portsmouth Harbour, the maxima there being 1,150 in February and 1,350 in March 1970 (*H.* 1970); Newtown, where the species has become more numerous since the marsh was flooded in 1954, winter peaks subsequently exceeding 100 quite often and even exceeding 200 on occasions, with 400 on 29 January 1967 the most (*I.o.W.* 3. Part 2).

Elsewhere on the coast in winter, with the possible exception of Calshot and Ashlett, it is usually absent or perhaps present on occasional dates, but every now and again a sizeable flock may appear at a high tide roost or feeding ground. Thus at Needs Oar in 1968, the only records were of two single birds until 150 appeared at a high tide on 21 December (*H.* 1968) and 300 were present at the same locality, also at a high tide roost, on 17 January 1965 (*H.* 23. Part 3). Sometimes these isolated counts can be very large, 1,500 being seen at Needs Oar on 9 October 1957 (*W.*) and ca. 1,000 at Hamble on 16 March 1955 (Dennis).

Spring migration in April/May is small; a few are seen passing E. along the Solent coast and at times passing St. Catherine's Point, and birds are seen to leave northwards from Langstone Harbour in the evenings (e.g. 15 left NNE over Portsdown Hills at 18.03 G.M.T. on 6 May 1953).

Few are seen in June or early July, though groups have occurred at these times e.g. 40 in Langstone Harbour on 4 June 1961 and 50 there on 1 July 1961 — *H.* 22. Part 2). They may be in full summer plumage. From August to September and continuing into October, there is a larger return passage and at this time small flocks are likely to be seen all along the coast other than the beaches west of Hurst.

The only inland records have been one in puddles on a barrack's square at Barton Stacey on 13 September 1960 (Rees) and one at Alresford on 22 March 1962 (*H.* 22. Part 3).

170. Purple Sandpiper. *Calidris maritima*: K & M say 'a winter visitor to our coasts but not in large numbers and less common in the Isle of Wight'. Not much of our coast is suited to this species and an analysis of records for the winters 1959/60 to 1970/71 shows the following:

1. Only two mainland sites are used regularly, Hengistbury and Southsea Castle. Four was the maximum at both localities until the last two winters of the series when the maxima at Hengistbury were six and 11, and at Southsea seven and 10. Birds were recorded at Hengistbury every winter and at Southsea Castle on all but one of the last 10 winters of this period. The first usually arrive in October or November but they have been as early as August. The last are in April or May.

2. Elsewhere on the mainland coast, single birds were recorded on about a dozen isolated dates from six localities within the above period except for one at Pennington on 7 July 1969 (Wiseman), and 1970 at Hurst when 11 were present in January and up to three on six other dates (*H.* 1970).

3. On the Island it seems as uncommon as on most of the mainland but seven at Old Pepper Rock (Main Bench) on 30 March 1964 (*H.* 23. Part 2) suggest that this rather suitable area could be a haunt of the species. Most of the rocks at Main Bench are almost impossible to cover regularly so birds could be missed.

171. Little Stint. *Calidris minuta*: Most records are of birds on autumn passage from late July to late October with the peak usually occurring in September. Numbers at one locality are typically below 10 but they may be a little higher on occasions and exceptional years occur when greater counts are made, such a time being 1960 when as many as 56 were at Pennington on 4 October, 50 at Dibden Bay on 26 September and 30 at Langstone Harbour on 9 October (*H.* 22. Part 1). On this passage they may be seen at all suitable points on the mainland and north Island coasts, though Island records are fewer and concern *very* small counts.

Less than 10 a year would be typical on spring passage and some years produce none at this time. They would be in April/May. June birds are rare but they have occurred (e.g. one at Farlington Marshes on 2 June 1968 — *H.* 1968).

All recent years have produced a few wintering birds from November to March, especially at Black Point. The largest winter counts have been 12 at Christchurch Harbour on 4 December 1960 (*H.* 22. Part 1) and 10 at Gilkicker on 4 February 1962 (*H.* 22. Part 3).

Inland in autumn, up to three were at Winchester sewage farm in 1966 and one was at Woolmer in 1970.

173. Temminck's Stint. *Calidris temminckii*: K & M give four mainland and two Island records. There have been no subsequent Island records, but from the mainland there have been quite a few, especially since 1954 when observer coverage has been much more complete; indeed since 1954, most years have produced a few records.

Between K & M and 1954 there were: four at Keyhaven on 12 May 1935 and one on 25th (*B.B.* 29. 324 and *H.* 13. 221); three possibles near Beaulieu on 1 October 1942 (*W.* 1949. 13); two at Titchfield Haven on 30 October 1948 (*H.* 17 219); one on four dates in late September 1951 at Dibden Bay.

From 1954–1970 inclusive, at least 27 individuals were seen on the mainland coast. All but five years produced birds but three was probably the most for any one year. They were mostly in May or September with records also from July, August and October. In 1971, one was at Farlington Marshes on 6 June (*H.* 1971).

175. White-rumped Sandpiper. *Calidris fuscicollis**: One at Titchfield Haven on 17 October 1963 (Cheke, Davison and Suffern — *B.B.* 57. 269).

176. Pectoral Sandpiper. *Calidris melanotos**: At least one of the two Sussex birds reported in *B.B.* 41. 186/7, was seen on 12 October 1947 to fly across the Emsworth channel well into Hampshire (Ferguson-Lees *in litt.*), though it was not seen to land.

One, Farlington Marshes, 7/11 September 1952 (Billett and Rees, *B.B.* 47. 279).
One, Farlington Marshes, 29 September/6 October 1957 (*H.* 20. 26).
One, Farlington Marshes, 26 July/6 August 1959 (*B.B.* 53. 418).
One, Farlington Marshes, 6/29 September 1961 (*H.* 22. Part 2).
One, Redbridge, 6/8 October 1961, was probably the same one recorded at nearby Eling Great Marsh 8/10 October in the Southampton N.H.S. report (*H.* 22. Part 2).
One/two, Pennington, 25 August/8 September 1962 (*H.* 22. Part 3).
One, Dibden Bay, 27 October 1963 (*H.* 23. Part 1).
One, Keyhaven, 10/17 September 1964 (*H.* 23. Part 2).
One, Stanpit, 9 October 1966 (*H.* 1966).
One, Stanpit, 7 September 1968 (*H.* 1968).
Two, Keyhaven, 11 September 1968 (*H.* 1968).
One, Farlington Marshes, 25/27 October 1969 (*H.* 1969).
At least five (two caught and ringed) in the Hurst/Pennington area, 5/26 September 1970 (*H.* 1970).
One, Dibden Bay, 11 September 1971 (*H.* 1971).
One, Farlington Marshes, 3/17 October 1971 (*H.* 1971).

178. Dunlin. *Calidris alpina*: K & M say 'a very common visitor to all our coasts.' Subsequently, observers have from time to time reported local changes but today it it still a very common winter visitor to suitable coasts, becoming abundant in the harbours of the east. At Langstone Harbour (including the area round Portsmouth airport which is used at high tide), numbers have reached or exceeded 20,000 in December 1959, December 1966, January 1968, January 1969 and January 1970, with 24,000 the maximum. At Portsmouth Harbour numbers have reached 15,000, and at Hayling Island 12,000. Elsewhere on the mainland and north Island coast, winter groups are widespread and may reach 1/2,000 at favoured places such as Warsash, Dibden Bay, Calshot, Needs Oar, Pennington, Christchurch Harbour and Newtown. At such places counts may very occasionally be even higher (e.g. 7,000 have been recorded at Pennington), especially at high tide roosts.

Spring movement is from March to early May, the bulk in April. Birds may be seen moving E. past St. Catherine's Point (e.g. 450 E. on 27 April 1960 — *H.* 22. Part 1) or through the Solent (e.g. 455 E. at Hurst between 7 April/3 May 1969 — *H.* 1969), they may be heard at night (e.g. a vast easterly movement took place all night at St. Catherine's Light on 30 April/1 May 1965 — *H.* 23. Part 3) or they may be seen leaving Langstone Harbour between ENE and WNW over Portsdown Hills in the evenings (e.g. 554 left between 19 April/16 May 1959, all but six in April — *H.* 21. Part 3). These birds leaving Langstone are not seen to return and they coincide with lower counts in the area.

Numbers are lowest in late May and June but even then they are by no means uncommon. In Langstone Harbour, for instance, 1,000 may be present in May —

though around 300 would be more usual later in the month — and 50/60 would be quite usual in June. The only suggestion of possible breeding is contained in a note of Munn's for his second edition, as follows: 'In July 1919 in the SE corner of Hampshire, W. Rowan disturbed a bird that shammed lameness and displayed every sign that it had young there. Little doubt that it nests but nest not yet found.' And no nest has been found yet.

Autumn migration is from July onwards with the peak usually in September. (For details of autumn migration in Christchurch Harbour see the paper by Rogers and Webber in *H.* 1970). At Hengistbury in August 1958, two flocks of 11 and 18 were seen to leave S. at a great height in the evening of 16th and 11 did the same on 17th (C.H.O.S.G.)

Inland records have occurred at times on both migrations, and on rare occasions in winter. Up to 12 at Winnall between 7 May and 24 June 1962 (*H.* 22. Part 3) were the most at one place, whilst 10 on flooded meadows at Blashford on 11 January 1968 (Rycroft) has been the highest count in winter.

Birds recovered in Hampshire during winter have been ringed between July and October in Sweden (nine), Norway (three), Finland (one), Denmark (one) and Heligoland (one). The Danish bird was a nestling whose ring was found in the pellet of a Short-eared Owl at Farlington Marshes (*H.* 1966). Two birds ringed at Stanpit in August 1960 were killed in the Gironde department of France in late April 1962 (*per* Wise).

A nationwide estuaries count in mid-December 1971 showed Hampshire holding 55,000 Dunlin, some 19 per cent of the total for England, Scotland and Wales.

179. Curlew Sandpiper. *Calidris testacea*: K & M described it as 'a common visitor to the coast on the spring and autumn migrations.' It can no longer claim such a status. In spring it is scarce — absent in some years — whilst in autumn numbers are usually very small.

An analysis of the years 1959/70 inclusive for the mainland and north Island coasts gives the following pattern which is typical of today. Isolated birds occurred on rare occasions in winter, e.g. at Dibden Bay on 28 December 1966 (*H.* 1966); at Stanpit on 22 January 1961 (*H.* 22. Part 2); at Wootton Bridge on 5 February 1967 (*I.o.W.* 6. Part 2). Spring passage was in April/May (very occasionally March), no year's total reaching double figures and three years producing no records. Only one bird was seen in June, and that was on the 1st at Hurst in 1963 (*H.* 23. Part 1). Return passage started as early as 9 July and usually ended in October (very occasionally November). September often saw the peak. At this time numbers were highest, but the total seen in a typical year would only be 20/30. Some years (1959, 1960, 1969) had larger movements, the highest counts being: 34 at Pennington on 31 August 1969 (*H.* 1969), 34 at Farlington Marshes on 21 September 1959 and at Hayling on 16 September 1959 (*H.* 21. Part 3), and 26 at Hurst on 3 September 1960 (*H.* 22. Part 1).

EC in *B.o.H.* said: 'Very few records from the Island'; but for the period analysed above the species occurred every year, mostly at Newtown.

All records were coastal.

181. Sanderling. *Crocethia alba*: K & M call it 'a common winter visitor to all our coasts.' This is certainly not true today. The only places now where one could *expect* to meet a flock in winter are: around Hayling Island, particularly at Black Point, the maximum being 280 on 5 January 1970 (*H.* 1970); the Bembridge/Ryde stretch of coast, the maximum being 140 on 29 December 1971; to a lesser extent,

Christchurch Harbour, where up to 50 have been seen. Elsewhere on the coast in winter it is usually absent with occasional records only.

It is much more widespread on spring passage in April/early June (mostly May), when birds are seen moving E. e.g. 148 flew E. at Hurst on 9 May 1968 (*H.* 1968), 120 flew E. — also at Hurst — on 22 May 1961 (*H.* 22. Part 2) and 50 flew E. at Needs Oar as late as 1 June 1963 (*H.* 23. Part 1). They have also been heard at night at St. Catherine's Light.

Return passage from July to October is much smaller.

Birds are occasionally seen inland, e.g. singles at Winnall on 7 May 1966, at Ash Vale gravel pit on 22 May 1966, at Fleet Pond on 4 November 1966 (*H.* 1966), at Yateley gravel pit on 12 September 1965 (*H.* 23. Part 3), at Winchester sewage farm on 8 May 1964 (*H.* 23. Part 2) and at Winnall on 8 May 1962 (*H.* 22. Part 3).

183. Broad-billed Sandpiper. *Limicola falcinellus*[*]: The first one recorded in the county was seen at Farlington Marshes on 5 October 1957 by Billett and Henty, and on the 6th by many other observers; a full description appeared in *B.B.* 51 for May 1958 and a correction of the date in December 1958.

184. Ruff. *Philomachus pugnax*: K & M say: 'A winter visitor, rare inland.' The status has changed markedly within the last few years. Through the 1950s and early 1960s, the greatest number of records was during autumn passage in August and September with frequent sightings in spring and only isolated occurrences in winter. The largest gathering was 33 at Keyhaven in April 1957 (Boys *et al.*). Inland records were scarce (EC in *B.o.H.* gives five) and the same source states that 'there are only about half a dozen records from the Island' between K & M and 1960, all since World War II.

From about 1965, the bird has become a regular winter visitor in increasing numbers to a few localities. Pennington/Keyhaven is easily the main area and in the last few winters the flock has exceeded 100. In 1966, numbers there increased to 61 on 13 March (Green) and monthly maxima at the same locality for 1967/71 were:

1967	18	93	40	13	0	0	1	15	7	4	1	32
1968	90	120	130	31	1	0	1	2	30	2	26	101
1969	150	130	120	30	4	0	0	6	4	2	8	120
1970	100	171	40	9	1	1	1	3	4	–	35	40
1971	150	130	70	1	1	0	1	7	6	4	–	50

At the same time, Farlington Marshes, Titchfield Haven and to a lesser extent Dibden Bay have had wintering birds with counts in the 20s or even a little higher. Other coastal localities have had more frequent though irregular records. On the Island, they have appeared every year since 1962 in increasing numbers — mainly at the Medina, Brading and Newtown — with 17 at the Medina in 1968 and 40 there in 1969. Inland birds are no longer unusual with as many as 35/40 at Ibsley on 25 March 1967 (Brice), 11 at Winchester sewage farm on 3/4 September 1966 (*H.* 1966) and records in every year from 1965 to date. All this increase is probably related to the species expansion on its breeding grounds. The recent winter population represents around 10 per cent of the national total.

A male ringed in Northumberland on 1 September 1960 was found dead in Chichester Harbour on 25 November 1962 (*B.B.* 56. Ringing Supplement).

185. Avocet. *Recurvirostra avosetta*: Of 31 mentioned by K & M as seen, no less than 22 were shot. Happily, those that appear today are allowed to live.

76

Between K & M and 1959, the mainland had a number of records from February to December, mostly of three birds or less, but 12 were in Christchurch Harbour from 8 to 10 August 1936 (Jourdain in *B.B.* 30. 196). Numbers in late October/November 1958 were remarkable, viz. — 50 flying E. at Black Point in October and 35 at Langstone Harbour on 23 November (wrongly reported as 23 October in *H.* 21. Part 2). Two single birds in 1919 and 1954 were the only Island birds whilst inland on the mainland, two at Oakhanger Pond near Selborne on 25 August 1908 (Munn in *H.* 9.1) and the remains of one near Otterborne on 28 January 1942 (it had been ringed in Denmark on 15 June 1941 *B.B.* 36. 201) were the only reports.

From 1959 to 1971 there have been three more Island reports, one inland at West Wellow in March/April 1969, and an increasing number of records from the mainland coast where birds have occurred every year. Most of the records are in March/May and October/December. The totals each year have been (1959—1970): 3, 14, 1, 3, 3, 3, 31, 3, 20, 38, 19, 14. Most sightings have been of very small numbers, but flocks are occasionally seen flying E. in the early months, e.g. 15 past St. Catherine's Point on 27 April 1968 (*I.o.W.* 6. Part 3); 12 past Hurst on 16 April 1968 (*H.* 1968); 12 past Gilkicker on 11 May 1967 (*H.* 1967); 25 past Gilkicker on 14 March 1966 (*H.* 1966); 13 past Titchfield Haven on 14 February 1960 (*H.* 22. Part 1).

186. Black-winged Stilt. *Himantopus himantopus*: K & M list four, all procured. Subsequently there have been:

Black-winged Stilt

One, Beaulieu, 23/26 November 1923 (Troubridge in *B.B.* 17. 212).

Up to four, mid-May 1945, Warren Flats (*H.* 16. 304).

Two males and three females, West Yar, 18 April 1949, the first Island record since the early nineteenth century (Adams *et al.*).

One, Stanpit, May 1939, seen by an inexperienced observer and not reported until 1952, must be considered 'possible' (*B.* 43. 37).

One, Bursledon, 3 October 1962 (*B.B.* 56.11.401).

Three (one male and two immature males), Dibden Bay, 10/13 April 1965 (*H.* 23. Part 3).

187. Grey Phalarope. *Phalaropus fulicarius:* An almost annual visitor in very small numbers, principally in September but quite often in October/November. It has also occurred from December to the end of January, whilst the first spring record was a bird at Ryde on 3 March 1966 (*H.* 1966). Birds as early as August are rare.

In common with other parts of the south coast, Hampshire had far more than usual in the autumns of 1957 and 1960; in the former, 20 occurred between 8 September/21 November including six on a pool in Stokes Bay on 3 October (Mole); the 1960 influx was caused by gales on 8/9 October and produced 20 at Southbourne (17 on the sea and three in a car-park puddle — JHT), 18 between Hurst and Pennington and 17 at Ryde, all these on 9th; several were found dead (*H.* 22. Part 1).

There have been eight inland records from the southern half of the mainland. A bird will often frequent the same area for several days after its arrival.

Between 1936 and 1957, it was only reported eight times from the Island, but in the 1960 invasion there were 15 at various places in addition to the 17 at Ryde.

188. Red-necked Phalarope. *Phalaropus lobatus:* K & M give one authenticated record. Subsequently, apart from four 'possibles', there have been:

One, Titchfield Haven, 14 October 1950 (Suffern).

One, Farlington Marshes, 10/12 September 1955 (Truckle *et al.*).

One, Stokes Bay, 10/12 September 1957 (Mole).

Two, Dibden Bay, 26 October 1958 (Brice and Suffern).

One, Dibden Bay, 19 August 1964 (Glue).

One, Compton (I.o.W.), 2/3 July 1966, the first Island record (Phillips and Stafford).

One immature, Pennington, 7 September 1968 (Bowers, Green and Hobby).

One on a paper mill effluent lagoon at Overton, 20 September 1968 (Mann).

One, Dibden Bay, 14 September 1969 (Martin).

One, Whitecliff Bay (I.o.W.), 12 November 1969 (Gough).

189. Stone Curlew. *Burhinus oedicnemus:* In all months except December and January; as it has been heard at the end of February, it may occasionally winter. The first migrants usually arrive towards the end of March or in the first half of April — over seven consecutive years the first date was 12 April (six times) or 13 April (Meinertzhagen) — but there are a few records for the first few days of March. The departing birds assemble in flocks in the neighbourhood of the breeding areas in August and September and migrate in the second half of October or early November. Flocks assembling prior to departure have numbered between 50 and 100, but recent years have produced smaller counts, viz. — 18 at Andover on 20 September 1959 (*H.* 21. Part 3), up to 25 at Barton Stacey in 1960 (Rees) and 23 at Twyford in October 1961 (*H.* 22. Part 2). As many as 37 were seen together immediately after arrival on 30 March in one place. Numbers in breeding localities (on the chalk running across the county) seem to fluctuate, decreases in certain areas having been reported in 1933–6, 1938, 1944, 1956 and 1967, but increases in other places in 1939 and 1941. Modern reclamation of down-land drives them out of former haunts and, where they do continue to nest, early eggs are often rolled in; they will often lay again, however, and in places farmers have helped by rolling around nests that had been marked (*H.* 23. Part 1). Egg collectors have been responsible for further losses. On one occasion a clutch was taken from the top of an old straw-stack 10 feet above ground, a most unusual site (Munn). EC asked Dr. Ash for his opinion and his reply is worth quoting in full:

'My impression is that this species is just hanging on (i.e. may be holding its own or decreasing slowly). They are certainly able to breed successfully on cultivated land, but only at the cost of repeated layings (presumably more often than on their downland habitat). They are known to have hatched as late as September. Like several other local elusive species, one has no idea of their population size until one begins to study them more closely (thus it was a surprise to me to find a density as high as a pair to 200 acres locally). Unless one is making annual counts a reduction of 50 per cent or more in total population would pass unnoticed, especially if spread over two or three years.

As time goes on the species is bound to become more closely linked to and affected by agricultural practices and it will be most interesting to see if it can adapt itself accordingly. For example, several years ago on a local farm where Stone Curlews bred on both down and agricultural land, they were forced to breed only on cultivated land after a few years, for all the down had disappeared under the plough. The farm switched to dairying and Stone Curlews seemed to be most successful on ploughed ground following a long ley. This was ploughed in autumn and not sown with kale until the following June, after which the only operation was hand-hoeing. Now with improved mechanisation the same ley would not be ploughed until May, sown in June, then probably machine-hoed and/or sprayed. The former method provided long undisturbed periods when a brood could be reared successfully; the latter hardly gives them a chance. A major change in agricultural practice might make all the difference one way or the other to this species'.

A bird ringed as young near Fordingbridge on 24 July 1951 was recovered at Durango, Vizcaya (Spain), on 1 November 1952 (*B.B.* 46. 314).

Munn wrote that records from the Island were scarce, but that Isaacs of Alum Bay had noted the species there in winter. Since then no records from the Island, until that of one flushed from a field at St. Catherine's Point on 18 April 1957. Another was reported there on 3 May 1958 (Bowers) and another on 12 March 1961 (*I.o.W.* 5. Part 6). One was near St. Helens on 8 April 1966.

191. Pratincole. *Glareola pratincola*: K & M list two examples on the mainland and one in the Island.

Since then there are only two acceptable records — a pair in the week of 15 May 1944 at Somborne near Stockbridge. They were seen by a rabbit-catcher who noticed their swallow-like tail feathers and sharp call-note in flight, and at once recognised them from an illustrated book (*H.* 16 noticed in *B.B.* 40. 31). And one at Stanpit on 14 September 1957 (Bowers and E. L. Jones), a full description which appeared in *B.B.* March 1958.

192. Cream-coloured Courser. *Cursorius c. cursor.* K. & M. give one, shot in 1845. None since.

193. Arctic Skua. *Stercorarius parasiticus*: K & M knew it as an occasional visitor to the coast during autumn and winter. Today it is a regular migrant in modest numbers on spring and autumn passage both through the Solent and past St. Catherine's Point.

Spring passage begins in April, at some time from the end of the first week onwards, and continues through May and even into June at times. March birds are rare but have occurred (e.g. 1963). During this passage, over a score are typically seen each year flying E. past St. Catherine's and a similar number move through the Solent, the most seen in any one year being 52 passing St. Catherine's in 1966 (*H.* 1966) and 49 passing Gilkicker in 1967 (*H.* 1967). June records are infrequent.

Return passage is from July to October/November with over 50 seen in some years. Reports are mostly of single birds but there have been as many as eight, e.g. in a large tern flock off Hengistbury in September 1970 (*H.* 1970). On several occasions they have been reported after gales. One dark phase adult flew E. near Quarr on 18 December 1967 (*I.o.W.* 6. Part 2).

Colour phase has not always been recorded but where it has, dark phase birds are more frequent than light phase individuals.

One inland record omitted by K & M was a bird shot at Ashmansworth (seven miles SW of Kingsclere) in 1883. The only other inland birds were an immature shot at Longparish in the autumn of 1910 (*H.* 9. Part 1), and one which flew SW over Amberwood Inclosure on 19 August 1961 (Clay *et al.*).

194. Great Skua. *Stercorarius skua*: Only four records in K & M. Very few down to the mid 1950s but the better observer-coverage from that time has shown the species to be a regular passage bird in spring in small numbers and a fairly regular autumn bird of passage in very small numbers. In winter and mid-summer, it is rare.

Spring passage is from late March to mid May when birds fly E., more moving past St. Catherine's Point than through the Solent. The most seen in one year passing St. Catherine's was 20 in 1962 (*H.* 22. Part 3) but typically there have been fewer than 10. Five in 1971 was the most in one year from the mainland.

Return passage is from late July/November, when birds mostly fly W., more recorded from the mainland than St. Catherine's Point though this may be due to lack of autumn coverage at the latter place. The highest total for any one year has been six and some recent autumns have produced none.

One at Hurst on 27 June 1966 was the first June record for Hampshire (Wiseman), the bird appearing after SW gales.

One flying E. off Hengistbury on 3 January 1969, after W. gales, and one at Pennington on 9 January 1971 were the only recent winter records (*H.* 1969 and 1971).

There have been inland records. One flew over Hazeley Down camp near Winchester on 3 February 1918 (Munn in *H.* 9. Part 1). One was found near Freshwater on 1 October 1954 being tossed by cows! It was cared for by Mrs Williams, but died from pneumonia (*I.o.W.* 4. Part 9). One was picked up alive on a rubbish tip near Alton in October 1963, where it had been killing rats disturbed by workmen, and kept by Mr. John Burkett (*Hampshire Chronicle*, 12.10.63).

195. Pomarine Skua. *Stercorarius pomarinus*: Four in K & M. The next was an immature picked up dead at Mudeford on 14 December 1946 and identified at the British Museum (*H.* 17. 93), followed by an adult in Langstone Harbour on 10 October 1957 (Bowers).

Then from 1959 to 1971 recorded every year — like the previous species, it must have been overlooked and its status revealed by better coverage. Well over half of the records have been in April and May (especially May) and nearly all the rest spread through August/November. Eight has been the greatest total for any one spring (1969) and eight also the highest total for any autumn (1961). On both passages, birds have been seen moving past St. Catherine's Point and through the Solent, more at the latter than the former in both spring and autumn. Most records have concerned single birds but five adults were off Hurst on 6 May 1969 (*H.* 1969).

One off St. Catherine's in 1959 was the first Island record since 1844 (*I.o.W.* 5. Part 4).

Other than passage: one dead at Thorness Bay in the cold spell early in 1963 (*I.o.W.* 1963/4); three adults flying E. at Keyhaven on 18 June 1969 (*H.* 1969); in December, one at Langstone Harbour in 1960 on 25 (*H.* 22. Part 1) and one flying W. at Hurst in 1964 on 7 (*H.* 23. Part 2), the second and third December records for Hampshire.

196. Long-tailed Skua. *Stercorarius longicaudus*: One should be added to the few recorded in K & M, an immature female that was obtained on the River Medina at Newport on 20 February 1899 (Munn).

The next was an adult at Hurst on 5 October 1963 (*H.* 23. Part 1), followed by one at Ryde on 5 October 1964 (*I.o.W.* 1963/4).

The latest record is of one flying E. off Gilkicker on 20 May 1967 (Terry). This was the first spring record for Hampshire, the earliest record by one day for anywhere in Britain from 1958 to the date of sighting, and only the second spring record anywhere in southern England during that same period (*H.* 1967).

Long-tailed Skua

Gull spp. *Larus:* For a detailed study of the movements of gulls to and from Southampton Water, see the paper by Crook in *B.B.* 46. 385—97.

In the winter of 1950 up to the end of December, the roosts at Dibden Bay and Cadland Creek consisted mainly of Black-headed Gulls with some Herring, Common and Great Black-backed. Some came from Alresford and on the River Test from apparently as far as Andover. Routes of the Itchen birds over Southampton were studied from Swaythling. The up-river gulls and the estuarine gulls apparently mix at the roost but only the latter feed nearby on the falling tide in Southampton Water, the former having fed by day on inland fields. When the tide is high birds roost on the water; when low on the foreshore.

198. Great Black-backed Gull. *Larus marinus*: K & M call it a winter visitor 'but not very common'. It must have increased considerably since then for every winter produces several gatherings of 50 or more from the mainland coast, and counts of 100 or more are by no means uncommon from places such as Langstone Harbour, Portchester, Southampton Water, Pennington and Christchurch Harbour. As many as 300 have been recorded (e.g. at Langstone Harbour) and 370 were at roost at Titchfield Haven on 15 January 1960 (*H.* 22. Part 1). Island numbers in winter tend to be lower than those on the mainland.

During these winter months, a few are likely to occur inland up the river valleys and as far north as Fleet Pond.

Small numbers are seen moving past St. Catherine's Point in spring and autumn but it is difficult to separate real migrants from birds on local movements.

A few pairs nest on the cliffs from the Needles to Freshwater Bay, eight pairs breeding in 1958 (*I.o.W.* 5. Part 3) and 12 pairs in 1964 (*I.o.W.* 1963/4). In 1950 and 1951 a pair nested at the edge of spartina grass in the Pennington Black-headed Gull colony, apparently the first breeding record for the mainland. In 1971, a pair held territory in fields at Needs Oar in the Herring Gull colony that is developing there.

Gatherings of immature birds are present through the summer months. Between 20 and 300 have frequented Langstone Harbour in June and July, and up to 120 have been reported regularly in recent years living on the fringe of the Black-head colony at Needs Oar throughout the nesting season.

A nestling ringed at Sogndal (Norway) on 15 July 1955 was recovered at Southampton on 2 February 1957. Another Norway-ringed nestling (27 June 1957) was recovered at Havant around the following November. A nestling ringed on 17 June 1959 on the Great Ainou Islands (U.S.S.R.) was found dead at Gosport on 24 March 1962.

199. Lesser Black-backed Gull. *Larus fuscus*: A small but increasing number are now recorded between November and February (see *Bird Study* 8. 130/1), from inland as well as the coast. Numbers in November and February may be migrants rather than wintering birds, e.g. 320 flying W. as far inland as Yateley gravel pit in fifteen minutes on 20 November 1970 (*H.* 1970), 100 plus at Stanpit on 8 November 1959 (*H.* 21. Part 3) and 30 plus at Fleet Pond on 22 February 1970 (*H.* 1970).

Spring passage is in March/May. Again, it is observed inland as well as on the coast, e.g. at Basing in April and May (P. E. Brown); a party flew north at night over Damerham on 26 March 1959 (*H.* 21. Part 3); along the Test and Itchen valleys. The largest numbers are seen on the coast however, especially passing St. Catherine's Point where birds are often seen coming in from the south and turning E. or W. on reaching land. In most years the movement is mainly to the E. (e.g. 233 moved E. — 210 adults — in 1966 compared with two flying W. — *H.* 1966) but a few years have produced westerly movements (e.g. 1962) and Nicholson observed westerly passage along the Freshwater coast in April including many *L.f. fuscus*.

There are no mainland breeding records and June records are typically rather sparse. On the Island cliffs at Culver and around Main Bench, never more than a very few pairs appear to have nested since K & M (strong doubt was cast by Witherby on the report — *B.B.* 4. 182 — that there was a remarkable increase to 50 pairs in the one year 1910). Recent examples of breeding numbers are: one pair at Main Bench in 1966 (*I.o.W.* 6. Part 1); two pairs at Culver and one pair at Main Bench in 1965 (*I.o.W.* 5. Part 10).

Autumn passage is in July/October. Again, it is overland as well as coastal (e.g. at Baughurst and Basing — P. E. Brown — and a marked southerly passage down the Avon — Ash). On the coast, movement is predominantly E. to W. (e.g. at St. Catherine's Point, 642 flew W. compared with 191 E. in 1959 — *H.* 21. Part 3 — whilst similar numbers there in 1961 were 302 W., 50 E. and 100 S. — *H.* 22. Part 2). Easterly movement is also recorded however, and 420 were recorded flying E. off Hill Head in the autumn of 1959 when birds at St. Catherine's were mostly flying W. 160/180 were at Blackgang Chine on 5 September 1954 (Adams).

The species has been seen on regular SW evening flights over Fleet Pond, monthly maxima there for August/December 1969 being: 12, 37, 39, 4 and 8.

199. Scandinavian Lesser Black-backed Gull. *Larus f. fuscus*: This race is not distinguished in K & M, but Meinertzhagen saw a small party which stayed for two days at Mottisfont in December 1896. They were the only gulls of any species which he saw there all through the nineties!

Mostly an autumn passage migrant seen at times both on the mainland and the Island. Most of the reported occurrences have been in the past two decades; as usual with this race identification has not always been positive, but some have been certain. EC watched 120 with only two *graellsii* at rest on Stanpit on 23 October 1958, and the autumn passage seen from St. Catherine's Point in 1957 was almost entirely of this race, some 1,350 — and probably thousands more (*I.o.W.* 5. Part 2) — being involved between 17 August and the end of October. In 1959, 90 per cent of 420 passing Hill Head were *fuscus*, but of 833 passing St. Catherine's Point, most were *graellsii* — all in August/November (*H.* 21. Part 3). However, in the same year at St. Catherine's, 50 which came in from the sea and coasted west on 5 September were mainly *fuscus*.

They might also be seen occasionally in spring and mid-winter, e.g. 18 out of 21 at Brownwich on 12 December 1957.

200. Herring Gull. *Larus argentatus*: Outside the breeding season there are daily movements up the river valleys from coastal roosts. The resulting inland gatherings are sometimes quite large, especially in autumn, e.g. numbers built up at Winchester sewage farm from late August to 500 on 28 September 1963, decreasing to 150 by mid-October (*H.* 23. Part 1); 350 plus at Beacon Hill on 25 August 1964 (*H.* 23. Part 2); the commonest gull in the regular SW evening flights over Fleet Pond in 1969, the maximum being 150 plus on 16 November (*H.* 1969).

Gatherings on the coast from mid-August onwards are sometimes very large, the biggest counts in recent years being 2,500 in Portsmouth Harbour on 15 October 1971, 2,286 at Stanpit on 1 January 1971 (*H.* 1971), 1,650 at Stanpit on 16 September 1950, 1,600 at Browndown tip on 4 February 1970 (*H.* 1970), 1,450 plus at Langstone Harbour on 14 March 1956, and 1,300 at Pennington on 31 December 1966 (*H.* 1966). The main body of adults begins to arrive back in coastal areas from mid-July.

Spring movement in the Solent and past St. Catherine's Point is mainly to the

E., e.g. a continual stream, mostly of immatures, came in from the SE at St. Catherine's and turned W. on reaching the shore on 31 March 1956 (Rees); 450 flew E. at Hurst on 20 April 1963 (*H.* 23. Part 1); 150 flew E. at St. Catherine's on 21 April 1962 (*H.* 22. Part 3).

They seem always to have bred in large numbers on the chalk cliffs of the Island. Between 700 and 800 pairs nested between Freshwater Bay and the Needles in 1955, and in 1957 the breeding population for the Island was at least 1,130 pairs (Bowers, Rees *et al.*). 300 pairs nested at Culver in 1963 (*H.*23. Part 1). In 1957, a pair nested at Newtown on flat ground only a few feet above sea level (*H.* 20. Supplement) and three pairs nested there in 1958 and 1959 (*I.o.W.* 5. Parts 3 and 4). One pair attempted to breed in 1960, unsuccessfully (Mrs. Seabroke).

On the mainland, it is a new breeding species since K & M, the first eggs being found on the shingle near Needs Oar on 7 June 1938 (Heycock in *W.* 1949, p.12). The next nest at Needs Oar was also on shingle in 1966 and the species has gradually built up a colony there in every subsequent year, reaching 17–23 pairs in 1971. By that time, a few pairs were still nesting on shingle but most were in grassy fields, pools and rushes in farmland (a description of the colony is in *B.B.* 65. 168 – JHT). Single pairs have also nested in spartina at Pennington in 1950 (Hook, Day and Goodhart) and 1971, and three pairs bred at Fawley in 1957.

Small numbers of adults and several hundred immatures gather in the breeding season at various coastal localities, including the fringe of the Black-headed Gullery at Needs Oar. For example, 400 (mainly immatures) were at Bembridge Down on 28 June 1968, and 1,000 (mostly immatures) were in Portsmouth Harbour on 6 July 1970 (*H.* 1970).

Autumn movement from the coast is mainly to the W., e.g. 146 in one hour on 27 October 1956 (Bowers) at St. Catherine's Point and 100 flew W. there on 16 September 1962 (*H.* 22. Part 3).

A nestling ringed at Ushant on 19 June 1959 was recovered at Portsmouth on 1 December 1959 (*B.B.* 53. 509). A nestling ringed at the Needles on 11 June 1927 was recovered near Broadstairs (Kent) in January 1929 (*B.B.* 23. 125). One ringed at Skokholm on 24 June 1963 found dead in Christchurch Harbour on 17 October 1969 (*H.* 1969).

200. Scandinavian Herring Gull (*Handbook*) or **Karelian Herring Gull** (Bannerman) *L.a. omissus*: K & M omit one bird of this yellow-legged race which was shot on Hayling Island 27 December 1895 (*Handbook*).

On 26 April 1957 there was a yellow-legged adult with a normally coloured mantle in Langstone Harbour (*H.* 20. Supplement. 30), and one was at the Foreland on 18 August 1962 (*I.o.W.* 5. Part 7).

201. Common Gull. *Larus canus*: There are few records for May or June, most birds leaving in March/April with the first returns usually in July. 10 immatures in Brading Harbour on 10 June 1953 were unusual, for example (Curber).

In the winter months it is present in large and sometimes enormous numbers. The birds occur inland by day, being common daily visitors to places such as Winchester, Alresford and Anton, returning to coastal roosts (e.g. Southampton Water) in late afternoon. Thousands may be seen in the course of a winters day on downland fields in the Damerham area (Ash) and smaller numbers are recorded right to the north of the county. The *really* large gatherings are all coastal however, particularly at roosts such as Langstone Harbour. Counts of birds flighting in there at evening from inland feeding grounds have produced 10,000 in early November 1952, 12,607 on 21 February 1953, 14,150 on 31 March 1953 and 6,500 on 25 October

1953 (P.G.). Similar numbers have been counted since.

Apart from these roosts, some large numbers have been seen at Hengistbury attracted by sprat shoals, e.g. 1,000 on 29 December 1967 (*H.* 1967), 3,000 on 29 December 1968 (*H.* 1968) and 500 in January and December 1969 (*H.* 1969).

Apart from movement inland, these winter numbers sometimes give rise to local coastal movements that are probably not true migration, e.g. 1,000 flew E. at Gilkicker on 27 February 1962 (*H.* 22. Part 3). On the Island in winter, the species is commoner in the E. with flocks of up to 300 in Osborne Bay and 400 plus there on 29 January 1955; it is rather irregular in the W. of the Island (Adams).

The direction of spring movement is confused. At St. Catherine's Point, movement has sometimes been to the W., especially in a westerly wind (e.g. 210 flew W. there in westerly winds on 6 April 1967, movements becoming easterly when the wind changed to the E. — *I.o.W.* 6. Part 2). At other times, movement is to the E. (e.g. 683 flew E. at Gilkicker between 13 and 17 April 1962 — *H.* 22. Part 3).

One ringed at Lübeck on 4 July 1911 was recovered at Portsmouth on 3 February 1912 (*B.B.* 5. 317). One ringed at Heiligenhafen (Germany) on 21 June 1949 was found dead at Wootton on 20 August 1956. A nestling ringed in S. Sweden on 4 July 1955 was found dead at Alverstone (Isle of Wight), on 24 December 1955. One found at Farlington Marshes on 29 April 1957 carried a Finnish ring. A nestling ringed on Texel (Netherlands) on 15 June 1969 was found dead at Ryde in April 1970.

202. Glaucous Gull. *Larus hyperboreus*: K & M say: 'An occasional winter visitor to the coast.'

One, not quite adult, in Sandown Bay from 13 January to 21 February 1908, seen by Fox (Munn, in his notes for a second edition of K & M). Two near Lymington on 24 May 1921 (*B.B.* 35. 39). One adult at Titchfield Haven on 16 October 1948 (*H.* 17. 222). One in its third or fourth winter at Yarmouth from 13 January to 15 February 1953 (Adams *et al.*). An adult in Langstone Harbour on 3 October 1953 (Billett and Rees). A first-winter bird at Black Point on 16 December 1956 (K. Brown and Henty). One on four January dates in 1957 at the mouth of Langstone Harbour (Billett *et al.*). One off Hayling Island in January 1958 (Brice). A probable third-winter/summer bird was at Hurst from 23 April to 18 June 1961, and what must have been the same individual returned as a fourth-winter bird from 13 January to 15 April 1962, and as an adult from 1 January to 23 February 1963 and from 23 November 1963 to 29 February 1964 (*H.* for those years).

From 1962 onwards (apart from the Hurst bird), most years have produced records, viz. — 1962, one; 1963, three; 1964, two; 1967, two; 1969, four; 1970, one; mostly of immature birds and in all months other than January, though this last fact cannot be significant as shown by previous birds in January.

203. Iceland Gull. *Larus glaucoides*: K & M's latest of only three instances is for February 1883 — shot off Freshwater.

One, probably in its second year, near Bournemouth on 6 April 1934 (Rooke in *B.B.* 28. 29). One, almost adult, at Beaulieu on 31 January 1937 and one, possibly the same bird, 15 miles to the east (i.e. Langstone Harbour) on 14 February 1937 (*B.B.* 30. 353/4). One at Damerham near Fordingbridge for one or two days, 21/2 February 1955, fed round the site of a threshed stack (Ash). In 1958, an adult at Langstone Harbour on 4 August (Henty *et al.*) and an immature on Bedhampton rubbish tip on 13 December (Rees). In 1959 a second-winter bird on 3 May at Farlington Marshes, and another on 3 November. Four in 1960. One at Farlington Marshes on 10 December 1961 (*H.* 22. Part 2). The second record from the Island is of an immature

1. *Norman Orr*

echat (above), a typical bird of the Hampshire heaths. However, the status of the Long-eared Owl (below)
t really known.

2.*Eric Hosking*

3. *Geoffrey F*

Bishop's Dyke (above), New Forest heath and **bog bordering on greenwood**, a habitat for such speci
Woodlark (below).

4. *Norma.*

5. *Norman Orr*

acked Shrikes (above) and Nightjars (below) might also be found here. A distinctive habitat, that together
adjoining heaths is unique in lowland England.

6.*Eric Hosking*

7.Geoffrey F

Chalk down and farmland (above) near Farley Mount. Lapwings (below) are common in such ha

8.Norma

9. *Eric Hosking*

is also one of the few remaining British haunts for Stone Curlews (above), whilst the occasional pair of
:agu's Harrier (below) may still breed.

10. *Norman Orr·*

11. *Geoffrey F*

The lush vegetation of the River Itchen (above), one of Hampshire's distinctive chalk streams. Kingfis (below) occur at intervals.

12. *Norman*

13. *Norman Orr*

land around the River Itchen is also the haunt of Grey Wagtails (above), whilst Great Crested Grebes (below)
d on some of the lakes.

14. *Norman Orr*

Four rather special Hampshire birds. Mediterranean Gulls (above) nested in Britain for the first time in 19€
Needs Oar. Collared Doves (below) have also arrived and are now common in places.

17 *Geoffrey Fisher*

oshire is the only south coast county with breeding Sandwich Terns (above) and one of the few with
ord Warblers (below).

18. *Geoffrey Fisher*

19. *Aerofilms*

Hurst Castle and Keyhaven (above) an area of spartina flats. Large colonies of Black-headed Gulls (below) situated on such habitat between Hurst and Southampton.

20. *Geoffrey F*

21. *Geoffrey Fisher*

non Terns (above) and waders such as Oystercatchers (below) breed in these areas, their numbers steadily ising where wardening gives them protection.

22. *Geoffrey Fisher*

23. *Aerofilms*
Hengistbury Head (above), a headland that attracts large numbers of small migrants such as Redstarts (be
24. *Norma*

25.*Norman Orr*

headland also attracts Warblers (Whitethroats above), whilst sea birds like the Great Skua (below) also pass
• enough to be seen from such points.

26.*Geoffrey Fisher*

27. *Geoffrey Fi*

Hampshire is well endowed with deciduous (above) and coniferous woodland, a rich habitat for Nuthatc
(below) and kindred species.

28. *Geoffrey Fi*

29. *Eric Hosking*

...ies (above) and Lesser Spotted Woodpeckers (below) might also be found in such woodlands which occur parts of the county.

30. *Norman Orr*

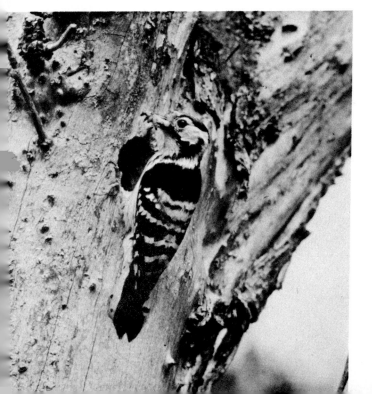

31. *Geoffrey Fi*

Hampshire's impressive list of species is made up of a good rarities list (e.g. Sabine's Gull, above) and a selection of commoner species (e.g. Meadow Pipit and young Cuckoo, below).

32. *Norman*

flying past St. Catherine's Point on 18 April 1960 (*I.o.W.* 5. Part 5) and the third is of one at Main Bench on 1 July 1961 (*H.* 22. Part 2).

From 1962 onwards, records each year have been: 1962, three; 1963, one; 1966, two; 1969, one; 1970, three. Adults and immatures have occurred and the records have been in all months except February, June and August, though as in the above species this is probably not significant. One was inland, at Rownhams Mount on 2 November 1966 (*H.* 1966).

The Hayling Island bird of 1952 mentioned in *B.o.H.* has since been rejected as the description was not quite conclusive.

204. Great Black-headed Gull. *Larus ichthyaetus**: At the end of November and beginning of December 1924 one frequented Poole Bay, chiefly to the western side of Bournemouth pier between that and Durley Chine; it was fairly tame, allowed approach to within 50 yards and did not mix with the other gulls. It was seen to catch sprats on several occasions. (Parkinson Curtis in *B.B.* 19. 28.)

205. Mediterranean Gull. *Larus melanocephalus**: Rees was skilful enough to identify the first at Eastney Point near Portsmouth on 27 April 1954 (*B.B.* 48. 89) and the following year saw the first in Island waters with one about two miles off the East Foreland on 5 August (*B.B.* 48. 547). It has been recorded in every subsequent year except 1963, and in 1968 added itself to the list of British breeding birds by nesting at Needs Oar Point.

Mediterranean Gull

An analysis of the records from 1956 to 1970 shows that they have been recorded in every month, but in June only from the Needs Oar colony. Monthly and annual totals, *excluding* Needs Oar birds, are: January, five; February, two; March, two; April, three; May, one; June, nil; July, three; August, three; September, two; October, three; November, four; December, three. 1956, one; 1957, one; 1958, one; 1959, two/three; 1960, five; 1961, three; 1962, one; 1963, nil; 1964, one; 1965, three; 1966, two; 1967, three; 1968, two; 1969, two; 1970, nil. Adults, second-summer/winter and first-year birds have all been recorded, and two of the above records were for the Island including the only inland record of a bird at Godshill on 4/6 April 1969 (*H.* 1969). Some birds have remained for days or even weeks, but others were seen on one day only.

The Needs Oar *colony* has been fully described elsewhere (JHT in *B.B.* 63. 67/79, *B.B.* 63. 380/382, *B.B.*65.185/6, and *Animals* December 1971). The first bird was seen over the Black-headed gullery late in 1966 and then an adult was present on two weekends in late April 1967, apparently holding a territory, but it was not seen subsequently. In 1968, a pair successfully raised two chicks, a second-summer male paired with a Black-headed Gull and raised three chicks, an adult nested unsuccessfully with a male hybrid Mediterranean/Black-head, and various other adults and a first-summer bird were seen about the gullery. In 1969, an adult pair appeared but did not stay, three males held territories for most of the season but failed to attract mates, the hybrid nested with a Black-head, and other individuals were at times seen flying round. Males held territories again in 1970 and 1971, again failing to attract mates, and in both these years the hybrid nested unsuccessfully with Black-headed Gulls, whilst other birds appeared occasionally around the colony. Perhaps the most interesting feature of these later years was that in 1970 a second-summer male defended a territory on the 1968 nest site, and in 1971 and 1972 an adult male with exactly the same bill markings defended the site again. It must surely have been one of the 1968 chicks.

206. Bonaparte's Gull. *Larus philadelphia* *: Although seen by two very competent observers the first occurrence cannot be considered as completely proved. Their description was: 'Newtown Marshes, 9 August 1948, after a gale. Very long bill. No black head (? immature). Up-ended like a duck. Made a different noise from the other gulls. Wings very long and pointed and crossed beyond tail. Much larger than Little Gull. Mobbed by Black-headed Gulls. Was later compared with skins in the British Museum.' They concluded: 'As reliable as any sight record of a bird the observer has never before seen alive.' — Dr. and Mrs. D. A. Bannerman. A rather fuller account appears in Vol. XI of Dr. Bannerman's *Birds of the British Isles.*

One in Langstone Harbour on 6 October 1956 (Le Brocq and Rees whose description was accepted but·not published by *B.B.*). (*H.* 19. 330).

207. Little Gull. *Larus minutus*: K & M say: 'A rare occasional visitor in winter', and give some 14 instances between 1855 and 1894. EC in *B.o.H.* gives about 80 between K & M and 1961, mostly between late September and mid April and mostly from the last few years of that period, viz. — 1956, 16; 1960, about 30, mostly in October gales and 1961, 11. This suggests that the species has become much more numerous.

An analysis of records from 1959 to 1970 supports this view for nearly 300 were reported with about 50 in 1970. They were recorded in all months but no longer mainly in winter. Indeed, January, February and December had fewer than 10 birds each. The vast majority of birds occurred on spring and autumn migration in April/May and August/October. March, June, July and November each had between 10 and 20 records. More immatures were recorded than adults and nearly all were from the mainland coast. From the Island, four were at Freshwater on 8 October 1960 (*I.o.W.* 5. Part 5) and one was at Freshwater on 1 January 1963, injured. Two were inland, at Sowley Pond and Winnall. Most records concerned single birds but as many as seven were seen together (at Hengistbury beach on 30 September 1962, *H.* 22. Part 3), and nine were seen to fly E. at Hurst on 4 May 1967 (*H.* 1967).

In 1971, 23 flew E. at Hurst from 3/7 May (*H.* 1971).

208. Black-headed Gull. *Larus ridibundus*: Has increased enormously as a breeding species since K & M. The oldest colony is the Newtown (I.o.W.) one that was in existence at any rate as far back as 1884 (Munn), although mention of it was omitted in K & M. Therefore the claim by Kelsall (*B.B.* 4. 182) that the first Island breeding record was in 1910 was erroneous. The first breeding record for the mainland was a pair which nested in a bog near Hurn Station in 1891 (Munn) which antedates the first recorded breeding in K & M by 12 or 13 years. Today, many thousands breed in the spartina between Hurst and Needs Oar, the Newtown colony is still in existence and birds have nested at times around Ashlett and Fawley. It is best to take each colony in turn and describe its growth, starting with the one that has become by far the largest.

1. Needs Oar, on an island in the river mouth and on spartina to the east and west of the river. It dates back to at least 1913 and in the comprehensive survey of Black-headed gulleries for the whole country in 1938 (Hollom, *B.B.* 33. 302), 75 pairs were reported. The numbers had increased to 200 plus by 1948 (Rooke) and 274 in 1952 (Rees *et al.*). By 1957, the number of pairs had increased to 1,130 and it stayed around the 1,000 mark until the area became a wardened Bird Reserve in 1962. Numbers then rocketed, the pairs breeding from 1963 onwards being: 1963, 3,900; 1964, 4,000 plus; 1965, 6,516; 1966, 6,706; 1967, 9,676; 1968, 10,500; 1969, 14–16,000; 1970, 17,000; 1971, *ca.* 20,000. The eggs are collected until early May but this has obviously not hindered expansion in any way. The increase has coincided with a marked increase in terns which breed amongst the gulls. For a full account of the gullery, see the paper by JHT in *H.* 1965.

2. Hurst to Lymington. Also in existence in 1913, the colony had 50 plus pairs in the 1938 census. Numbers have also rocketed here and it has also been wardened over the past few years, though as at Needs Oar, controlled egg collecting is allowed early in the season. Numbers of pairs breeding have been: 1959, 558 plus; 1962, 2,000; 1966, 3,500; 1968, 5,000; the colony covers a much more extensive area than the one at Needs Oar and is much more difficult to count.

3. From Lymington to Tanners Lane. Birds nest in the spartina along this stretch but there is no information on numbers.

4. Fawley/Calshot. A colony used to be situated in the spartina, just north of the refinery, and 500 pairs were there in 1963. Refinery activities have probably wiped out the colony, the birds probably moving to Needs Oar. In 1969, 68 pairs nested at Calshot so a colony may develop there in the future.

5. East Parley. In 1906 and 1907 there were about 500 pairs (Munn) but it was entirely destroyed in 1908. 80–100 pairs were nesting again in 1910, but the colony was subject to periodical disturbance and numbers fluctuated enormously (Munn). In May 1942 about 60–70 birds were seen in the air but the colony was again subject to interference (Rooke) and there has been none in the last 22 years or more.

6. Newtown. This gullery was often robbed so that from 'large numbers' in about 1900 it slumped to three pairs in 1912 (Munn) and recovered to 28 pairs in 1928 (*I.o.W.* 1929) when it was again robbed. The 1938 census showed 40–50 pairs but EC in *B.o.H.* gives 52 nests in 1958 and says that they 'were possibly the first for

88

20 years' so the colony may have ceased to exist in the meantime. In 1959, there were 352 nests (*I.o.W.* 5. Part 4), only 55–60 in 1962 (*I.o.W.* 5. Part 7), but then 500 pairs in 1965 and 450 in 1966 (*I.o.W.* 5. Part 10 and 6. Part 1). In 1972, *ca.* 250 pairs nested (Mrs. Seabroke) so the colony has not experienced the explosive increase of the major mainland ones. It suffers from high tides.

Isolated pairs have occasionally nested at other sites (e.g. Yarmouth).

Outside the breeding season, enormous roosts gather in the main harbours on the coast (e.g. Southampton Water and Langstone Harbour), 10,000 being at Langstone in December 1955 and 12,000 at Dibden Bay in February 1957. From these roosts, most of the birds fly inland to feeding grounds in the early morning, returning in the evening, often using the river valleys as flight lines. They penetrate well north of Winchester. These flights begin in July and mostly end in March. The species is now common along the Test at Mottisfont where it was not seen by Meinertzhagen in the nineties, further evidence of how much more numerous in the county it has become. They move to inland feeding grounds in the Island as well, and Island birds feeding by day in December 1953 along the Medina nearly all flew to roost on the mainland at the mouth of the Hamble.

For a detailed study of the movement of gulls to and from Southampton Water, the reader is referred to a paper by Crook in *B.B.* 46. 385–97.

A mass of ringing returns show several features:

1. Most of the birds in the Needs Oar colony join the winter roosts in Southampton Water and our eastern harbours. Most Needs Oar returns come from there.

2. A few of the birds ringed as nestlings in Hampshire are recovered in *other* counties shortly after flying (e.g. Devon, Shropshire, Lincoln and Essex) so that not all the birds winter in the Hampshire harbours, and some are recovered abroad (e.g. a nestling reared at Needs Oar on 26 July 1967 was recovered near Babate — Spain — on 31 January 1968).

3. Birds found nesting at Needs Oar were born in other colonies (e.g. from Kent and France), so the Hampshire increase is partly due to immigrants.

4. Birds recovered in Hampshire in summer and winter have come from a wide variety of places. Some have been ringed abroad (e.g. Finland, Sweden and Holland), others in Britain (e.g. Cumberland and Essex).

For a fuller report on ringing recoveries see the article by Mrs. Radford in *Bird Study* 9. 42.

Munn noticed in November 1913 that a steamer getting into Southampton after dark is surrounded by flocks of gulls as in daylight; they feed on the refuse from the ship by the aid of the large lights used for disembarking passengers.

In recent years a considerable number have frequented the open spaces of the New Forest in summer, attracted by the scraps from the ever increasing number of picnic parties.

Another interesting local habit is that of the Black-headed Gulls in the Lymington River estuary which regularly accompany the I.o.W. ferry steamer as it moves up and down the river when the mud at the edges is exposed by the tide; as the wash approaches the shore the gulls settle for a few moments and feed on small marine life which has been disturbed, and then fly on a few yards to anticipate the wash farther along.

Franklin's Gull. *Larus pipixcan**: An adult which frequented Farlington Marshes and the surrounding area from 21 February to 16 May 1970 was the first of its species to be seen in Europe. A full account appears in a paper by Billett and Grant (*B.B.* 64. 310/313).

209. Sabine's Gull. *Xema sabini*: Four occurrences in K & M, two adult and two immature. Since then there have been: an immature on 6 November 1905 at Cowes (Nicholl in *Ibis* of October 1906), and an immature male shot in Christchurch Harbour on 31 August 1921 (Jourdain in *B.* 23. 44); an adult at Warden Point off Hurst Castle on 28 November 1954 (Adams in *B.B.* 48. 83); an immature flying E. three miles off St. Catherine's Point on 16 October 1959 (*B.B.* 53. 420); one at Eastney on 4 December 1960 (*B.B.* 54. 187); an immature flying E. off Gilkicker on 6 September 1965 (*H.* 1966. p.44); a first winter bird at Hurst from 12 September to 11 October 1970 and an immature off Hengistbury on 19 September 1970 (*H.* 1970).

Two others are reported to have been shot by Rogers of Freshwater, but it has not been possible to trace the year; the skin of one of them is said to have been given to a local school by the widow of Dr. Hollis of Freshwater into whose possession it had come.

Sabine's Gull

211. Kittiwake. *Rissa tridactyla*: Its inclusion in K & M as a very scarce breeding species in the Island must be corrected, because the egg found on the Culver Cliffs in 1908 (on which the inclusion is based) is now considered to have been a dwarfed Herring Gull's egg (*B.B.* 2. 425). Breeding at Main Bench was suspected in 1967 and 1968 when birds were seen flying in and out of the cliff face and a sea cave during the breeding season (*I.o.W.* 6. Parts 2 and 3). In 1969, breeding was first proved there when 33 adults and eight nests were found in a sea cave (*H.* 1969), whilst 25 occupied nests were found at the same site in 1970 (*H.* 1970) on 21 June, and 20 nests could be seen from the cliff-tops in 1971 (*H.* 1971).

Birds have been recorded passing St. Catherine's Point throughout the year but particularly in spring and autumn when coverage has been most complete. Passage there in March/May tends to be mainly easterly (e.g. 272 flew E. and 98 W. from 25 March to 5 May 1968 — *H.* 1968 — and 152 flew E. and 31 W. from 16 March to 19 May 1963 — *H.* 23. Part 1), but it is occasionally in an indefinite direction (e.g. 195 flew E. and 212 W. from 29 March to 7 June 1969 — *H.* 1969). The largest autumn movement at St. Catherine's was 671 flying E. on 22 October 1961, 70 per cent of which were immature (*H.* 22. Part 2), though this number seems to be exceptional.

From the mainland, it is not often reported *in* the Solent. In the winter months, birds are sometimes seen passing Hengistbury, especially after gales, e.g. — 200 flying W. there on 24 December 1969 (*H.* 1969), 600 flying W. after severe westerly gales on 22 December 1968 (*H.* 1968), and 200 after gales on 31 December 1966 (*H.* 1966). Hurst and Gilkicker may also record movements in winter, e.g. — 400 flew E. at Hurst on 15 October 1971 (*H.* 1971), 145 flew W. at Hurst on 16 November 1963 (*H.* 23. Part 1) and 153 flew E. at Gilkicker on 6 November 1961 (*H.* 22. Part 2). These winter movements have either become more frequent or have been revealed by better coverage for 'probably over 200' off Boscombe on 9 and 10 December 1942 (Gooch in *H.* 15. 326) was unique at that time. Otherwise, small numbers are seen from places such as Hengistbury, Hurst and Gilkicker on spring and autumn passage, mainly moving E. in spring.

In the first days of February 1957, a 'wreck' took place on the southern and western shores of Britain (*B.B.* for July 1958). The wreck was most marked in the west of Hampshire: 25 plus on 9 February, and 108 plus on the 10th, nearly all bearing traces of oil; still 27 there on the 17th; 40 in the Hurst area on 9 February, and some dead birds. Much fewer further east. In all, a minimum of 320 birds were involved on Hampshire mainland coasts and 31 on the Island. Nearly all died.

The Birds of Milford (1913) described it as a regular winter migrant, but no particulars are given.

Three 'scavenging on the main road' at Swaythling on 21 December 1928 (Arnold) were unusual.

An adult ringed on Lundy Island on 15 July 1954 was found newly dead on the shore at Bonchurch, Isle of Wight, on 31 July 1956 after gales.

212. Black Tern. *Chlidonias niger*: Between K & M and 1961, it had been reported on one or more occasions in 20 years on spring and in 15 years on autumn passage. Observer coverage for much of that time was very thin. Today it is a regular migrant in both spring and autumn, sometimes in quite large numbers, most records being from the coast but a few usually appearing inland, probably migrating along the main river valleys. In view of the numbers seen on the mainland coast, remarkably few are recorded on the north Island shore and only a few go round past St. Catherine's Point, 27 flying E. on 4 May 1967 (*I.o.W.* 6. Part 2) and 18 flying E. on 31 August 1963 (*I.o.W.* 1963/4) being the most recorded there on spring and autumn passage. 30 at Fleet Pond on 31 May 1966 is by far the highest number inland (*H.* 1968. p.39).

Spring passage to the E. is in April/May, mostly in early May. In 1970, the first was as early as 4 April. The largest movements in recent years were 439 flying E. at Farlington Marshes on 1 May 1965 (*H.* 1965), 173 flying E. at Titchfield Haven on 11 May 1960 (*H.* 22. Part 1) and 90 flying E. at Hurst on 6 May 1971 (*H.* 1971). More normal peaks in recent years at Hurst were 60 flying E. from 4 to 10 May 1970, 48 flying E. on 2 May 1969, and 47 flying E. on 8 May 1968 (*H.* 1970, 1969, 1968). Some years see very few and in 1963 only two birds were seen throughout April/May (*H.* 23. Part 1).

A few birds are seen in June, e.g. six in 1970, seven in 1969 and one in 1968 (*H.* 1970, 1969, 1968).

Return passage to the W. is from July to October (very occasionally November — 1971, 1967 and 1960). 205 were seen at Calshot through autumn 1970 (*H.* 1970), whilst at Titchfield Haven in 1960, 40, 41 and 59 flew W. on three days in August and September (*H.* 22. Part 1). Large gatherings were a loose flock of 27 seen from the Ryde to Portsmouth ferry on 10 September 1956 (Marr *et al.*) and 60 in a flock going SW over Hengistbury on 21 September 1957 (C.H.O.S.G.). As in spring, some years produce very few in autumn.

213. White-winged Black Tern. *Chlidonias leucopterus*: Only one occurrence in K & M.

On 29 May 1937, two small parties at some hours interval on the River Avon were 'positively identified' by Neville Gladstone ('who knows Black Terns well') as this species (*H.* 14. 100). Jourdain, who was editor at that time, did not comment on the record though he accepted it, but as already mentioned under Great Snipe, he was a sick man at the time.

In 1959, a number of marsh terns without shoulder patches were seen at Titchfield Haven on 1 September by Suffern who thought they might have been this species (*H.* 21. Part 3), whilst one at Farlington Marshes on 20 August was rejected by *B.B.* but accepted by the Hampshire Editorial Committee (*H.* 21. Part 3).

Otherwise, birds accepted by *British Birds* Rarities Committee are:

One, Langstone Harbour, 14 September 1959 (*H.* 21. Part 3).

One, Lee-on-Solent, 11 May 1960 (*H.* 22. Part 1).

One, Hurst, 11 and 18 August 1963 (*H.* 23. Part 1).

One immature, S. Hayling, 1 September 1964 (*H.* 23. Part 2).

One, Farlington Marshes, 22 October/15 November 1967 (*H.* 1967).

One, Hengistbury, 2/3 November 1967 (*H.* 1967).

One, Titchfield Haven, 18 August 1971 (*H.* 1971).

One immature, Keyhaven area, 28 September and 4 October 1971 (*H.* 1971).

214. Whiskered Tern. *Chlidonias hybrida*: Kelso (1912, p.379) says 'has been obtained' from Hayling Island, which statement, without any data, is of course valueless and no record from Hayling Island is given in K & M whose only record (June 1875) is the only one mentioned for Hampshire in the *Handbook*.

Birds accepted by *British Birds* Rarities Committee are:

One, Stanpit, 13/16 August 1967 (*H.* 1967).

One, Newtown, 26 September 1969 (*H.* 1969).

One, Hurst, 12 May 1970 (*H.* 1970).

215. Gull-billed Tern. *Gelochelidon nilotica*: K & M give one from the mainland in 1872. A bird on 27 September 1953 at Newtown was put in square brackets by Stafford, the Island Report editor (*I.o.W.* 4.8.295) and rejected by the editors of *British Birds*.

One, St. Catherine's Point, 27 August 1956 (E. L. Jones, *H.* 19. 330).

An adult in winter plumage followed by a juvenile calling to it, flew E. at St. Catherine's Point, 29 August 1957 (Dennis).

One, Hayling Island, 18 May 1958 (*B.B.* 53. 166).

One, Stanpit, 2 September 1959 (*B.B.* 53. 421).

One, St. Catherine's Point, 30 August 1964 (*H.* 23. Part 2).

Two flying E., Farlington Marshes, 1 May 1965 (*H.* 1965).

One flying W., Gilkicker, 15 July 1966 (*H.* 1966).

One, Hurst, 5 July 1966 (*H.* 1966).

Two, Farlington Marshes, 29 April 1967 (*H.* 1967).

One, Langstone Harbour, 9 June 1968 (*H.* 1968).

One, St. Catherine's Point, 18 April 1971 (*H.* 1971).

One, Langstone Harbour, 31 May 1971 (*H.* 1971).

One, St. Catherine's Point, 19 June 1971 (*H.* 1971).

All the recent records were accepted by *British Birds* Rarities Committee.

216. Caspian Tern. *Hydroprogne caspia*: K & M give one in 1852.

Two probables near Damerham on 17 April 1954 (Ash in *H.* 19. 87, from which the following description is copied):

'Two very large terns flying east near Damerham at about 300 feet directly overhead. Strong *ca.* NNE breeze blowing at the time, overcast, slight haze. Following points noted: silent: appeared definitely larger than Sandwich Tern, having markedly heavier build. No other birds nearby for size comparison, but impression of larger size and more robust appearance AT ONCE noticed. Definitely terns and not gulls. Watched by my wife and me through 8 x 30 binoculars (two pairs) for about one minute as they flew steadily on. Long head and neck noticeable ('heavy-headed'), angled, broad wings, relatively short tail, which was forked but *not* deeply. Typical tern flight but less graceful than Sandwich, i.e. stronger, heavier, more powerful.'

One possible, Mudeford, 11 June 1958 (Forster).

One, Mudeford, 7 September 1958 (Adams — *B.B.* 53. 4).

One, Christchurch Harbour, 20 July 1968 (*H.* 1968) was accepted by *British Birds* Rarities Committee.

217. Common Tern. *Sterna hirundo*: The earliest date is 14 March (two found dead). The earliest living bird was on 18 March (Miss Popham in *H.* 17. 195) but April generally sees the first arrival.

In April/May, a heavy passage of *Common/Arctic* Terns to the east is recorded in most years, more moving through the Solent than past St. Catherine's Point. The peak is typically in the first 10 days of May, examples of high counts being: 1,738 flying E. at Gilkicker on 4/6 May 1969 (*H.* 1969); 1,670 E. at Hurst on 4 May 1967 (*H.* 1967); 1,553 E. at Gilkicker on 1 May 1965 (*H.* 1965); 1,246 E. at Hurst on 8 May 1968 (*H.* 1968). The highest counts at St. Catherine's were 619 flying E. on 1 May 1969 (*H.* 1969) and 437 on 4 May 1967 (*H.* 1967), but numbers there are usually *very* much smaller than this. Birds were heard at St. Catherine's Light on the night of 19/20 May 1961 (*H.* 22. Part 2) and a few are occasionally seen well inland on spring passage.

K & M said that it nested rarely on the mainland, but 13 years later (1918—19) Munn himself wrote that it did not nest (*H.* 9. 1). Over the past 20 years, breeding numbers have increased to reasonable proportions at several mainland sites and a few have nested on the Island. The two main colonies on the mainland are: Needs Oar (a Bird Reserve since 1962) where the number of pairs has increased from 48 in 1957 to

160/200 in 1971 (*H*. 1971 and a paper on the ternery by JHT in *H*. 1965); Hurst to Lymington (part of which is also a reserve) where numbers have increased from 69 pairs in 1959 (*H*. 21. Part 3) to *ca*. 140 pairs in 1970 (*H*. 1970). Both these terneries are in Black-headed Gull colonies. A few pairs also bred in the gullery at Fawley until the early 1960s when activities at the refinery probably drove them away. One curious record is of two pairs that nested on duck rafts well inland at Blashford gravel pits in 1967 (*H*. 1967), one pair raising two young. On the Island, a pair nested unsuccessfully at Newtown in 1958 (*I.o.W*. 5. Part 3) and one or two pairs have nested there in some subsequent years, and possibly by the Medina.

Return passage is over a longer period than in spring, so numbers each day are usually fewer. Large counts (again of *Common/Arctic*) do occur however, e.g. 1,700 flying W. at Titchfield Haven on 3 September 1960 (*H*. 22. Part 1) and 1,000 W. at Hengistbury on 26 August 1969 (*H*. 1969). As in spring, more move through the Solent than past St. Catherine's Point and odd records occur inland. At Stanpit in 1967, Common were said to outnumber Arctic in late July but Arctic outnumbered Common by 100:40 by mid August (*H*. 1967). A roost of *Common/Arctic* at Calshot reached 700 on 14 August 1970 (*H*. 1970). For details of autumn movement in Christchurch Harbour, see the paper by Rogers and Webber in *H*. 1970.

The latest record is 17 November 1958 at Newtown.

Amongst the more interesting ringing returns are: one *pull*, ringed Needs Oar on 16 July 1967 recovered Finisterre (France) on 31 August 1967; one *pull*. ringed Needs Oar on 16 July 1967 recovered Ghana on 14 March 1968; one *pull*. ringed Needs Oar on 27 June 1965 found breeding in Poole Harbour on 18 July 1968.

Evidence gained from nestlings ringed at Needs Oar suggests that the first dispersal from the colony is to the east for recoveries in Kent and further east in Hampshire have occurred shortly after young have flown. Evidence is not sufficient on this point to allow a definite statement however.

218. Arctic Tern. *Sterna macrura*: See the previous species for data on passage. Earliest date 29 March, in 1958 at Langstone Harbour (*H*. 21. Part 2) and in 1968 at Newtown (*H*. 1968). Last date 4 November, at Southsea (Conchie *et al*.).

As most passage terns are recorded as Common/Arctic, details of the species in the county are inadequate.

Nesting now known. Occasionally seen inland on passage.

219. Roseate Tern. *Sterna dougallii* *: As the species occurred almost annually in Sussex and occasionally in Dorset, it must have been overlooked in Hampshire before our first record which was of four flying NE at 100—200 feet over Titchfield Haven on 24 July 1955 (Suffern *et al*.). In the same year, five flew over Hurst from E. to W. on 4 September (Ballantyne). A few have been recorded from the mainland coast in *every* subsequent year. The earliest were two at Needs Oar on 22 April 1966 (*H*. 1966) — the only April record for Hampshire, — and the latest on 29 October 1967 at Hengistbury (*H*. 1967) — the only October record for Hampshire. Nearly all the records have been of birds flying E. in May or of return passage in July/August, with very few in September. Most years have produced fewer than 10 birds on passage, but over 30 were recorded in 1966 (*H*. 1966). Records are mostly of single birds but a flock of eight flew E. at Needs Oar on 2 May 1971 (*H*. 1971) and seven flew E. at Hurst on 3 May 1969 (*H*. 1969). There are no records from the Island.

In 1958, Dennis found the first newly hatched chick at Pennington on 6 July, and on the 12th he and three others saw three sitting Roseates in a colony of *ca*. 50 Common Terns but unfortunately at least one of the nests was flooded. The account in *H*. 21. Part 2 of only one nest is incomplete because the information was withheld

94

for security reasons. Nesting has occurred in the area in subsequent years, e.g. 1967 (two pairs), 1968 (one pair) and 1969 (one pair), though with little success. The only other breeding has been at Needs Oar where a pair nested in 1969 (probably successfully) and 1970 (raising two chicks — JHT).

The only inland record was one at Frensham Great Pond on 7 May 1971 (*H. 1971*).

Roseate Tern

220. Sooty Tern. *Sterna fuscata* *: An adult was seen on 17 June 1961 by D. Poole, E. J. Williams and D. B. Wooldridge (*B.B.* 55. 575). One was found dead at Fawley Refinery on 18 August 1969 and sent to the Natural History Museum (*B.B.* 64. 369). This species is normally confined to tropical waters.

222. Little Tern. *Sterna albifrons*: The first date, an exceptionally early one at Hurst on 24 March 1957 (Bowers). Usually not seen until the second week of April. Spring passage is to the E., nearly all the birds moving through the Solent with *very* few passing round St. Catherine's Point (e.g. eight on 3 May the only St. Catherine's record for 1970). Numbers on the mainland suggested by the following counts passing E. at Hurst: 80 between 3 and 9 May 1970 (*H.* 1970); 127 between 20 April and 6 May 1969 (*H.* 1969); 145 between 13 April and 9 May 1968 (*H.* 1968). 100 were in Christchurch Harbour on 14 May 1966 (*H.* 1966).

K & M did not know it as a breeding species, though Munn in 1918—19 said: 'possibly still nests but only on extreme eastern border of county; not nested at Mudeford for some years' which suggests that K & M probably missed some or that today's colonies are new since then. For at least the past two decades, birds have bred regularly on the mainland at: Needs Oar (a bird reserve since 1962) where from 20 plus to 34 pairs bred each year between 1963 and 1971, with considerable success over the last six years though with losses to high tides and trespassers prior to that; the stretch from Hurst to Lymington where up to 56 pairs bred each year from 1961 to 1970, again with considerable success over the last five years of that period but with losses due to tides and egg collectors at times. Birds nested at these colonies before the years given above; the years were chosen just as examples of most recent numbers. In 1961, birds nested on Hurst shingle spit but all the eggs were trampled, so in 1962 the county Naturalists' Trust erected a fence round the site and breeding was successful. The site is now abandoned and all the birds at the above site nest on shingle patches on the salt marsh.

An older colony at the western end of the coast was harried out of existence in 1938, and odd pairs return at times to attempt nesting at two other sites where they have little chance of success due to beach huts, visitors and their dogs.

One pleasing development was the nesting in 1971 of 20 pairs on reclaimed land in Portsmouth Harbour (Duffin and Miss Jones), which raised 18 young with the co-operation of the Portsmouth City Council.

On the Island it has bred sparingly in two small colonies until 1953. The next was in 1958 and subsequently a few pairs have nested at Newtown (8/10 pairs in 1961, *I.o.W.* 5. Part 6, the maximum in any one year) with limited success due to Foxes and other unknown predators (e.g. *I.o.W.* 6. Part 3).

Return passage mainly in late July/August. High numbers have been: 190 at Langstone Harbour on 5 August 1957 (P.G.); 180 roosting at Portsmouth Harbour on 11 August 1971 (Duffin); 135 in Langstone Harbour on 1 August 1955 (P.G.). The latest date is 26 October 1955 when one was in Shanklin Bay but few are seen after mid September.

Inland records occur but are rare, e.g. one flying SW over Hampton Ridge (New Forest) on 9 May 1964 (*H.* 23. Part 2) and one at Badshot Lea on 13 August 1969 (*H.* 1969).

For an account of the Needs Oar colony see the paper by JHT in *H.* 1965, and for migration in Christchurch Harbour see the paper by Rogers and Webber in *H.* 1970.

223. Sandwich Tern. *Sterna sandvicensis*: K & M describe it as an occasional visitor to the coast on spring and autumn migration. From 1935 onwards it was reported with greater frequency and for the past 20 years at least, it has been a regular migrant in some numbers on both passages and has bred in steadily increasing numbers since the first nesting in 1954.

The first birds usually appear around the end of the third week of March with some regularity and the earliest record was within this period, i.e. one flying E. at Gilkicker on 18 March 1969 (*H.* 1969). Passage to the E. is mostly in April/May, through the Solent and past St. Catherine's Point, the present species using the St. Catherine's route much more than do the other terns. Numbers involved in spring migration are suggested by the following examples: 481 flew E. at St. Catherine's Point from 17 to 27 April 1962 with 250 on 19 alone (*H.* 22. Part 3); 576 flew E. at Gilkicker on eight dates in 1969 (*H.* 1969); recent years have all produced several days when over 100 have passed points such as Hengistbury, Hurst, Gilkicker and St. Catherine's (see *H.* 1970, 1969 etc.).

Odd birds were seen in June until 1954 when 10 pairs bred, followed by 17 pairs in 1955 (W. D. H. Brown), suspected breeding in 1956 and *ca.* 80 pairs which reared some 50 young in 1957. In 1958 the nests were all washed out by high tides. These early colonies were in the Keyhaven/Pennington area and birds have continued to nest there in varying numbers, the most being *ca.* 100 pairs in 1967 (probably birds washed out at Needs Oar) but only two pairs nested in 1970 (*H.* for recent years). Eggs and young have sometimes been lost to high tides, and on one occasion (1969) to Foxes.

The main colony has become established on the gullery island at Needs Oar (see paper in *H.* 1965 for a detailed description). From a beginning in 1961, the colony has built up as follows: 1962, 2; 1963, 45; 1964, 5; 1965, 127; 1966, 128; 1967, 112; 1968, 167; 1969, 179; 1970, 228; 1971, 242 (these numbers are breeding pairs). Except for 1967 when they were washed out by tides, they have had a tremendous breeding success in this wardened Bird Reserve. They seem to thrive amidst the ever growing population of Black-headed Gulls.

Autumn passage is mainly in August/September, numbers involved suggested by the following examples: 462 flew W. at Gilkicker on 1 September 1968 (*H.* 1968); 300 at Pennington on 5 August 1967 (*H.* 1967); 250 at Hengistbury on 7 August 1965 (*H.* 1965); 996 seen from Alum Chine (Bournemouth) in 39 hours of watching from 28 July to 15 August 1958, the stronger the wind was from the W. the higher the percentage of birds moving W. (JHT — see *B.o.H.* p.170 for details). The last are usually in October, but one flying W. at Hengistbury on 28 November 1970 (*H.* 1970) was the latest, and the only November record to date. For details of passage at Christchurch, see the paper by Rogers and Webber in *H.* 1970.

Inland birds are rare but one was at Badshot Lea on 13 and 17 September 1969 (*H.* 1969); Common and Little Terns were also seen there on autumn passage in 1969.

Ringing returns of Hampshire nestlings show the expected movement along the west coast of Europe and Africa. One ringed in Holland on 28 June 1947 was caught by a wing in a fishing hook while diving for small fish which were being chased by bass in the western approaches to the Solent on 12 June 1956, and released unharmed (Thomas). One ringed as a nestling off the mouth of the Elbe on 11 June 1964, was found dead at Barton-on-Sea on 18 August 1964.

224. Razorbill. *Alca torda*: Apart from Hengistbury, where birds occur occasionally (mainly in winter), very few are seen from the mainland and those that are reported are often oiled or dead. At Hengistbury, a total of 68 was seen in 1969 (*H.* 1969) whilst the highest count for one day there in 1967 was 13 on 16 December (*H.* 1967). For the rest of the mainland, numbers seen are suggested by the following yearly totals: 1969, 12; 1970, 6.

As early as 1923 it was stated that many were destroyed by oil (*I.o.W.* 1. Part 4). Mortality from this cause was heavy in February 1957, 28 being found on 10th alone between Hengistbury and Bournemouth Pier (Miss Brotherton), and 17 at Hurst on three dates (Bowers *et al.*). 30 dead or oiled birds were found at Hengistbury in February/March 1967 (*H.* 1967). With all the marine pollution today, the species is subject to many hazards and numbers of dead such as the 25 found at Hengistbury on 9 September 1970 (*H.* 1970) are likely to become more frequent.

Breeding numbers on the Main Bench cliffs have steadily declined. A rough count on 25 April 1937 gave about 1,000 (Hollom) but by 1946, Bannerman only counted *ca.* 200 from a boat. Estimates of pairs at the breeding site in 1955/6/7 were 45, 80 and 60 (Bowers and Wiseman) but cliff top counts are very inaccurate as only birds on the water can be seen. From 1959 to 1971, no estimate of birds on the water has exceeded 90 and the annual maximum has been below 50 at times. In 1967, only three nests could be counted from a boat, though up to 50 birds were seen on the water (*I.o.W.* 6. Part 2 and *H.* 1967).

A nestling ringed 30 June 1955 on Skokholm found long dead at Hengistbury on 9 February 1958. Another ringed 16 June 1959 at Cap Fréhel, Côtes du Nord, found dying at Titchfield Haven on 16 October 1959 (*B.B.* 53. 509). A nestling ringed 30 June 1966 on Alderney found dead at Hengistbury on 15 August 1966 (*B.B.* 61. 72).

Razorbill

226. Little Auk. *Plautus alle*: EC in *B.o.H.* said most records were of dead or dying birds found on the coast and occasionally far inland and that it is not often seen swimming or flying off shore. An analysis of records from 1959 to 1970 shows a slight change with live birds seen every year except 1967, 1969 and 1970, never more than five in one year and some years producing only one bird. Nevertheless, the period produced 18 apparently healthy birds compared with eight stranded (seven of which were dead or dying). Half of the live birds were seen at St. Catherine's Point, and all but one of the rest from Hurst, Hengistbury and Gilkicker; all were from October (one) to February (one) except for St. Catherine's where four flew E. on 17 May 1959 (*I.o.W.* 5. Part 4), one flew E. on 28 March 1962 (*I.o.W.* 5. Part 7) and another flew E. on 18 April 1963 (*H.* 23. Part 1). Two of the birds that died were well inland, one found walking in the road at Alresford on 16 November 1960 (*H.* 22. Part 1) and one at Kingsworthy on 1 November 1967 (*H.* 1967).

'Wrecks' occur at times. Four were reported from the Island and four from the mainland in such a 'wreck' in mid-February 1950 (*B.B.* 45. 132), and four were 'wrecked' on the Island (three died) in gales during November/December 1959 (*I.o.W.* 5. Part 4).

98

227. Guillemot. *Uria aalge*: Apart from small numbers at Hengistbury (mainly in winter), not often seen from the mainland in a satisfactory condition, e.g. only seven recorded from the whole of the mainland in 1969 (*H.* 1969), and away from Hengistbury, only three in 1970 (*H.* 1970). More often found when washed ashore dead or dying, oiled or storm driven, e.g. 25 found dead or oiled at Hengistbury in February/March 1967 (*H.* 1967).

At the breeding colony on the Freshwater Cliffs, Heycock in 1935 found them in far fewer numbers than Razorbills, but in 1937 (Hollom) and 1947 (E. White) they were said to far out number the latter. On 25 April 1937 Hollom counted roughly 3,000 there as against 1,000 Razorbills; on 14 April 1946 he counted about 1,200 and found no 'bridled' birds among the 130 or so which he examined. Big decrease since, viz. — 1955, 50 to 90 birds on various dates between 17 April and 25 June; 1956 *ca.* 80 pairs on 12 May (Bowers); 1957 *ca.* 80 pairs on 25 May (Bowers); *ca.* 90 occupied nests were counted in 1967 and cliff top counts of birds on the water revealed maxima of 234 and 105 in 1969 and 1970 respectively (*H.* 1969 and 1970). No longer breeds at Culver as in K & M.

The first complaint of destruction by oil comes from as long ago as 1923: 'seem to keep up their numbers but many destroyed by oil' (*I.o.W.* 1. 4. 180).

One ringed Heligoland on 28 February 1927 recovered Hayling Island on 10 January 1929 (*B.B.* 23. 305).

A bird ringed as young in Cruden Bay (Aberdeenshire) on 10 July 1951 was recovered at Hayling Island on 15 March 1953 (*B.B.* 46. 317). Two ringed on Lundy Island were recovered in September 1956 at Southbourne and Portsmouth, and a third ringed there as a nestling on 26 June 1955 was recovered at Shanklin, about 160 miles ESE on 23 April 1958. A nestling ringed 30 June 1963 on the Calf of Man found dead at Sandown on 27 November 1963 (*B.B.* 57. 557).

229. Black Guillemot. *Uria grylle*: Some eight specimens obtained are recorded in K & M, the last being in 1891. None since.

230. Puffin. *Fratercula arctica*: Very few recorded from the mainland, e.g. 1970, two; 1969, none; 1968, three; 1967, five; 1966, four. Occasionally blown ashore and even as far inland as Alton and Baughurst by gales.

Numbers breeding on Freshwater Cliffs appear to have declined almost to vanishing point; indeed, there is some doubt as to whether or not it still breeds. In 1905 they bred 'in fair numbers' (K & M); in 1913 'a fair number breed' (*B.o.M.* possibly copying K & M) and 'crowds' (Munn); in 1918/19 'still abound in nesting season on Freshwater Cliffs' (Munn); in 1923 'seem to keep up numbers' (*I.o.W.* 1. Part 4); on 25 April 1937, about 300—500 (Hollom); in 1941 'breeds sparingly' (*Handbook*); on 14 April 1946, about 24 (Hollom); on 21 April 1950, about 30 (Adams and Mrs. Bannerman); in 1951 'nest in small numbers' (Adams); on 11 June 1955, 16 plus (Adams); *ca.* 10 pairs on 12 May 1956 (Bowers). Since then, 12 has been the most seen in any one year except for 1968 when 20 were reported together in the breeding season (*H.* 1968). However, these are just birds on the water and one seen entering a burrow on 30 May 1964 (*I.o.W.* 1963/4) was said at that time to be the only recent evidence of actual breeding. Today it is quite possible to spend a day searching from the cliff tops and not see a single bird.

One ringed Alderney on 23 June 1955 found dead at Hengistbury on 13 September 1964 (*H.* 23. Part 2).

231. Pallas's Sandgrouse. *Syrrhaptes paradoxus*: According to K & M only two of the previous irruptions resulted in birds being obtained in Hampshire, those of 1863 and 1888.

During the 1908 irruption five were seen near East Liss (near Petersfield) in mid April (*The Field* 20 June 1908), two flew over Havant on 8 July (*B.B.* 2. 98) and five were clearly identified in early August by Lyon (*ibid.*).

232. Stock Dove. *Columba oenas*: K & M call it a universally distributed resident, nowhere very plentiful. Today it is certainly well spread all over the mainland and Island, the *Atlas* survey showing breeding proved in most 10-kilometer squares and probably missed in squares where breeding was not fully proved. Within this general picture however, the exact status is not fully known but evidence suggests a patchy distribution. In some areas it is common, e.g. in 1953 over 100 pairs were nesting on 1,000 acres near Micheldever, mostly in ivy covered trees and rabbit burrows in railway cuttings (Jenkins); one of the characteristic birds of the wooded area behind St. Catherine's Point (JHT). In some places, loose 'colonies' seem to exist, e.g. St. Leonards, near Beaulieu. In other areas it is very sparsely represented, whilst some districts do not have any breeding pairs. Much more detailed information is needed.

Outside of the breeding season flocks assemble, but here again they are found somewhat locally and often in the same spots year after year, e.g. the Needs Oar/St. Leonards area. The flocks appear in all quarters of the county and numbers up to 100 are reported in most years. The largest flocks recently were: 400 at Sowley on 27 December 1966 feeding on young corn (*H.* 1966); and about 250 feeding on chickweed in the Martin/Damerham area in June 1952 (flocks also occur in May/June at feeding areas), apparently coming from the New Forest since not many breed locally (Ash). Desertion of breeding grounds to form flocks is no doubt responsible for the statement in *W.* 1931 that birds round Winchester are entirely absent from summer haunts in winter 'as though it were a migrant.' Some movement has in fact been seen on the coast, e.g. 37 flying W. at St. Catherine's Point in 1961 and 90 flying NE in cold weather at Titchfield Haven on 31 December 1961 (*H.* 1961).

One ringed as a nestling at Sway on 29 April 1955 shot at Ryde on 15 August 1953 (*B.B.* 47. 384).

233. Rock Dove. *Columba livia*: 'A rare accidental visitor, always in winter' (K & M). As Colonel Meinertzhagen was not one of their correspondents, K & M did not know of the following occurrence: 'On 8 November 1898 a small flock appeared at Oakley, near Mottisfont, feeding on crop land. They were extremely wild and unapproachable and nobody in the neighbourhood kept such birds. We supposed they were a straggling flock from the coast. They all appeared to be pure wild birds.'

The only subsequent references are as follows: 1910 Freshwater Cliffs, 'A few rock-doves and kestrels completed the avian scene' (White: *Some Changes in Island Bird Life during the Past 50 Years. I.o.W.* 1947); and on 26 August 1944 one at Hengistbury with a query as to whether it was a purely wild bird (*H.* 16. 215).

It is as certain as can be that no pure wild birds may now be included in the county avifauna.

234. Woodpigeon. *Columba palumbus*: K & M say: 'A very common resident in all districts in the county and in the Isle of Wight.'

Notes or complaints of their abundance crop up frequently in the literature from 1918 to the present day. Flocks up to 500 are commonly reported, particularly from November to March. The largest gatherings have been: 10—12,000 at Pitts Wood on 6 November 1969 (*H.* 1969); 10,000 at Amberwood and Islands Thorns Inclosures on 30 November 1968; 10,000 flighting to roost from Alice Holt Forest in November/December 1968 (*H.* 1968 — acorn crops were very heavy in 1968 and 1969); 5,000 around Islands Thorns Inclosure in December 1964 (*H.* 23. Part 2);

5,000 at High Boulsbury, near Fordingbridge, on 6 November 1953 (Ash).

Evidence of breeding numbers: 200 pairs found in 500 acres at Ampfield Wood in 1967 (*H.* 1967); 6,000 eggs were destroyed during 1959 in the NE of the Island by a Rabbit Clearance Society (*I.o.W.* 5. Part 4); the *Atlas* survey showed the species to be present in every corner of the county. Eggs or newly-fledged young have been seen in November, December and January on several occasions.

These numbers continue despite the war waged on the species, e.g. 7,335 'pigeons' (which may include Stock Doves) were shot on the Island in organised shoots from 1 September 1953 to 1 April 1954.

Hardly any spring movement seen but heavy autumn movements observed on a number of occasions, e.g.: at St. Catherine's Point, 10,040 flew W., 1,050 from N. to SW, and 1,190 from S. to N. on 4 November 1961, whilst on the following day 2,755 flew W. and 700 S. (*I.o.W.* 5. Part 4); sometimes there is movement to the E. *ca.* 800 flying E. on 9 November 1957; 4,135 flew N. over Weston Shore in one hour on 4 November 1959, and on the following day 8,400 flew NNW in one and a half hours at Titchfield Haven (*H.* 21. Part 3). Similar though smaller movements have occurred in several recent years. For a very full discussion of Woodpigeon movements the reader is referred to a paper by Murton and Ridpath in *Bird Study* 9.1.7/41. They attribute the increase along the south coast in November partly to 'a general movement south of a small proportion of the British population' and partly to passage of Continental immigrants which move south across the Channel as soon as the weather is favourable.

Birds suffering from 'pigeon-pox' are met with at times and in 1907 there was a large scale epidemic of *bacillus diptheriae columbarum* among winter flocks, during which numbers were found dead at Kingsclere, Burghclere and elsewhere (*Bull. B.O.C.* 15.5.07).

A nestling ringed Andover on 14 August 1925 recovered at Ripon (Yorkshire) on 26 January 1926 (*B.B.* 20. 49).

235. Turtle Dove. *Streptopelia turtur*: A common summer resident, as in K & M's time, breeding in all parts of the mainland and Island. Breeding density suggested by 100 plus pairs on an estate of some 4,000 acres near Damerham in 1952 (Ash) and 20—50 pairs on a 1,000 estate near Micheldever in 1953 (Jenkins). However, there would appear to be marked fluctuations in numbers from one summer to another. Munn found a considerable increase in 1918/19 over 1905, and it was reported as having greatly increased in the Alton area in 1944 (*H.* 16. 215); on the other hand 1947, 1949 and 1950 were very poor, at least in the southwest of the county; 1955 and 1956 were better. On the Island it was described as 'abundant as ever' in 1923 (*I.o.W.* 1. Part 4), but in 1951 Adams said that it was a summer visitor 'in small numbers.'

Flocks around 30—50 assemble in late summer, occasionally reaching 100 or more, e.g. 110 at Keyhaven on 29 August 1968 (*H.* 1968), 110 plus at Winchester sewage farm on 10/11 August 1964 (*H.* 23. Part 2) and 100 at Botley on 20 August 1962 (*H.* 22. Part 3).

The earliest date was a bird at Chandlers Ford on 25 March 1970 (*H.* 1970). The last are usually in October, late birds being at Farlington Marshes on 7 November 1970 (*H.* 1970), one at Titchfield Haven on 6 December 1966 (*H.* 1966), and the latest date, one at Weston from 15 to 26 December 1969 (*H.* 1969).

Thirteen were killed at St. Catherine's Light on various dates in May 1906, 1907 and 1908, and one on 19 September 1905. Autumn movement was seen at St. Catherine's Point in 1956 and 1957, 151 flying E. between midnight and 06.00 hrs. on 9 September 1956 in a very strong NE wind (*I.o.W.* 5. Part 1).

Three nestlings ringed in Hampshire have been recovered in Portugal, viz. — ringed 9 August 1913, recovered September 1913; ringed 7 June 1950, recovered 1 September 1952; ringed 9 July 1961, shot 12' September 1964 (*B.B.* 8. 162 — 46. 318 — 58. 563).

Turtle Dove

Collared Dove. *Streptopelia decaocto* *: One on 30 August 1957 at Gosport (Mole — *H.* 20. Supplement) was the first for the county. Breeding occurred at Hayling in 1961, and on 23 July 1961 one was feeding at Stanpit with Turtle Doves (*H.* 22. Part 2). 1962 saw the first real influx with the first Island records (at Wootton, Sandown, Shanklin and Totland), the first Island breeding records (at Wootton, Sandown and Shanklin), a spread of mainland breeding (at Totton), and reports from a dozen localities with eight at Totton in December and eight at Sandown (*H.* 22. Part 3 and *I.o.W.* 5. Part 10, pp.465—7, a paper by Stafford on the spread of the species in the Island).

Since then it has shown the explosive increase that it has shown all over the country (for an account of the early spread in Britain, see Hudson's paper in *B.B.* 58. 105/139). The main features in Hampshire have been:

1963. Several small colonies were established in the coastal area of the mainland from Totton to Hayling Island with 20 adults at Hayling. A few records from Winchester, Andover and Stratfield Saye represented the first small penetration inland (*H.* 23. Part 1).

1964. A colony of 16/18 at Barton showed a spread westwards along the coast from the stronghold around Portsmouth, and 25 plus near Winchester at Morestead Down showed a further push inland (*H.* 23. Part 2). On the Island, birds nested at Luccombe, Sandown, Shanklin, Ventnor and Wootton, 20 birds being seen at Ventnor (*I.o.W.* 63/64 and 5. Part 10).

1965. Nesting took place in at least 10 Island localities and over 40 were reported at Sandown (*I.o.W.* 5. Part 10 and 6. Part 1). 30 at Havant and Portsmouth were the highest mainland counts (*H.* 1965).

1966. Nesting in at least 14 Island localities (mainly coastal) with *ca.* 60 at Sandown on 24 August. The breeding distribution on the mainland was still heavily centred on the SE corner. Maximum gatherings were 82 at Titchfield Haven on 27 November, 74 near Holdenhurst on 26 August, and 60 plus at Totton on 20 September where it was described as a garden pest (*H.* 1966 and *I.o.W.* 6. Part 1).

1967. Still concentrated in the SE corner of the mainland but spreading inland and 100 estimated at Winchester (Fisher).

1968. The first year of the *Atlas* survey showed breeding proved or suspected in 24 of the 57 mainland 10-kilometer squares, heavily concentrated in a 20 mile wide coastal belt with penetration particularly along the Test and Itchen valleys. Still missing from some inland areas in the east. On the Island, distribution also markedly coastal (*H.* 1968).

1969. The largest gatherings were 180 at Lainston (near Winchester) on 23 December, 130 at Mersley Farm (I.o.W.) on 13 December, and 120 at Browndown on 19 October (*H.* 1969). It had become very common as a breeding species in several parts of Bournemouth, including areas in the centre of the town (JHT).

1970. The Lainston flock reached 250 plus on 25 February, all sitting on one barn roof (Fisher).

1971. The *Atlas* survey showed breeding widespread all over the mainland and Island. Numbers had increased so much that records such as 32 in one small Bournemouth garden were no longer notable.

One imagines the spread continuing so that this account will be out of date within a few years.

One ringed as fully grown in Gelderland (Holland) on 2 January 1965 was killed at Marchwood on 31 August 1968 (*B.B.* 63. 251). A juvenile ringed at Broadstairs (Kent) on 30 September 1967 was killed at Petersfield on 10 April 1968 (*B.B.* 62. 422).

237. Cuckoo. *Cuculus canorus*: Widespread throughout the county as a summer visitor, though numbers vary between one locality and another, as well as from season to season. Birds arrive in some strength usually about the middle of April — the 14th was known round Mottisfont as 'Cuckoo Day' (Meinertzhagen) — but March birds have occurred with the earliest on 16 March 1938 (*Handbook*). However, records even in the first week of April are not common. In 1958 the first was as late as 19 April whilst the average first date over the past 20 years has been 8/10 April. It is of interest to note that two centuries ago Gilbert White gave mid-April as the usual time for arrival at Selborne, while the earliest date in his *Naturalist's Calender* is 7 April.

Records in late summer and autumn, almost always of juveniles, are most frequent in coastal districts. Stafford, on 17 September 1953, watched eight birds arrive from the N. at sunset and settle to roost in Kingston Copse (I.o.W.). At Titchfield Haven on 19 September 1957, Bowers recorded a bird flying off in a SE direction at dusk. In 1959 there were several interesting records at St. Catherine's Point: on 1 August a juvenile flew off SSW and on the 3rd one flew in from the sea. The latest admissible date is one on 26 September 1971 at Bishop's Waltham (*H.* 1971). The average last date for the years 1951/59 was 19 September (the above based on a summary by P. E. Brown).

Females of the rare rufous phase were seen at Timsbury on 26 June 1970 (Thelwell), and in 1971 at Steep (on 27 April) and Old Winchester Hill (on 23 May — *H.* 1971).

239. Yellow-billed Cuckoo. *Coccyzus americanus*: Two in K & M, one dead at Ventnor in October 1896 and one shot near Avon Castle on 30 October 1901. None since.

241. Barn Owl. *Tyto alba*: This species, if hardly common, is well-distributed throughout the county and Island. There was little evidence until 1957 of any significant change in status since K & M wrote in 1905. From 1957, however, there were persistent reports of a marked decline in some south-eastern parts of the county (*H*), and in 1964 a decrease was noted in the Basingstoke area. This decline could have been due to birds taking prey containing chemicals, the apparent cause of so much raptor death around that time, but the *whole* county did not seem to be affected for some areas maintained numbers, e.g. said to be widespread and not uncommon on the Island in 1961 (*H*. 22. Part 2). The first year of the *Atlas* survey (1968) showed a more encouraging picture and a recovery seemed to be under way that has continued to the present day. The final picture obtained from the *Atlas* was of breeding proved or suspected in most of the 10-kilometer squares, and allowing for pairs that were overlooked, its status seems to be back to that described in the opening sentence.

Examples of numbers in particular areas are: 3/4 pairs in the Micheldever area in 1953 (Jenkins); 2/3 pairs in the parish of Old Basing during 1954/9 (P. E. Brown); 13 hunting in daylight near Damerham in March 1958 and 'exceptional numbers' also hunting there in daylight in March 1962 (Ash).

Young have been recorded fledging as late as December (*W*. 1966).

A young bird ringed at Fordingbridge on 22 June 1952 recovered at Hampstead Norris (Berkshire) on 1 February 1953 (*B.B.* 46. 319).

242. Scops Owl. *Otus scops*: K & M admitted four, all last century. One at Totton in October 1950 had probably escaped after being brought in by a seaman. One found dead at Highclere on 11 May 1968 was accepted by *British Birds* Rarities Committee (*B.B.* 62. 474).

243. Eagle Owl. *Bubo bubo*: K & M admit one shot in the New Forest in 1855. They mention another killed at Paultons near Romsey in 1891 but suggest that it might have escaped from captivity. None since.

244. Snowy Owl. *Nyctea scandiaca*: K & M admit one, shot in 1848. One seen by Goddard near Southampton on 22 January 1946 was accepted by *British Birds* (*B.B.* 39. 216). In 1965, what was presumably the same bird was seen at Brightstone (I.o.W.) from about 20 February to 13 March, at Pennington on 14 March, and at Brading on 28 March (*I.o.W.* 5. Part 10 and *H*. 1965). The unusually large number of records from southern England in 1965 are considered suspect as Snowy Owls were imported for sale (*B.B.* 59. 291/2). One reported on the mainland and at Bembridge in July 1966 was not accepted by *British Birds* (*B.B.* 59. 352 and 60. 337).

246. Little Owl. *Athene noctua*: This introduced species was probably just starting to spread into the county when K & M wrote in 1905. There were, however, remarkably few records up to the outbreak of the First World War. A bird was shot near Petersfield in December 1908 (*B.B.* 2. 310) and the species was reported nesting near Portsmouth in the following year. By 1912 it was certainly nesting in the New Forest and even west of the Avon (*B.B.* 7. 271). The first pair to breed at Mottisfont was in that year (Meinertzhagen). It reached the Isle of Wight by 1916, when it was also noted round Winchester and in the north of the county where there had already been records of birds shot near Overton in November 1911 and at Basingstoke in August 1913 (*H.*). By the 1920s it was obviously widespread in some strength, though the peak population was probably not reached until some 10 years later.

The little Owl remains well distributed throughout the county and the Isle of Wight, although in many areas, especially in the north of the county, there has been a marked decline compared with the thirties. E. L. Jones has found several gibbeted throughout the fifties and says 'this persecution continues'. In very recent years this fall in population has been even more marked in areas in the north-east and south-east of the county, so that in a few places it is now almost scarce. EC also noticed a decrease in the south-west and in the late 60s it was not to be found in some of its regular haunts on the Island. Reports from recent years suggest that numbers have been maintained in the north of the county much better than they have in the south, though the *Atlas* survey (1968/72) showed breeding proved or suspected in nearly all the 10-kilometer mainland squares. There is little quantitative data on the extent of the decline but some does exist, e.g. in 1966, Glue found that only one of five known breeding sites in the lower Test valley was occupied (*H.* 1966). (Most of the above written by P. E. Brown.)

A young bird ringed at Sibford Ferris (Oxon.) on 11 June 1952 was recovered near Hursley on 16 December of the same year (*B.B.* 46. 319); another ringed at Sunninghill (Berkshire) on 4 June 1949, was recovered at Lee-on-Solent on 27 December 1949 (*B.B.* 43. 317); another nestling ringed at Calcombe (Oxfordshire) on 14 June 1964 was found dead at Milford-on-Sea on 19 May 1965 (*B.B.* 59. 469).

247. Tawny Owl. *Strix aluco*: Widely distributed throughout the county but scarce on the Island. It seems that this species is more common than it was when K & M (1905) described it as 'sparingly' distributed on the mainland. The *Atlas* survey showed proved or suspected breeding in every part of the mainland and records occur in the middle of even our largest towns (e.g. Southampton and Bournemouth). On the Island however, the first four years of *Atlas* work revealed just two cases of birds present in suitable breeding habitat. Stafford reports that a typical year's total of Isle of Wight reports would amount to two or three, almost all of them from the northern half of the Island. This scarcity is strange in view of the suitable habitat and the bird's status on the mainland.

248. Long-eared Owl. *Asio otus*: K & M described the species as widely distributed, except on the Island, and 'common' in suitable localities. The extreme paucity of records, however, suggest that this is not the case today, though it is important to bear in mind that this nocturnal and relatively quiet owl can be easily overlooked. There are records in the last 20 years from woodland districts throughout the mainland, perhaps most frequently from the New Forest, but seldom more than two or three in any one year, and no reports at all in some years. On the Island, the species is not mentioned in the Bird Reports for 1958/68, though a pair was found nesting at one locality in 1969 and 1971. Mainland breeding was proved by Ash near Martin Down in 1953 and by Orr at the same place in 1963 (*H.* 23. Part 1), but in the first four years of the *Atlas* survey, breeding was not fully proved in any of the mainland 10-kilometer squares, though birds were suspected of breeding in two squares and seen in four others. As P. E. Brown said in *B.o.H.*, 'one feels bound to admit that the available information makes it impossible to assess accurately the present status of this species.'

One ringed as a nestling in Overijssel (Holland) on 8 June 1968 found sick near Southampton on 29 December 1968 (*B.B.* 63. 251).

Long-eared Owl

249. Short-eared Owl. *Asio flammeus*: A regular winter visitor in some numbers to many parts of the county and the Isle of Wight, more especially (but not by any means exclusively) to coastal districts. It has bred in the county, but only sporadically and almost certainly not in any recent years. Most of the acceptable nesting records are confined to the northern half of the county. A pair nested near Ropley in 1882 (not recorded in K & M), whilst between 1928 and 1930 birds bred regularly and in some numbers in the Overton-Whitchurch-Micheldever areas. Portal (*B.B.* 22. 263 for this and other breeding records) reported two or more nests on the Laverstoke estate in 1928 and this is confirmed by Arnold (*per* Miss Barraud) who was told by the keeper at Laverstoke that there were in fact three pairs nesting in that year. In 1930 Portal (*B.B.* 24. 296) reported no less than seven nests in the Laverstoke area. Apart from a pair reported by Stevenson Clarke to have nested near the centre of the Isle of Wight in 1939 (*I.o.W.*) there appear to be no other authentic breeding records.

The north-central part of the county continues, however, to be one of the favourite wintering areas for this species, though numbers certainly fluctuate from year to year. Jenkins described the bird as an 'irregular' winter visitor to the Micheldever area in 1954, but had recorded up to 20 there in some years, the birds appearing from August onwards. On 22 November 1953, Robertson and Powell counted 26 hunting over about 100 acres of stubble near Chilbolton, and such numbers were frequent there in the mid-fifties (E. L. Jones). Arnold (*per* Miss Barraud) saw 11 in the air together during a shoot near Overton on 7 January 1929 and counted seven at the same place in 1934. Captain Bacon of Burghclere (*in litt.*) said that about 1940 a Mr. Paginton, shooting over his ground at Doiley Hill, between Andover and Hurstbourne Tarrant, put up six or seven birds, whilst seven were present for several weeks in the winter of 1942 at Ibthorpe Farm, Hurstbourne Tarrant (*H.*). Nine were in a small plantation near Whitchurch on 22 December 1966, and Danebury was much favoured by the species until much of the yew was destroyed for farmland. Inland wintering birds have also been recorded fairly frequently in the Damerham area (Ash) and occasionally elsewhere (e.g. two near Winchester early in February 1946, the first for the century recorded by Winchester College). Not many are reported from the New Forest.

In coastal localities the birds are frequently recorded outside the breeding-season, most often on marshes like Farlington and Pennington. At Farlington, where one or two are most usual, up to nine have occurred (*H.* 1970), very early birds arriving in September (19 August 1957) and lingering until late March or even April (27 April 1966). Other places where these wintering birds occur with fair frequency include: Hayling; Southampton Water; Keyhaven; and Dibden Bay. Not many recently from the Island.

We are indebted to P. E. Brown for most of the above summary.

252. Nightjar. *Caprimulgus europaeus:* K & M call it a regular summer visitor to all parts of the county and the Isle of Wight. The status does not appear to have altered significantly since then though the amount of suitable habitat has dwindled due to afforestation and ploughing of heathlands. The *Atlas* survey showed breeding proved or suspected in just over half of the 10-kilometer squares, more detailed surveys of particular areas being: 26 pairs found in Ampfield Wood (400 acres surveyed out of 800 acres) in 1967 (Green in *H.* 1967); 27 pairs found in 10 localities in a fairly full survey of the Island in 1957/8 for the British Trust for Ornithology (*I.o.W.* 5. Part 3); 12 pairs at Sheddon Oak in 1963 (*W.* 1963). Tubbs in *The New Forest* (1968) says that it remains numerous there despite a decrease in other parts of southern England.

The earliest date is one at Hengistbury on 27 April 1968 but the first usually arrive in May. The last are normally seen in September but we can trace two October records and the latest occurred on 23 November 1958 when one was seen at Farlington Marshes.

A nestling ringed at Damerham on 28 June 1953 was killed by high tension wires at Nantes (France) on 8 September 1954 (*B.B.* 48. 489).

255. Swift. *Apus apus:* Although there are occasional notes of decreases locally in certain years, it is still a very common breeding species.

The earliest date is 3 April 1968 when one was at Seaview (*I.o.W.*) (*H.* 1968), other early arrivals being two at Ryde on 5 April 1954 (*H.* 19. Part 1), and on 5 April 1964 at Nursling (*H.* 23. Part 2). First arrivals on average are at the end of the third week or beginning of the fourth week in April. Peak passage is often in early May, e.g. 1,172 flying N. at Gilkicker on 2 May 1962 (*H.* 22. Part 3).

There are many notes of migratory or mid-season movements, e.g. 350 flying SW at Gilkicker on 25 July 1966, 450 flying S. there on 13 August 1966, and *ca.* 1,000 flying S. at Hurst in thundery weather on 6 July 1966 (*H.* 1966). A small W. to E. passage along the coast has also been observed in some years.

Return passage is mainly from early August to mid-September, October records being rather few in number. The latest was at Farlington Marshes on 11 November

1969 (*H.* 1969).
One ringed 19 June 1963 at Winchester recovered Walton-on-Thames on 27 June 1963 (*W.* 1963).

256. Alpine Swift. *Apus melba*: Under the name of White-bellied Swift, K & M admit two together near Basingstoke on 28 April 1886.
One, with Common Swifts, Mottisfont, 9/10 September 1894 (Meinertzhagen).
One, Brockenhurst, 28 May 1911 (Mitford — *B.B.* 5. 84).
One, Leckford, 18 July 1946 (Peter Scott — *B.B.* 40. 21).
One, St. Catherine's Point, 13 May 1962 (Wiseman *et al.* — *B.B.* 56. 402).
One near Winchester, from 30 April to 7 May 1964 (*H.* 23. Part 2).
One, Gilkicker, 4 October 1965 (*B.B.* 59. 292).
Two, Locks Farm (I.o.W.), 19 May 1967 (*H.* 1967).
One, Bouldnor (I.o.W.), 27 May 1967 (*B.B.* 61, 347).
One, the Needles, 18 May 1969 (*B.B.* 63. 282).

257. Needle-tailed Swift. *Chaetura caudacuta*: A specimen of this Asiatic species was obtained near Ringwood in July, 1879 and was said to be flying with another one (K & M).

258. Kingfisher. *Alcedo atthis*: K & M say: 'Resident and universally distributed throughout the county and the Isle of Wight'. This is still the position although it is nowhere numerous and in some parts (particularly coastal areas) it is strictly a winter visitor. Records for the southern half of the Island are scarce, some years producing none. An indication of the distribution was given by the *Atlas* survey which showed the species breeding or suspected of breeding in nearly all the mainland and north Island 10-kilometer squares. There is little detailed information on breeding numbers but nine pairs were located in the New Forest in 1961 (*H.* 22. Part 2).

There is some movement to the coast every winter, though many remain in their breeding areas. This may help to offset the effects of severe winters though the species suffered heavy losses in the cold of 1962/3, being almost exterminated in the south-east. For a more detailed account of that winter's effect, see *H.* 23. Part 1. Recovery was rapid however; mainland numbers approached normal by 1965, and the recovery seemed complete by 1968. Recovery on the Island was slower, numbers still being down in 1966.

They are not popular on some stretches of trout stream though there is little recent evidence of persecution.

Meinertzhagen noted that all nests on the Mottisfont estate were in holes in the banks of small water cuts, none in the banks of the Test itself.

One ringed Stanpit on 25 June 1960 recaptured at Latchmore Bottom (New Forest) on 17 August 1960 (*H.* 22. Part 1). One ringed Britford (Wiltshire) on 7 April 1961 found dead at Emsworth about 8 January 1962 (*B.B.* 56. 504 — this bird had moved 40 miles, a long-distance recovery for British-ringed Kingfishers). One ringed Stanpit on 5 July 1964 found dead at Botley on 18 January 1969 (*H.* 1969). An adult male ringed Totton on 15 July 1967 killed at Whyke (Sussex) on 20 January 1968 (*B.B.* 62. 423).

259. Bee-eater. *Merops apiaster*: K & M admit five on the mainland and one on the Island between 1885 and 1903, all but one of which were shot.
One killed at Shorwell (I.o.W.); no date available but Munn was satisfied as to the validity of the record (*H.* 8. 3).
Two at Bembridge (I.o.W.) on 16/17 May 1967 (*B.B.* 61. 347).

The one reported at Titchfield Haven on 11 May 1960 was not accepted by *British Birds* (*B.B.* 54. 199).

Bee-eater

260. Roller. *Coracias garrulus*: K & M admit three on the mainland and two on the Island between 1874 and 1904, all but the last being shot.

A female, shot at New Milton, 23 September 1918 (*B.B.* 12. 140).

A juvenile, near Fareham, from 15 to 21 September 1947 (*B.B.* 41. 119).

One, Butser Hill, 30 May 1955 (Billett, Bowers, Champion and Wiseman).

Two other recent records were rejected by the county Editorial Committee.

261. Hoopoe. *Upupa epops*: An uncommon but annual bird of passage, probably occurring more frequently in the last two decades though the increased number of bird-watchers may be the reason for this apparent increase. During the period 1951–70, about 120 birds were seen, principally on the Island and the southern part of the mainland. An analysis of records from 1959/70 gives the following monthly totals: March, six; April, 33; May, 19; June, three; July, one; August, eight; September, five; October, four. It will be seen that about two-thirds were in April/May. The lowest total for one year in this period was two birds in 1961; 13 birds in 1964 was the highest.

In 1940, one was at Swanmore in January. It died of starvation during a frost (*B.B.* 33. 315).

Hoopoes have bred in the county on a number of occasions, the most recent being near Sherfield-on-Loddon in 1953 and at Middle Wallop in 1956. On both occasions breeding was successful, though only with human help in the latter case (see *B.B.* 49. 454 for a full account of the Middle Wallop nest).

262. Green Woodpecker. *Picus viridis*: In 1905 K & M described this species as 'very rare' in the Isle of Wight, when they knew of only three occurrences there; two, rather vague, in the mid-eighties of last century and one shot at Wootton about 1899. The phenomenal spread of this species into the Island must have begun very soon after 1905. The first breeding record appears to have come from Briddlesford Wood, between Cowes and Ryde, in 1910. Breeding was first established in the Osborne district (Nicholl) in 1913, where the subsequent increase was said to be 'rapid'. In 1918 Shaw found birds nesting at Brook, at the western end of the Island, where it was described as 'common' a year later. At about the same time Goodall described it as well established and quite common near Bembridge, at the eastern end. It rapidly spread to all parts of the Island and it remains common there in all suitable localities.

On the mainland, where it is common and widespread, there is no indication of any change in status since K & M other than the temporary effect of the 1962/3 winter. Most observers on the mainland and Island noted a decline in numbers following the severe cold but recovery was rapid and probably complete by 1965. The *Atlas* survey showed proved or suspected breeding in every mainland 10-kilometer square.

Meinertzhagen writes that from nine to 11 pairs nested on the Mottisfont estate in the nineties but only from five to eight pairs between 1939 and 1945, and says that keepers shot them for their tongues which they used for 'gapes' in young Pheasants.

263. Great Spotted Woodpecker. *Dendrocopos major*: Although common only in a few favoured localities, this species is well-distributed throughout the county. K & M (1905) say little about this species; what they do say might suggest that it is now somewhat commoner than it was at the start of the century (P. E. Brown). Meinertzhagen, too, reports an increase at Mottisfont from two pairs in the nineties to eight to 11 pairs between 1940 and 1945. Like the Green Woodpecker, it appears only to have spread into the Isle of Wight during this century, though according to K & M a specimen was procured there in November 1889. Perhaps the earliest breeding record there is of a pair nesting near Bembridge in 1926, where it was reported to be nesting annually in 1939 (Rogers). It probably now nests in most suitable localities in the Island (Stafford).

In recent years some observations suggest that there may be small-scale migratory movements. In 1957, one flew west past Eastney Point on 2 October; on 20 October one flew west along the cliff edge at St. Catherine's Point (with Linnets), whilst on 16 November at the same place a bird flew in from the south-west and landed. In the same year Dennis recorded birds at Titchfield Haven on 27 October, one; 4 November, two; and 27 November one which were 'in exposed positions by the shore, appeared restless and flew about a lot; seemed to be migrants'. In 1959 a single bird was recorded at St. Catherine's on 27 March and two on 2 August, whilst one was seen on Farlington Marshes on 17 September. Subsequent years have produced similar records, e.g. several at Hengistbury from September to December 1966 appeared to be associated with influxes of tits (*H.* 1966).

264. Lesser Spotted Woodpecker. *Dendrocopos minor*: This inconspicuous little woodpecker is probably rather more common than the records might suggest, though it is almost certainly the least common of the three breeding woodpeckers and probably more local in its distribution. K & M however described it as the commoner of the spotted woodpeckers. In 1955 in the parish of Old Basing, P. E. Brown and Miss Davies found three nesting-pairs of this species, the same as for *D. major*. Meinertzhagen reports an increase on the Mottisfont estate from none between 1891 and 1896 to two pairs in 1897, four in 1899 and at least seven between 1935 and 1945. In the *Atlas* survey, breeding was proved or suspected in over three-fifths of the mainland 10-kilometer squares, and birds were probably overlooked in some of the *blank* squares.

For the Isle of Wight, K & M give only one certain record: a bird shot at Swainston in September 1893. It has subsequently spread into the Island, but on a much smaller scale than either of the two preceding species. The first record of breeding appears to be of a pair near Cowes in 1921. E. H. White, writing in 1947 of changes in the bird-life of the Island over the previous 50 years (*Proc. I.o.W. Nat. Hist. & Arch. Soc. 1948*) wrote of this species: 'I rarely saw it, but it is on the increase. In our garden at Shanklin we frequently see it, and elsewhere, and for four years running I knew a tree in Whitefield Woods where it nested in the same hole.' C. Smith found it nesting in Tollbar Plantation in 1952. However, the first four years of the *Atlas* survey failed to reveal one case of even suspected breeding, even though coverage was fairly full.

Lesser Spotted Woodpecker

265. Wryneck. *Jynx torquilla*: K & M describe the Wryneck as a common visitor to all parts of the county and the Isle of Wight but they added that 'it is not an equally common bird in all parts, but is perhaps most plentiful along the south coast and in the Island'. They quote no nesting records in the northern half of the county, so that it may well have been rather scarce as a breeding-species even in 1905. However, in the three years 1906/08 at least nine have been found killed at St. Catherine's Light (Poole); all those records refer to April (though there are others between 14 March 1910 and 19 September 1945) and it seems probable that the species entered the county in some numbers 60 or so years ago, though many may have passed through. There are a number of breeding records in the 1920s, when it was even said to nest 'freely' in the Stockbridge area (Miss Chawner). As regards breeding during the past

30 years, the story is easily if sadly told. Pairs are said to have bred near Hinton Admiral in 1940 (Meyrick), at Crondall in 1944 (*H*. 16. 212), near Petersfield in 1946 (*H*. 17), at Aldershot in 1950 and at Drayton near Portsmouth in 1954 (the last two *per* Dr. Monk), with the possibility of six more between 1954 and 1958 (Monk). Since then one calling continuously at a locality in the NE from 22 May to 3 July 1966 (*H*. 1966), and one at a nesting hole in a dead Scots Pine near Burley in June 1968 (Betts and EC) are the only suggestions of nesting.

A few passage birds occur almost every year, reports coming from all over the mainland and Island, annual totals for 1959/70 being: 1959, one; 1960, two; 1961, three; 1962, none; 1963, three; 1964, four; 1965, seven; 1966, eight; 1967, seven; 1968, eleven; 1969, eight; 1970, five. All of these were between April/October, with about half of them in September; May and August accounted for most of the rest, with two to four in each of the other months.

An adult ringed at Petersfield on 28 June 1915 was found nesting at Steep on 17 June 1917 (Blagg).

269. Short-toed Lark. *Calandrella brachydactyla*: Two or three in K & M, 1861/2 and 1890 of which two are mentioned in *The Handbook*.

271. Woodlark. *Lullula arborea*: K & M described this species as 'a resident, of local distribution, both on the mainland and in the Isle of Wight'. Since then, numbers have decreased seriously, especially since the late 1950s, and it has disappeared from some areas as a breeding species. There are no recent breeding records from the Island, for instance; indeed, even isolated sightings there have become *very* few, the Island Bird Report recording a complete blank in some years. In the Martin/Damerham area, Ash reported a decline in the early 1950s and it is doubtful if the species now breeds there. It disappeared from parts of Chandlers Ford as habitat was destroyed for building purposes, and it has probably disappeared from the Farley Mount area where it could always be found in the mid 1950s. The same story can be told from site after site, and it seems clear that some other factor than habitat destruction is present, for even in its stronghold of the New Forest numbers have much declined, viz. — 1957, 46 pairs; 1959, 41 pairs; 1962, 38 pairs; 1963, *ca*. 20 pairs; 1965, eight pairs; 1969, a minimum of 13 pairs; 1970, minimum of 12 pairs (*H*. for the various years). However, Orr found 30 pairs in the Forest and surrounding heaths in 1971 so perhaps the decline has been exaggerated. The *Atlas* survey showed proved or suspected breeding in about a quarter of the mainland 10-kilometer squares, very few of these squares being in the north so that the decline seems to be affecting those areas, though a survey of the Hampshire heathland along the Surrey border in 1971 revealed eight pairs (*Hants/Surrey Border Bird Report 1971*).

For a review of its status in the New Forest, see Chapter 12 of *The New Forest* by Tubbs.

There is some recent evidence of migratory movements on a small scale, e.g.: Ash reported single birds flying S. over Damerham on 26 September 1957 and over Fordingbridge on 7 October; seven were at St. Catherine's Point on 16 and 23 March 1968 (*I.o.W*. 5. Part 3); one at Hengistbury on 22 March 1968 (*H*. 1968); one at Hill Head on 1 November 1969 (*H*. 1969).

272. Skylark. *Alauda arvensis*: A very common breeding species throughout the county and the Isle of Wight. Enormous numbers winter on arable land on the downs, especially when local birds are augmented by immigrants, e.g. 10,000 estimated in one square mile of farmland to the east of Freshwater in a cold spell on 31 December 1961 (*I.o.W*. 5. Part 6).

There is a good deal of movement in October and the first half of November, especially along the mainland coast and past St. Catherine's Point. Most move in a generally westerly direction, though at St. Catherine's they have been noted moving in most directions at various times, especially north and north-west and occasionally going out to sea. Examples of such movements are: movement N. at Farlington Marshes all day on 30 October 1959 (*H.* 21. Part 3); 585 flying NW at Hurst on 16 October 1960 (*H.* 22. Part 1); a flock of 500 flying S. out to sea at St. Catherine's Point on 30 October 1967 (*H.* 1967); 200 flying E. at Hengistbury on 2 November 1969 (*H.* 1969).

Enormous cold weather movement occurs at times, the direction often confused, e.g. in cold weather on 31 December 1961, 40,000 flew SE at Gilkicker, 37,000 flew E. at Titchfield Haven, and 23,000 flew W. at Hengistbury (*H.* 22. Part 2).

The return movements in spring are nothing like so well-marked.

An adult ringed Micheldever on 2 February 1954 alighted on a fishing boat W. of Rauma (Finland) 61.08°N 21.33°E on 5 May 1954 and was released. One ringed at St. Catherine's on 15 October 1960 found dead at Exmouth about 18 January 1963 — movements of British-ringed Skylarks over five miles are seldom recorded (*B.B.* 57. 559) but this bird was recovered in very severe weather.

273. Shorelark. *Eremophila alpestris*: K & M admit two which were in the Hart collection, said to have been obtained near Christchurch on 21 October 1875.

Five, Pennington, 31 October 1955 (Kinsey).

One, Warsash, 9 November 1955 (Dennis — *H.* 19. Part 2).

Three, Black Point, 23 November 1959 (*H.* 21. Part 3).

Three, Sinah Common, 29 December 1959 (*H.* 21. Part 3).

Two/four, Main Bench, from 26 to 30 October 1969, and three — probably the same birds — Hurst Spit, from 10 December 1969 to 7 April 1970, one staying until 16th (*H.* 1969, 1970).

One, Hayling Island, 10 January 1971 (*H.* 1971).

Two, Main Bench, from 22 to 24 October 1971 (*H.* 1971).

274. Swallow. *Hirundo rustica*: Though still quite common there would seem to be no doubt that the number of breeding pairs has diminished quite substantially. The first observation to this effect goes back as far as 1918 when Munn (*H.* 8. 3) said that they had 'decreased the most' of the hirundines. In the Island report also one reads (1923) 'undoubtedly decreased — I think every year', and (1927) 'still decreasing'. Similar remarks come from Fareham (Suffern referring to the years from 1920 until about 1950), Winchester, Burghclere (Bacon) and Wickham (Arnold), the last two observers referring to the years from 1936 to about 1950. In the north of the county, evidence suggests a decline in the first 30 or 40 years of the century followed by a marked increase following the Second World War (P. E. Brown). The above decline refers to an overall trend, now happily halted it would seem, and not to dramatic drops in local populations in one year which are probably due to disasters on migration.

The *Atlas* survey, as expected, showed the species breeding in every corner of the county.

Most years produce March records, though very few in number, the earliest record of all being a bird on 16 February 1967 at Iford (*H.* 1967). Considerable passage is seen in April/May, e.g. 600 flying N. in three hours at St. Catherine's Point on 20 April 1968 (*I.o.W.* 6. Part 3) and 1,900 flying N. at Gilkicker on 2 May 1962 (*H.* 22. Part 3). In 1971, a small reed-bed roost was found at Farlington Marshes on

15 May, something not previously recorded there in spring.

Numbers on autumn passage are very large, moving in a variety of directions, e.g. NW, N., NE and E.; indeed, from 23 August to 10 September 1955, a watch kept at St. Catherine's Point showed movement in *all* directions *except* N. to S. (Rees *et al.*). Examples of large movements in recent years are: *ca.* 30,000 flying W. at Titchfield Haven throughout the 25 September 1958 (S. L. White *et al.*); on 28 September 1958 at St. Catherine's Point, when passage E. increased from 600 an hour at dawn to *ca.* 6,000 an hour by midday, decreasing to nothing when the wind veered from NE to SW (*I.o.W.* 5. Part 3); 6,000 moving W. at St. Catherine's Point on 19 September 1965 (*I.o.W.* 5. Part 10). Examples of more normal movements are: 1,500 flying SE at Gilkicker on 24 September 1966 (*H.* 1966); 1,510 flying SE at St. Catherine's Point in one and a half hours on 17 September 1965 (*I.o.W.* 5. Part 10).

During the autumn movement, some large roosts develop in reed beds, e.g. at Brading Marsh, 5,000 on 23 September 1955, 10,000 on 7 September 1966, and 7,500 on 21 September 1967 (*H.* and *I.o.W.* for those years); 4,500 at Titchfield Haven on 7 September 1969 (*H.* 1969); 3,000 at Farlington Marshes on 19 September 1969 (*H.* 1969). Ash has also reported small roosts in trees on two occasions in the New Forest (*H.* 19. Part 1 and 21. Part 2).

A few birds are seen in November in most years, the latest record being on 22 December 1906 at Havant (*B.B.* 1. 127).

They have been recorded at night at St. Catherine's Lighthouse (*H.* 23. Part 2).

A number of ringing returns show expected movement to and from South Africa, e.g. a nestling ringed at Sherfield on 7 June 1962 found dead in South Africa near Kimberley on 17 November 1962 (*B.B.* 56. 505). Other returns show movement E. and N. in autumn, as already mentioned, e.g. one ringed Farlington Marshes 23 August 1968 recovered at Andover on 28 August 1968; one ringed Weymouth on 29 June 1968 recovered Farlington Marshes on 23 August 1968 (both *H.* 1968); juveniles ringed at Farlington Marshes on 9 August 1967 and 25 July 1967 recovered respectively at Burham (Kent) on 27 August 1967 and in Norfolk on 25 August 1967 (*H.* 1968 p.44).

Swallows

276. House Martin. *Delichon urbica*: It remains a widespread and common breeding species though there is a little evidence suggesting some decline in numbers. Meinertzhagen reported a drop in breeding pairs on the Mottisfont estate from *ca.* 70 in the nineties to 58 in 1941, 49 in 1942 and 38 in 1945, whilst a decrease in *towns* was noted on the Island in 1947 and attributed to the increase of tarmacadam roads which reduced the availability of mud for nest building. On the mainland however, some new housing estates have been colonised very rapidly (e.g. Winchester).

The earliest migrants were three on 5 March 1952 at Stockbridge (Acton-Davis), and several years afterwards one could see the first arrive at the end of March. There are wintering records however, e.g. one at Christchurch on 1 January 1967 (Miss Wren) and one at Gilkicker in January/February 1967 (*H.* 1967).

Heavy autumn passage is seen from August/October, birds moving E., W., S. and in all directions within that arc, e.g. *ca.* 12,000 flew SE at St. Catherine's Point on 15 September 1962 (*I.o.W.* 5. Part 7); birds were passing E. at St. Catherine's Point at a rate of *ca.* 375 per hour all morning on 19 September 1959, whilst at the same place on 26 September 1959 a flock of *ca.* 300 flew SE out to sea at a great height (*H.* 21. Part 3); 1,000 flew W. at Quarr (I.o.W.) on 21 September 1968 (*H.* 1968). The dates of peak movements often coincide with Swallow peaks.

A few stragglers are seen well into November in some years and there has been a handful of December records with the latest on 13 December 1960 at Titchfield Haven (*H.* 22. Part 1).

Six were killed at St. Catherine's Light between 1905/08, in April, May, October and November (*I.o.W.* 1922).

Reed-bed roosts were seen at Fleet Pond in 1970 and 1971 (*B.B.* 65. 126 and *H.),* a habit apparently not recorded anywhere previously.

277. Sand Martin. *Riparia riparia*: An account of this species' breeding distribution over the years would fill a book. Colonies are frequently deserted, usually due to human disturbance, and so new ones are taken up, e.g. a colony in the cliffs at Brownwich was started in 1956 when Suffern counted 108 nests, but it was completely deserted in 1961 (*H.* 22. Part 2); 120—150 pairs were in a gravel pit on St. Catherine's Hill (Christchurch) in 1963 but tipping destroyed many nests (*H.* 23. Part 1); the once flourishing colony at Rockford (W. edge New Forest) was cut by half in 1961 to *ca.* 500 pairs and in 1962 most of it had moved to a nearby site; *ca.* 440 pairs were in recent diggings near Romsey in 1970 (*H.* 1970). Sometimes the desertion is temporary, e.g. in 1957 no birds nested in the quarry at Petersfield Hospital for the first time in living memory, but it was recolonised the following year.

The largest colony at the moment is at Casbrook Common (Timsbury), 1,142 pairs in 1963, 1,500 in 1965, 1,150 in 1967 and 1,085 in 1970. At Fair Oak, three colonies totalled 1,150 pairs in 1966 (see *H.* for the years in question). Other large counts in recent years have been 300 plus at Bramshill through the latter half of the 60s, 500—600 pairs in two colonies near Kingsley in 1966, and 300 at Curbridge in 1968 (*H.* for those years).

Two less usual sites: in holes under the bridge taking the Winchester bypass over the Itchen near Kingsworthy (28 pairs in 1961, 12 in 1963, but deserted in 1965), and in the sandy cliff tops at Hengistbury and Southbourne (78 pairs in 1967, and 75 in 1970).

For all information on breeding sites, see the Hampshire Bird Reports.

On the Island, the only regular colony is on the Sandown golf course. In 1955, 16 pairs recolonised the site after temporary desertion, but in 1957 it was interfered with and probably no young were reared. Subsequently it has been in constant use with 12 pairs in 1963, 10—15 in 1966 and 20 in 1968 (*I.o.W.*). Otherwise on the Island, odd pairs occasionally nest in the same rock outcrop that stretches from the golf course across the middle of the Island (Stafford), and a colony was near Shanklin in 1961 but deserted in 1962 (Machin *in litt.*).

The first birds usually appear in March, the earliest date being 4 March 1936 at Winchester. Stragglers are occasionally seen well into November, the latest being 5 December 1936 at Lake.

As with the other hirundines, considerable autumn movement is seen. Examples are: *ca.* 20,000 flying W. at Titchfield Haven on 25 September 1958 (S. L. White); heavy SW movement all day at Farlington Marshes on 18 July 1959 (*H.* 21. Part 3); 2,000 flying down river and out over the Solent at Titchfield Haven on 3 September 1961 (*H.* 22. Part 2); strong movement to the E. at Titchfield Haven in late July 1968 and at Gilkicker on 7/8 September 1968 (*H.* 1968).

Large reed-bed roosts develop in autumn, e.g. 2,000 at Titchfield Haven on 12 August 1968 (*H.* 1968); 2,300 at Wick Hams in 1969 (*H.* 1969); 1,400 at Fleet Pond on 17 September 1970 (*H.* 1970); 2,000 at Winnall on 21 July 1970 (*H.* 1970).

A mass of ringing recoveries resulting from the B.T.O. drive to ring the species revealed the general E. movement in autumn, e.g. one ringed at Otterbourne on 2 July 1963 recovered 29 August 1963 at Sandwich Bay and four other birds ringed at Otterbourne in June/July 1963 were controlled in Chichester Harbour in August/September 1963 (*H.* 23. Part 1). Other interesting returns are: a juvenile ringed at Timsbury on 28 July 1962 recovered Loch Lomond on 25 May 1965; an adult ringed on Jersey on 8 May 1965 retrapped at Timsbury on 29 May 1965; a juvenile ringed at Binnegar (Dorset) on 4 July 1965 retrapped five days later at Timsbury; an adult ringed at Timsbury on 2 August 1964 controlled in Morocco on 4 May 1965 and again at Timsbury in August 1965; one ringed Stanpit on 11 August 1965 controlled at Chichester two hours later; one ringed at Wick Hams on 21 July 1965 recovered in Norfolk on 7 August 1965 (all *H.* 1965); one ringed on Malta on 22 April 1966 recovered at Romsey on 18 July 1966 (*B.B.* 60. 457); one ringed as adult at Timsbury on 2 August 1964 retrapped in Norfolk on 29 August 1964, then retrapped near Romsey on 8 July 1967 and again at Horton Heath on 9 July 1967 (*H.* 1968. p.44); an adult ringed at Waltham Chase on 24 July 1968 was caught alive at Djanet (an oasis in the Sahara region of Algeria) on 3 May 1969 (*B.B.* 64. 172).

These are just a few examples of the ringing returns. Several pages could be filled with others, equally interesting. A paper by Thelwell summarising ringing returns from the Casbrook (Timsbury) colony appears in *H.* 1971.

278. Golden Oriole. *Oriolus oriolus*: K & M admit about 16 between 1824 and 1905 and one record of breeding near Christchurch, the egg or eggs, one need hardly say, being taken. They did not know of a pair at Mottisfont from mid May till 21 August 1897 when, although no nest was found, three juveniles appeared at the end of July (Meinertzhagen), and they missed one case of a male near Milford on 19 March 1901 (*B.o.M.*).

Since then there have been about 45, the majority in May/June but a male was at Highclere on 1 December 1947 (*B.B.* 42. 53) — one of K & M's was also in December.

Cases of proved or possible breeding since K & M are: a pair near Christchurch in 1916 (Munn in *H.* 8); a pair nested unsuccessfully near Owslebury around 1920 (G. W. Pierce in *W.*); 'information was received with confirmation from a different source' of breeding in the New Forest in 1929; the pair were reported to return regularly to the same locality (Jourdain, *B.* 23. 42); a pair were in Avington Park in 1934; a pair bred on the Island in 1935 (*Oologists' Record*, February 1964, reviewing *B.o.H.*); a pair nested successfully near Wickham in 1969 (*H.* 1969).

279. Raven. *Corvus corax*: K & M say: 'A scarce resident now confined to I.o.W.', adding that it used to nest on the mainland in several localities, the last time being in 1887 when one of the adults disappeared, 'probably shot'. They recall that Gilbert White recorded a flock of 46 over the hanger one 24 October, showing to what a sorry state man has reduced this fine bird in the county.

Near Freshwater (I.o.W.), the last breeding pair was robbed and then shot in 1909. A few years later fresh birds were introduced (Munn in *H.* 8). In 1910 a pair raised young in another part of the Island. In 1913 there were two pairs on Culver Cliffs and two or three pairs apparently bred almost annually in the 20s and 30s and perhaps until as late as 1951. But in 1953 the species was only seen twice in 20 or more visits. In 1954 one of a pair apparently came to grief in the breeding season and there was no evidence of breeding in the following year. However, young were being fed in 1956 — though the nest was inadvertently destroyed before they flew by the tipping of rocks from the top of the cliff (*I.o.W.* 5. Part 1) — and there was possibly successful breeding in 1957 and 1958. At Main Bench, there were several reports of small parties in 1958, including two adults and what were thought to be three juveniles on 20 April (*I.o.W.* 5. Part 3) and birds were seen at this site in the following years. In 1966, a nest was built at Main Bench but deserted — it was thought because of too many visitors (*I.o.W.* 6. Part 1) — but in 1967 a pair raised at least two young there (*H.* 1967), at least one young was reared in 1968 (*H.* 1968), whilst a pair present in the 1969 season and four on 1 June suggested further successful breeding (*H.* 1969). Two pairs were resident on the Island in 1970 (*H.* 1970) so with our conservation-minded public today, the species could increase its breeding numbers in the future.

One pair used to breed regularly at Hengistbury but not, apparently, since 1946 when boys disturbed the birds.

EC used to see occasional birds flying over Sway in 1944/5 and 1950 (maximum six flying E. on 7 August 1945), but mainland occurrences in recent years have been very few. From 1959 to 1970, a total of 13 was reported from the mainland, nearly all from the coastal strip with no more than three in any one year. They were nearly all between July and September, with odd records in April, November and December.

280. Carrion Crow. *Corvus corone*: K & M write: 'A resident, sparingly distributed in all the districts of the mainland, but more plentiful in the Isle of Wight.' Today, it is only *sparingly* distributed where gamekeepers are thick on the ground, and where keepers are few or missing the species becomes common, e.g. it is plentiful in the New Forest, this area perhaps holding the densest population of the species in the county; it increased during both wars when fewer gamekeepers were present; 'common round Kingsclere due to under-keepering' (Standford); not very plentiful in the heavily-keepered chalk areas north of Winchester (Taverner). The *Atlas* survey showed breeding in every corner of the county.

Considerable roosts develop at a few localities. The roost at Woolmer reached 300 on 30 January 1960 (*H.* 22. Part 1) and 330 on 18 November 1961 (*H.* 23. Part 2. p.25). Another roost at Quarr (I.o.W.) which is used through the summer numbered 116 on 19 February 1967 (*I.o.W.* 6. Part 2) and 125 on 5 January 1968 (*I.o.W.* 6. Part 3). Numbers are also seen scavenging along the quieter stretches of shore, e.g. Crows fed throughout 1966 at Quarr on crustacea, the maximum count being 90 on 13 December (*I.o.W.* 6. Part 1). The largest gathering in recent years however was 400 on Timsbury rubbish tip in the winter of 1963/4 (*H.* 23. Part 2).

At St. Catherine's Point in spring and autumn, there are several records of birds flying in from the sea and also leaving to the south. 'Birds of this genus have a disturbing habit of taking long flights out to sea at St. Catherine's Point, turning and coming in again, often on a different line. This could easily lead to records of migration that are erroneous. However, all birds seen flying out to sea and recorded as such are watched until out of sight' (*H.* 1965). Even these birds could turn in again over the Channel and so all such records are slightly suspect. Numbers involved have always been very low. The 38 recorded flying out to sea there on 8 October 1961 should have read three (*H.* 22. Part 2).

281. Hooded Crow. *Corvus cornix*: Apparently seen much less often than in K & M's time. They described it as 'of regular and fairly common occurrence in all our coasts but occurs only sparingly and occasionally in some inland localities.' Today it occurs *only sparingly and occasionally* over the whole mainland and Island, apart from the last few years in the Christchurch area where one (sometimes two) have been recorded regularly since 1967. (In 1969 one bred there with a Carrion Crow and raised hybrid offspring, and seven Hooded/Carrion hybrids were seen through 1970 — *H.* 1967 onwards.) These Christchurch birds could have been released from captivity in the area but no information on the subject has come to light.

An analysis of all records for 1959 to 1970 (excluding the Christchurch hybrids) shows a total of around 30 birds. No year has produced more than four, and two years produced none. They have been from the mainland coast, inland and on the Island, nearly all the records occurring from November/April.

282. Rook. *Corvus frugilegus*: A common resident everywhere, as in K & M's day. A mainland census of rookeries carried out for the Agricultural Research Council in 1945 gave a total of rather more than 32,345 occupied nests to which must be added 366 counted in 1946. A partial census organised by Standring in 1969 showed 2,019 occupied nests, and selected areas of this count compared with the 1945 census showed a 40 per cent decline (*H.* 1969) though the sample was probably too small to be significant.

Censuses of rookeries in the Island gave:

In 1932   4,209 occupied nests
1946   5,243 occupied nests
1954   4,892 occupied nests (mean of estimates)
1955   5,692 at 170 sites (470 at Westover, Calbourne, being the largest)
1956   5,858 at 172 sites
1957   5,047 at 180 sites
1958   4,751 at 185 sites

We are indebted to James Fisher for the first three figures and the 1945 mainland census.

Since EC first recorded it in 1949 a number of observers have seen cross-Solent flights each year in both directions between October and March and once on 26 June (1956). Most of the observations have been of flights in late afternoon or at dusk and the flight lines pass over Hurst Castle in the west to Hill Head in the east, the largest numbers involved being 200 to the Island on 14 October 1950, 500 to the mainland on 7 January 1952, and 173 to the Island on 1 November 1954. On 15 December 1956 a few were flying about the shore at Hill Head at 15.45 hours apparently unwilling to face a 30 knot SSW wind with rain and fog. A 'concourse' of birds on 26 June 1956 went to the Island at sunset (Day).

Return of birds that had presumably roosted on the Island was seen as follows: at 7.30 a.m. on 29 November 1957, 280 arrived at Hill Head, and at 19.45 hours on 14

December 1957 about 400 passed over there.

As the Hampshire report for 1955 put it, 'One would have supposed that there were plenty of feeding grounds in the Island or, alternatively, that there were plenty of roosting sites on the mainland, but presumably the birds ignore the fact that the waters of the Solent lie below the route from the feeding grounds to roost and treat it just as though it were land'.

In 1953 a new rookery of 15 pairs was formed in the heart of Portsmouth. Seven nests were built in 1954 but the site was deserted. There are several regular rookeries in the city of Winchester.

In 1959, 1960 and 1961, nests were built on pylons at Millbrook, some young being reared from the 10 nests in 1961 (*H.* 22. Part 2).

At St. Catherine's Point, birds are seen to leave out to sea and come in from the sea, but as with other corvids, they have a habit of leaving the coast, turning when some way out and coming back, so it is debatable whether any are really migrating over the water.

ca. 12,000 were roosting in beech trees at Upham on 10 December 1971.

Rook

283. Jackdaw. *Corvus monedula*: A very common resident, probably even commoner than in K & M's time. Increase was noted at Wickham in 1922, and at Fareham, Alresford and in the Isle of Wight in about 1950 compared with 20—30 years previously. That the increase dated from the 20s of this century receives confirmation from a note by Munn: 'Do not appear to be unusually plentiful; before the 1914 war they were killed ruthlessly by game-keepers' (*H.* 8).

By providing suitable nest-boxes at Sway, EC built up a colony in his grounds from one or two pairs to 16 pairs in 1961, the build-up taking only four or five years.

They were said to nest in the cliffs on the west side of Milford-on-Sea (*B.o.M.* — 1913), but they have not done so since at any rate 1940. They nest in numbers on some of the southern cliffs of the Isle of Wight.

Passage to the NE over Havant was observed in February 1912, March 1914 and March/April 1916 (Atkins in *B.B.* 13), local birds not being involved. In recent years, a small coastal passage has been seen in spring and autumn, a few birds being seen to come in from the sea at St. Catherine's Point, for example (see comment under Carrion Crow about corvids coming off the sea at St. Catherine's).

A bird shot at Fordingbridge on 26 February 1953 was identified as belonging to the Scandinavian race (*Corvus m. monedula*) by Ash and the identification was confirmed by Wagstaffe (*H.* 18. Part 3). The back of the head was considerably more silvery grey and paler than in the local race, there was a conspicuous white patch at each side of the neck and the under-parts were paler grey.

There was a large roost on the ground at Longwater Lawn, Ashurst, in September 1961 with a peak of *ca.* 5,000 on the 27 (*H.* 22. Part 2). *ca.* 4,000 were roosting in beech trees at Upham on 10 December 1971 (*H.* 1971).

284. Magpie. *Pica pica*: K & M describe it as a fairly common resident; it is very common now. There are a number of reports of increase in widely separate areas — 14 shot in half an hour at Milford in 1946 — from just before the last war until 1953 with several fairly large gatherings from December to early March, but none approaching a congregation of 136 or 142 (two counts) on downland near East Meon (Portal) in March 1944; a local man was said to have counted 240 at the time (*H.* 16. Part 2). Flocks of between 30 and 40 have been reported on several occasions in very recent years from various parts of the mainland and 28 were seen together near Newtown (I.o.W.) on 29 January 1966 (*I.o.W.* 6. Part 1).

P. E. Brown mentions (1944, referring to Baughurst) that locally bred birds stay until the middle or end of November and then disappear.

A nestling ringed 8 May 1962 at Winchester controlled near Andover about 19 September 1965.

285. Nutcracker. *Nucifraga caryocatactes*: K & M admit one in November 1868 (shot) and one in April 1886 (seen and heard).

Since then, one was shot at Hamstead, Isle of Wight, in February 1914, now in the Haslemere Museum (*I.o.W.* 1. 4); two in a garden at Bonchurch in the winter of 1936/7 (Miss Venables) and one in the same garden in December 1938 (Miss Thornycroft, *I.o.W.* 2. Part 7). The 1968 irruption produced only three reliable records, a bird at Fordingbridge from 6 to 28 December, when it was found dead (*H.* 1968), one at Osborne on 9 January 1969, and one at Brighstone on 14 and 20 February 1969 (*H.* 1969). One was at Stoke St. Mary Bourne from 5 to 24 November 1969 when it was killed by a cat (*H.* 1969).

Two other possibles on the mainland were not accepted in *B.B.*

286. Jay. *Garrulus glandarius.* Common and widely distributed as in K & M. Increases in the forties reported from Bournemouth, Hurn, Portchester and Fareham areas. Day reported a pronounced diminution in the New Forest in 1950/51 compared with the previous three to five years; keepers used to shoot them because they were so numerous but in 1950/51 they were not nearly so often seen and he thought that the increase of the Grey Squirrel might have had something to do with it. By 1953 it seemed their numbers were restored and they are certainly common enough there now.

There have been irruptions in 1902 (K & M), in October 1935 (*B.B.* 29 — large numbers seen flying high to the SSW and SW, mainly over the southern parts of the mainland, but also over Andover, the largest counts being: 250/300 just outside Southampton — *Bull. B.O.C.* 56. 24; 187 near Stoneham; on the Red Rice estate (Andover) there were fully 200 as late as 20 October where there had been scarcely any a month previously. A critical examination of birds shot from these flocks did not show the very definite characteristics of the typical Scandinavian bird, but most appeared paler and greyer than British birds and it was thought that they might be intermediate forms from Holland or N. France), in the winter of 1947/8 when it was estimated that 2,000 were on the Mottisfont estate, 47 being shot during a covert shoot on 3 December (Meinertzhagen), in September/October 1957 (*H.* 20. Supplement) and in September/November 1963 (small flocks moving or present at widespread localities including birds *coasting* e.g. 18 moved along the coast at Stone Point on 19 October and a loose flock of 35 flew E. along the downs at Main Bench on 20 October — for details see *H.* 23. Part 1).

Apart from these irruptions, several recent years have records of small but significant increases, or of small parties seen moving along the coast, between September/October which suggest almost regular autumn influxes on a small scale, e.g. in September/October 1962 (*H.* 22. Part 2), an increase at St. Catherine's Point from the usual three/four to six/eight in early October 1965 (*H.* 1965), an increase in the Bramley area in October/November 1966 (*H.* 1966), and birds seen at unusual coastal localities such as Quarr, Needs Oar and Hengistbury in October/November 1967 (*H.* 1967).

A full-grown bird ringed 29 November 1955 at Sway, shot at Mottisfont in November 1956.

287. Chough. *Pyrrhocorax pyrrhocorax*: Formerly resident in the cliffs of the Island. K & M state that they were last seen in 1882.

This is one of a list of birds mentioned in a gruesome paragraph in *The Strangers' Hand-book, Picture of the Isle of Wight*, by George Brannon, *ca.* 1850: The precipices of Freshwater ... the aquatic fowl furnish most amusing sport to numberless shooting parties during the season. The principal species are Puffins, Gulls, Cormorants, Cornish Choughs, the Eider Duck, Auks, Divers, Guillemots, Razorbills, Widgeons, Willocks, Daws, Starlings and Pigeons'. Hopkinson drew attention to this reference.

One stayed for two or three weeks at Cheesefoot Head about 1941. It was seen by a shepherd and a farm bailiff; it used to keep round the sheep-pen (Shelley *in litt.* 21st October 1949).

Mrs. Bannerman reported one dead in the Island in 1948.

One was seen at Hordle Cliff on 26 May 1963 (Riddick *in litt.*).

288. Great Tit. *Parus major*: A very common resident.

There is evidence of autumn influxes, usually on a small scale, e.g. noted in small numbers during the Blue Tit irruption of 1957; at St. Catherine's Point, one seen to arrive on 19 September 1959 and two likewise the following day (*H*. 21. Part 3); at Gilkicker, where the species is not normally recorded, five were present on 14 September 1962 and 10 the following day (*H*. 22. Part 3) — other such records in subsequent years. Some of these could be continental birds, for one ringed at Sway on 12 November 1959 was killed there on 6 January 1960 and was matched by Hazelwood with skins of October birds from Jämtland (Sweden), whilst a first-winter bird ringed at Brighstone on 20 February 1960 was found dead at Wassenaar (Holland) about 14 March 1960 (*B.B.* 54. 477), presumably at or on its way to its breeding area.

Movement also seen in spring, e.g. about 30 were recorded coming in from the sea at St. Catherine's Point on six dates in April 1958.

One ringed 24 February 1938 at Winchester recovered Liphook on 30 March 1939. One ringed as fully grown female 9 December 1963 at Sidmouth found dead near Andover on 10 July 1964 (*B.B.* 58. 565).

289. Blue Tit. *Parus caeruleus*: A very common resident. As an instance of the large numbers which may frequent gardens, Ash ringed 107 between 19 November 1961 and 26 December 1961 on the western edge of the New Forest and a further 41 between 6 January 1962 and 25 March 1962. Such numbers are only revealed by ringing.

All Hampshire had its share of a large irruption in 1957, there being many reports of unusually large numbers between the end of September and the beginning of November; thereafter numbers declined rapidly and several observers commented on the very low numbers in December. Evidence of movement through the country was provided by a bird ringed at Hengistbury on 8 October 1957 during the peak of the irruption and recovered 165 miles NNE at Rainworth near Mansfield, Nottinghamshire, on 27 November. Birds trapped at Southampton University during the period gave a ratio of 10 first-winter to one adult; but nearly every bird trapped there in November and December was an adult, suggesting that the first-winter birds moved on with the immigrants. Wing measurements of many of the birds suggested a continental origin (although this is not an infallible guide) and to support this are many records of birds seen flying in from the sea. 'Clouds' of Blue Tits were flushed from the reeds at Hengistbury in the early morning of 8 October. Large numbers were seen on the move and in the bushes at St. Catherine's Point, at Culver Down and at Newport in the Island and at Portsmouth, Gosport (120 in a garden from 28 September until 15 October — Searle) and Hurst on the mainland.

Before 1957 there had been evidence of irruptions, e.g. November—December 1949 when large numbers were recorded in unusual habitats such as 150 feeding in phragmites at Keyhaven on 20 November, and 100 plus in spartina at Hurst on 27 November. Better observer coverage revealed an influx in every year during the period 1959/1970, no movement reaching the proportions of 1957 and some years showing only very small movements. They could hardly be called irruptions, but it seems clear that an influx of some sort is quite normal from August to the end of year, September/Octoeber being the peak period, and that these occasionally reach such a size that the term irruption can be used. A few examples of such influxes are: 100 at Newtown on 13 October 1959 (*I.o.W.* 5. Part 4); at Gilkicker, peaks of 60 on 24 September 1966 and 70 on 8 October 1966 (*H*. 1966); a noticeable influx around Keyhaven from 23 October 1967 onwards, with most birds apparently of the continental race (*H*. 1967).

One ringed 8 March 1958 at Swansea found dead at Bembridge on 9 March 1959. One ringed 15 January 1961 at Fordingbridge in its first winter found dead near Teignmouth (Devon) on 29 March 1962. One ringed 13 January 1958 at

122

Tiddington (Warwick) found dead at Basingstoke on 5 April 1962 (*B.B.* 56. 507). One ringed 7 January 1961 at Sherfield in its first winter found dead near Weymouth around 5 February 1962 (*B.B.* 56. 507). An adult ringed 10 October 1961 at Portland found dead near Southampton around April 1962 (*B.B.* 56. 507). A juvenile ringed 29 August 1964 at Woldingham (Surrey) recovered at Farnborough on 3 December 1964 (*B.B.* 58. 565).

290. Coal Tit. *Parus ater*: The *Atlas* survey showed breeding in every 10-kilometer square of the mainland, but within this general picture the distribution seems patchy and much more information is needed on local population density. Only odd pieces of information are available, viz. — 18 pairs breeding at Mottisfont in 1941/2 (Meinertzhagen); 'frequent' around Droxford in 1946 et seq. (Miss Barraud); 'many' in Crab Wood (Winchester) in the spring of 1950; rare in the Fareham area (Suffern); 23 at a time coming to a bird table close to the house of Mr. and Mrs. Cobb at Setley near Brockenhurst in the winter of 1960/61 (EC), and similar numbers there subsequently. It appears to be common today in the New Forest.

In 1967, numerous records from the Island were all north of the downs (*I.o.W.* 6. Part 2 — *cf.* Marsh Tit).

There is some evidence that a few birds were involved in the large irruption of Blue Tits in September/October 1957. Most subsequent years have shown evidence of a *very* small influx around September/November, birds appearing at coastal localities where they are otherwise seldom recorded (e.g. at Farlington Marshes, Gilkicker, Needs Oar, Hengistbury and St. Catherine's Point), 13 in the Hengistbury area on 9 October 1966 being the most (*H.* for further details).

291. Central European Crested Tit. *Parus cristatus mitratus*: None since the two in K & M, one near Yarmouth before 1844 and the other, shot, near Stanpit in 1846.

292. Marsh Tit. *Parus palustris*: Like the Coal Tit, not enough is known of this species' distribution. *B.o.H.* said: 'Widely distributed and fairly common except (*Suffern*) in Fareham area and possibly in the Island. Colonel Payn in 1936 called it almost the commonest tit on high ground near Andover (*H.* 13).' The *Atlas* project suggested that this species might be less common in the county as a whole than the Coal Tit; it was shown to be breeding widely over the mainland, but more observers *proved* Coal Tit as breeding. In 1968, numerous records from the Island were all north of the downs (*I.o.W.* 6. Part 3 — *cf.* Coal Tit).

There is very little evidence of the autumn influx that most other tit species exhibit. The only suggestions of this in the years from 1959 to 70 are: one at Farlington Marshes on 27 and 29 September 1962, an unusual locality (*H.* 22. Part 3); one caught and ringed at Hengistbury on 22 September 1963 was the first record for that area (*H.* 23. Part 1); one at Needs Oar on 1 October 1967 and 5 November 1967 (*H.* 1967) and two there on 5 October 1969 (*H.* 1969) were also in a shore area where the species is not normally seen.

293. Willow Tit. *Parus montanus**: Not mentioned in K & M (1905) although the species had been discovered in this country in 1900.

The first mention which we can trace is in *H.* 13 (1936) when it was said to be widely distributed in NE Hampshire, where there was suitable timber, but not very numerous; and 'by no means common in the New Forest but a pair or two here and there among birches' (Jourdain).

A comprehensive review of its distribution in the country appeared in *B.B.* 30. 358 (May 1937) where it was stated that there were 'fairly numerous records through the Sussex Weald and the wealden or greensand areas of south Surrey and east Hampshire especially in the Farnham-Haslemere-Midhurst-Selbourne districts where the Willow Tit is believed to approach or even equal the Marsh Tit in numbers in suitable habitats'. And 'along the coastal plain from Brighton to Southampton the species appears to be rare. It has been seen in Bournemouth and infrequently in the New Forest. From here up to the extreme north of Hampshire Willow Tits have not hitherto been recorded, but they have been found in approximately equal numbers with Marsh Tits in autumn on the chalk hills near Highclere and along the ridge westward into Berkshire and Wiltshire.'

The position today is best judged from the *Atlas* survey and the annual bird reports. As a breeding species it is probably missing from a narrow belt along the mainland coast, is *very* scarce on the Island though possibly overlooked (the first Island breeding record was at Newtown in 1968 — Mrs. Seabroke — *I.o.W.* 6. Part 3), and thin on the ground in the New Forest and the nine 10-kilometer squares that form the SE corner of the county (i.e. squares SU 50, 60, 70, 51, 61, 71, 52, 62, 72). In the river valleys, on suitable parts of the chalk, and in the north of the county, it is well distributed as a breeding species. There are few reports that give any idea of breeding density — information is much needed — but in 1953 Jenkins estimated from five to 20 pairs near Micheldever, whilst in 1971 it was said to breed round Fleet Pond and Frensham Great Pond in greater numbers than does the Marsh Tit.

Outside of the breeding season it is more widespread, several reports suggesting dispersal movements, e.g. the only records in 1959 from a Chandlers Ford garden were on 5 April and 17 August (JHT); one at Fordingbridge on 17 December 1960 was the first there for 10 years (Ash). 20 plus were at Little Park and Stokes Wood (Purbrook) on 11 February 1967, and in several localities observers have reported it as more common than the Marsh Tit, viz. — at Alton, Alresford, Bramshill, Overton, Silchester, Stratfield Saye (all *H.* 1967) and Beacon Hill (1971) — all localities in the northern half of the county.

Although obviously overlooked, more so before the 1950s than today, it has clearly increased in numbers. Ash said in 1956/7 that it seemed to be increasing on the chalk west of Damerham and was noted in several localities where a few years ago it was unknown; in 1957 a similar increase was noted in the north of the county, particularly in autumn (*H.* 20. Supplement). It was probably overlooked on the Island as well where Mrs. Seabroke saw the first at Newtown on 15 November 1959 (*I.o.W.* 5. Part 4), though there have not been many Island records since then.

294. Long-tailed Tit. *Aegithalos caudatus*: A common resident, having recovered well in two or three years after each of the hard winters of 1916/17, 1939/40, 1946/7 and 1962/3. The very cold spell in 1946/7 lasted from the third week in January to mid-March without a break and P. E. Brown was satisfied that the breeding stock in the north of the county was reduced by at least 90 per cent. Severe losses were also suffered in the 1962/3 winter.

Outside the breeding season, flocks of up to 60 (at Shanklin and Fleet Pond in 1971) have been recorded.

As with most other tit species, most recent years have produced records showing an influx in autumn, particularly in October/November. With the present species, the influx is small, a few examples being: 40 at St. Catherine's Point on 19 October 1958 (*I.o.W.* 5. Part 3); six flew W. off the sea at the Foreland on 28

October 1961 and 22 were there the following day (*I.o.W.* 5. Part 6); 15 arrived from the S. at Hurst on 6 November 1960 (*H.* 22. Part 1); 40 at St. Catherine's Point on 9 October 1969 (*H.* 1970. p.38).

An adult ringed 2 July 1957 at Winchester and found dead 16 miles away at Stubbington *ca.* 24 January 1958 was 'the most distant recovery so far reported for this species' (*B.B.* 52. 472). Longer distance recoveries have occurred subsequently, one involving Hampshire, i.e. one ringed as adult at Stanwell (Middlesex) on 12 August 1961 found long dead near Gosport (52 miles SW) around 11 January 1965 (*B.B.* 59. 471).

Long-tailed Tit

295. Bearded Tit. *Panurus biarmicus*: K & M admit nine including two cases of breeding.

One on 3 July 1911 at Titchfield Haven (*B.o.H.* 209) and a male at the same place on 1 February 1922 (*B.B.* 15.2.69). Jourdain square-bracketed a pair at Hengistbury in early August 1935, 'accurately described and reported' by Miss Klamborowski (*B.* 27). An adult female was at St. Cross (Winchester) from 3 to 5 November 1956 (Martin — *H.* 19. Part 3). Three were at Titchfield Haven on 15/16 January 1960 and up to three were there until 3 April (*B.B.* 54. 189). Two (an adult male and an immature) were at Fleet Pond from 9 December 1961 to early March 1962 (Pratt — *H.* 22. Parts 2 and 3).

From 1964 onwards, the species has become a regular winter visitor to Farlington Marshes, Titchfield Haven, Keyhaven, Stanpit and possibly Fleet Pond with a few scattered records from other areas, especially the lower Test marshes. In the winter of 1964/5, records came from Farlington Marshes (maximum five), Titchfield Haven (maximum five), Nursling gravel pit (maximum five) and Keyhaven (maximum five), the first birds appearing in October 1964 and the last leaving in March 1965 (*H.* 23. Parts 2 and 3 — the coincidence of the maxima could have meant the same birds were seen at more than one locality but the same five were not involved in *all* the occurrences). There was a widespread influx in October 1965, the largest counts being 16 flying W. in the lower Test valley on 10 October, 17 there on 2 November, 20 plus at Stanpit in the latter half of October and 18 seen to fly in there on 31 October (*H.* 1965). During this influx, birds were recorded at Brading (12 on 12 October) and Yarmouth (two/three), the first Island records since two in the nineteenth century (*I.o.W.* 5. Part 10), and two were caught at Stanpit that had been ringed earlier in the year at Walberswick (Suffolk) (see paper by Husband in the Christchurch Harbour Report, 1965). Other parts of southern England were affected by this influx in 1965. In Hampshire, a few stayed until March/April and a pair possibly stayed to breed at Titchfield Haven in 1966 (*H.* 1966). (See *B.B.* 58. 527/8 for data on the influx into southern England.)

The most interesting features from subsequent years have been:

1. A number of ringing returns, either of birds ringed on their breeding grounds and recaught in Hampshire or ringed in Hampshire and recaught in their breeding grounds, have shown the source of our birds is mainly Walberswick and Minsmere (Suffolk). Other returns have shown Stodmarsh (Kent) and Alkmaar (Holland) as further sources of our Hampshire birds (See *H.* 1966, 1967, 1968 and 1970 for details).

2. Some have been caught on three or more occasions, e.g. one pair ringed at Farlington Marshes on 18 December 1966, both retrapped at Minsmere on 5 July 1967, again retrapped at Farlington Marshes on 25 November 1967, still together (*H.* 1967), and one retrapped yet again at Farlington on 17 December 1968 (*H.* 1968); one ringed at Minsmere on 27 September 1966 was retrapped at Farlington Marshes on 18 December 1966 and 25 November 1967 (*H.* 1967); one ringed at Farlington Marshes on 24 November 1967 was retrapped at Stodmarsh on 25 September 1968, again at Farlington on 8 December 1968 and yet again at Farlington on 8 November 1970 (*H.* 1970); one ringed at Farlington Marshes on 8 December 1968 was retrapped there on 22 March 1969 and 8 November 1970. It is obvious from this that at least some of the birds winter in the same area each year.

3. A pair bred at Titchfield Haven in 1967, 1969, 1970 and 1971.

4. The first birds usually appear in October but they may be as early as August. The last are usually in March though some have been in April/May.

For full details of the numbers, see *H.* 1965/1971.

296. Nuthatch. *Sitta europaea*: In K & M's time it was unknown on the Island which is curious because they are reasonably common on the mainland and have been seen in the last trees landward of Pennington only a few hundred yards from the coast and barely two miles from the nearest part of the Isle of Wight. To this day, breeding on the Island has never been fully proved, though there is a certain amount of circumstantial evidence of suspected breeding, and it is still scarce enough there for the annual I.o.W. Bird Report to state individual sightings.

It is found all over the mainland and is common in places where suitable habitat exists, e.g. Chandlers Ford, several localities around Winchester, and parts of the New Forest. Like so many of our small birds, there is practically no detailed information available on numbers, though in 1941/2 Meinertzhagen located 15 or 16 pairs at Mottisfont.

Most observers agreed that the species survived the 1962/3 winter very well.

298. Treecreeper. *Certhia familiaris*: K & M say: 'Resident in all wooded parts of the county and the Isle of Wight and not uncommon.' It may often be overlooked, but 'not uncommon' about describes its status today on the mainland and Island. This latest status report from the Island (Stafford) seems to suggest an increase there for the 1936 report said: 'Must now be considered as scarce'; and the 1940 report: 'Has been for some years quite uncommon'.

There is some suggestion of migrants appearing, e.g. apparent migrants were at Hengistbury on 1 and 18 September 1966 (*H.* 1966); single birds at Stanpit on 24 August 1967 and at Hengistbury on 28 October 1967 were most unusual for those places, as were single birds that appeared at Gilkicker on 13 and 17 September 1967 during a period of tit movement.

299. Wren. *Troglodytes troglodytes*: A very common resident. Numbers are sometimes much reduced by cold spells, the winter of 1962/3 taking a terrible toll for instance, though numbers had apparently fully recovered by 1966. An idea of the loss and recovery is gained from breeding numbers at Nursling gravel pit where only two pairs nested in 1963 following the hard winter but 21 pairs were nesting in 1967 (*H.* 1967). Breeding density can be gauged by sample counts, such as 32 and 48 pairs at Lord's Wood and Nightingale Wood respectively in 1967 (*H.* 1967 — woods in the Southampton area), and 59 pairs in 1.4 square miles of woodland at West Walk in 1968 (*H.* 1968).

As with some other species (e.g. tits), most years produce records that suggest an influx in the autumn and early winter, especially in October/November, e.g. in December 1893, about 180 — far exceeding the home population — were in reed beds at Mottisfont after a NW gale, the birds leaving suddenly on 17 January 1894 (Meinertzhagen); on 29 October 1955, the bushes at St. Catherine's Point were 'crawling' with Wrens (Rees) and *ca.* 250 were estimated to be in the lighthouse grounds and surrounding cliffs on 6 October 1957; numbers at Hengistbury were three or four times greater than normal on 10 October 1959 (*H.* 21. Part 3); at the Gins, Wrens were 'all over the place' on 4 December 1966 (*H.* 1966) and the same place was described as 'seething with Wrens' on 12 November 1967 (*H.* 1967).

Ten distinct territories were taken up on Beaulieu Heath at the end of September 1957 and kept till the end of the year where none was present in the breeding season; although local birds occupying wooded territories were singing freely, none of these newcomers was ever heard to sing (Palmer).

A juvenile ringed 1 July 1967 at Winchester found dead at Amiens (France) on 3 January 1968 (*B.B.* 62. 426).

A communal roost in a nest-box at Parkhurst contained 51 birds on the night of 8/9 January 1963 (*I.o.W.* 1963/4).

300. Dipper. *Cinclus cinclus*: K & M admit eight, all on the mainland between 1786 and 1893, with a doubtful breeding record in 1874.

Subsequently: one at Dunbridge for three days in January 1895, presumed to be of the Scandinavian race (Meinertzhagen) as it lacked chestnut on its breast.

One above Longparish on 26 April 1912 (Munn in *H.* 8).

One between Twyford and Bishopstoke on 28 May 1933 (Paulson in *B.B.* 27. 164).

In *B.B.* 36, four letters to *The Field* are quoted, two of which report breeding on the Test in 1942 (successful) and for three years in succession at Brambridge (Eastleigh) just prior to World War II.

There are nine other mainland records, including three of breeding on the Test near Stockbridge between 1938 and 1950. The latest of these nine records were single birds in 1969 and 1970 (*H.* 1969 and 1970).

In 1953, the Island report gives records for Isle of Wight in 1946, 1948 (four at Brighstone on 21 May) and 1951, all on dates falling well inside the breeding season, but they have not been reported subsequently.

301. Mistle Thrush. *Turdus viscivorus*: A common and increasing resident; perhaps commoner than the Song Thrush in some areas, e.g. the New Forest. Outside the breeding season, gatherings may exceed 100, e.g. 200 plus at Farley Mount in 1957; in the same year at the same place, 100 plus were at roost in yews on 26 October (Taverner); 150 at Ashley Walk on 20 October 1968 (*H.* 1968).

Most recent years have shown evidence of movement in autumn, particularly in October/November. Most of this has been seen at St. Catherine's Point and the mainland coast, some of the movement being W. to E., some E. to W., and some of the birds on the mainland coast moving in northerly directions, but inland movement has also been reported, e.g. 30 flew NW at Fleet Pond on 5 October 1969 (*H.* 1969).

Cold weather movements may concern larger numbers, such as 500 flying E. at Titchfield Haven on 31 December 1961 (*H.* 22. Part 2).

A young bird ringed 21 April 1951 in the New Forest recovered Icklesham (Sussex) on 5 January 1952 (*B.B.* 45. 271). A nestling ringed 17 April 1961 in Somerset controlled 13 May 1964 at Christchurch (*B.B.* 58. 565).

302. Fieldfare. *Turdus pilaris*: A common winter visitor though numbers vary very much from year to year. Earliest date 3 August (1968) though August birds are scarce; latest date 13 May (1961 and 1967 — but May birds also scarce) apart from one in the north of the county on 27 June 1967 (*H.* 1967). Flocks of several hundred are recorded in most winters, especially in the coastal belt, and over 1,000 have been recorded on occasions, e.g. 1,200 at Romsey on 14 February 1970 (*H.* 1970) and 1,000 plus at Yaverland (I.o.W.) on 25 January 1967 (*I.o.W.* 6. Part 2). By far the largest concentration however was 10/15,000 at Farley Mount on 29 November 1970 (*H.* 1970). Flocks of a few hundred are seen as late as April.

There are numerous records of movement from all years recently, some of the largest being connected with cold weather. Thus on 31 December 1961, at the start of a cold spell, about 30,000 flew ESE at Gilkicker, some 4,400 flew E. at Titchfield Haven, while 650 flew W. at Hengistbury in addition to 350 flying in there from the SW (*H.* 22. Part 2). In another cold spell, 2,300 flew S. at Timsbury and 1,000 E. at Hengistbury, both on 21 February 1969 (*H.* 1969). Other cold spells have produced movements, the birds generally moving S. over inland areas and E. along the coast, though directions are occasionally different and somewhat confused as shown by the Hengistbury movement above on 31 December 1961.

A good deal of movement however has nothing to do with hard weather, but is due to normal migration. 550 flew N. off the sea at St. Catherine's Point on 4

November 1961 (*H.* 22. Part 2).

A nestling ringed 25 May 1954 at Naerbo (Norway) recovered at Romsey on 10 March 1956. An adult ringed 23 January 1963 at Sandown recovered in Sweden on 27 July 1963 (*B.B.* 57. 565). One ringed fully grown 1 November 1966 at Texel (Holland) found dead Liphook on 16 March 1967 (*B.B.* 62. 20).

303. Song Thrush. *Turdus philomelos*: A common resident, but not as common as the Blackbird. At Bursledon it used to be as common but in 1940 it was estimated that there were 12 Blackbirds to one Song Thrush, and at the time of writing, a similar ratio would be found in the Winchester area. In the SE of the Island, the ratio of Blackbird to Song Thrush changed from five to four in 1941 to five to just under three in 1946.

The Song Thrush suffers more from hard winters, e.g. in the Island after 1916/17, in and around Bournemouth in 1929, in the Southampton area after the 1946/7 winter, and in the north of the county after the 1962/3 winter (*H.*). Cold weather movements are observed in such winters, e.g. on 31 December 1961, 3,000 flew E. at Titchfield Haven and 575 flew W. at Hengistbury (*H.* 22. Part 2).

Movements are recorded both by day and night in autumn in the coastal strip, e.g. nocturnal movement occurred over Portsmouth in late October 1963 (*H.* 23. Part 1), some 200 were at St. Catherine's Light on the night of 26/27 October 1968 (*H.* 1968), and 100 were at St. Catherine's Point on 30 October 1967 (*H.* 1967). 175 were killed at the Light in the months February/March and September/December between 1905/1908. Very little autumn movement has been recorded inland but 700 plus flew SW over Butser in 100 minutes late in the afternoon of 24 October 1964 (*H.* 23. Part 2).

Specimens of the continental race were first taken by Witherby at St. Catherine's Light on 22 and 24 April 1908 (*B.B.* 4) and were recorded there in the first 10 days of April 1910 (*B.B.* 5), and in large numbers on five dates in the second half of October 1910 and in March 1911 (*B.B.* 6). Since then they have been suspected (sometimes in large numbers) both on the southern part of the mainland and at St. Catherine's, larger numbers in autumn and in hard weather, fewer in spring.

At least two birds ringed as nestlings in Holland have been recovered in Hampshire the following winter, the Dutch race being the same as the British one (*B.B.* 38. 224 and 54. 504). Three birds ringed in Hampshire have been recovered during winter in Devon. One ringed at Sway in September had moved to Saint Pabu Finistère by the following February, a nestling ringed at Sherfield on 27 April 1961 was recovered in northern Spain on 17 December 1961, and one ringed at Fordingbridge on 22 December 1962 was found dead 100 miles S. in France on 17 January 1963. All this indicates a general movement E. and S. in autumn. A bird ringed 13 April 1956 at Sway and recovered in Suffolk on 4 May 1959 indicates the return movement W. in spring.

304. Redwing. *Turdus musicus*: A common winter visitor. Apart from one on Southampton Common from 17 May to 3 June 1965 (*H.* 1965), the latest date appears to be 27 April (1960) and the earliest 28 September (1962). Numbers vary considerably from year to year and gatherings may reach 1,000 even in normal weather, e.g. 1,000 plus at Butser on 24 October 1964 (*H.* 23. Part 2 — at that time thought to be the largest gathering recorded in Hampshire apart from cold spells) and 1,000 at Romsey on 14 February 1970 (*H.* 1970). The main influx is in late October/November. At this time, heavy nocturnal movements are recorded along the coastal stretch, e.g. over Portsmouth on the nights between 23 and 25 October 1963

(*H.* 23. Part 1) and about 400 at St. Catherine's Light on the night of 26/27 October 1968 (*I.o.W.* 6. Part 3). Movements by day are also observed, e.g. 1,380 flew WSW at Butser on 20 October 1968 (*H.* 1968).

Even larger movements occur in cold weather. On 14 February 1953, large numbers passed E. all day at Farlington where there were about two and a half inches of snow (Rees). The 'diversity and unpredictability of Redwing migration' (*B.B.* 53. 492) is exemplified by the report of *ca.* 30,000 flying ESE at Gilkicker in hard weather on 31 December 1961 when on the same day 1,200 flew W. at Needs Oar and *ca.* 345 W. at Hengistbury (*H.* 22. Part 2 — see also under Fieldfare and Song Thrush). Large gatherings also occur in cold spells, e.g. 2,200 at Dibden Bay on 10 January 1967 (*H.* 1967).

Return migration in spring is less obvious but many were recorded at St. Catherine's Light on the nights of 9/10 and 28/29 March 1962 (*H.* 22. Part 3). 96 were killed at the Light in March, April and October/December between 1905/08.

One picked up dead at Damerham on 18 November 1953 proved to be *T.m. coburni* (Iceland race), as was another picked up dead in the cold spell of February 1956.

One ringed 7 December 1958 in the New Forest recovered at Morcenx, Landes (France) on 21 October 1959 (*B.B.* 53. 492). One ringed 17 February 1969 at Farlington Marshes recovered at Francavilla Fontana (Italy) on 19 February 1970 (*H.* 1970).

307. Ring Ouzel. *Turdus torquatus*: K & M say: 'A regular spring and autumn visitor to the greater part of the county and Isle of Wight'. They did not know of an interesting inland record, a flock of about 20 at Mottisfont on 23 April 1892 when the valley was shrouded in mist, four staying until the 25th (Meinertzhagen),In *The Birds of Milford* (1913) it is described as 'an occasional visitor in spring and autumn'.

Ring Ouzel

An analysis of records between 1959 and 1970 gives a good idea of the species' status today. In spring, records were in the period March/May. March records were rather scarce, and May records very scarce, so the vast majority of birds were in April. The total number seen in any one spring varied from none (1962) to 15 plus. Far more were seen in autumn than in spring (though isolated years were exceptions to this, e.g. 1964), the records being in the period August/November. August records were very scarce; November records rather scarce. The vast majority of autumn birds were in September/October, with October alone having something like two-thirds of *all* the records (spring and autumn) for the period in question. Numbers seen in any one autumn varied from five to *ca.* 100 (1966, when many parts of Britain experienced a marked influx). Taking the period in question, most of the records came from the Island (especially at St. Catherine's Point); records from the mainland coast were quite frequent, and only a handful of reports came from inland on the mainland. The largest concentrations were all at St. Catherine's Point, i.e. 40/50 on 8 October 1966 (*I.o.W.* 6. Part 3), a total of 61 on 10 dates between 19 September and 24 October 1965 (*H.* 1965), 22 on 14 October 1962 (*H.* 22. Part 3) and 20 on 17/18 October 1970 (*H.* 1970).

The editors of *B.B.* (1.54 and 153) cast doubt upon the only two reports of breeding, both in the Island (1906 and 1907); in the second case a Ring Ouzel female was alleged to have bred with a Blackbird male.

308. Blackbird. *Turdus merula*: Abundant and widespread. Perhaps the commonest resident we have and certainly much commoner than the Song Thrush.

Large influxes and movements are typical between September/November, especially in October (see tits, other thrushes etc.). A few examples illustrating this: large nocturnal movements have been recorded over Portsmouth and Southampton; on 12 October 1956 they were heard passing all night at St. Catherine's Light, and on the 27th 16 came in off the sea there at 06.00; 'hundreds' at Farlington Marshes on 4 November 1961 (*H.* 22. Part 2); a marked increase at Farlington Marshes on 26 October 1963 coinciding with a heavy movement at St. Catherine's Light on the night of 25/26 October (*H.* 23. Part 1); an influx at Gilkicker of *ca.* 200 on 13 October 1969 (*H.* 1969). Most of these influxes have been on the coast but some have occurred inland, e.g. large nocturnal passage has been reported at Fordingbridge.

Smaller spring passage has been recorded, e.g. it was the commonest thrush at St. Catherine's Light on the night of 9/10 March 1962 (*H.* 22. Part 3); on 14 March 1962 there was 'an enormous influx' into the Fordingbridge area, the birds having mostly gone by the 15th (*H.* 22. Part 3); records from Stanpit in March 1966 indicate an influx (*H.* 1966).

There have been several records of nests with eggs or young in December; most came to grief.

One ringed 14 January 1951 at Highclere recovered Schleswig-Holstein on 3 June 1951 (*B.B.* 45. 273). One ringed 1 February 1954 at Sway found injured at Totes (Seine-Maritime) on 27 March 1955 (EC). One ringed 24 October 1955 at Dungeness found dead at Andover on 10 February 1956 (*B.B.* 50. 478). One ringed 27 December 1959 at Farlington Marshes recovered in Germany in June 1960 (*H.* 22. Part 2). One ringed 14 January 1960 at Sway found dead at Zuidlaren (Holland) on 4 March 1960 (EC). A first-winter female ringed 16 November 1960 at Dungeness recovered at Godshill Wood on 15 January 1963 (Ash). One ringed 10 January 1959 at Farlington Marshes recovered in East Flanders on 13 October 1962 (*H.* 22. Part 3). An adult male ringed 12 August 1961 at Södermanland (Sweden) found dead at Fordingbridge on 27 March 1962 (*B.B.* 56. 537).

309. Golden Mountain Thrush. *Turdus dauma*: One in K & M shot on 24 January 1828 by the Earl of Malmesbury was the first British record. None since.

311. Wheatear. *Oenanthe oenanthe:*
   Greenland Wheater. *O.o leucorrhoa:* This book follows *B.o.H.* in not differentiating between the races unless they have been handled because of the impossibility of drawing any sharp dividing line between them, a position which is further confused by intermediate forms from Iceland and the Faeroes (*B.B.* 42. 203).

As a breeding species it has decreased markedly, apparently as a result of ploughing up downlands during and after the Second World War (Goater *in litt.*). The first four years of the *Atlas* survey showed mainland breeding *proved* only in six southern 10-kilometer squares to the west of Southampton Water, in and around the New Forest, and possible breeding in several other mainland squares, mainly on the chalk. There is a need for more detailed information, but 11 pairs were found in 15,120 acres of New Forest heath and bog in 1966, half the total area of such habitat in the Forest (*H.* 1966), and at least 12 pairs bred in the Forest during 1968 (*H.* 1968). This suggests that the decrease has continued into quite recent years, for in 1957 no fewer than 34 pairs were located in the New Forest of which 12 (as against one in 1958 and one in 1959) were on the eastern half of Beaulieu Heath.

On the Island, a pair bred on Tennyson's Down in 1957 (*H.* 20. Supplement) but it is certainly no longer 'plentiful in most parts of the Central Hill district of the county and in the Isle of Wight' as described in K & M. It is even uncertain whether it now breeds regularly in the Island at all.

Two or three were reported as wintering at Highcliffe in 1932/3 (*H.* 12), and there was one (possibly wintering) on Freshwater Down on 22 February 1913 (*B.B.* 6). Usually, the first spring visitors arrive in mid-March and some fairly large influxes have been recorded, e.g. 161 arrived at Hengistbury in April/May 1962; 50 were at Hengistbury on 8 April 1963 (*H.* 23. Part 1); 60 were at Hengistbury on 8 April 1967 (only one next day), and 70 were there on 15 April 1967 (*H.* 1967). At St. Catherine's Light, this species has been present in several of the 'rushes' that have occurred on spring nights at the lantern. Similar numbers and movements have been recorded during the autumn migration, e.g. 85 flew in from the sea at St. Catherine's Point on 18 August 1957; ca. 180 were seen at the Light there on the night of 14/15 September 1958 (*H.* 21. Part 2); 100 plus were along a five-mile stretch of the Freshwater/Blackgang road on 26 August 1970 (*H.* 1970). Numbers were high in 1971, the peak count at Hengistbury being 500 on 12 August (*H.* 1971). The latest date is 26 November 1960 at Farlington Marshes (*H.*21. Part 3).

Between 1905/1908, 193 were killed at St. Catherine's Light in the months March/May and August/October (*I.o.W.* 1922).

Definite identifications of the Greenland race are as follows: two males 'obtained' near Oakley in May 1896 (Meinertzhagen); one at St. Catherine's Light on 22 April 1911 and another on 13 April 1913 (*Bull B.O.C.* 30 and 34 quoted in *B.B.* 6. 8); a female killed in a rabbit trap near Damerham on 21 May 1953 (wing 103.5mm.), (Ash in *H.* 18. Part 3); a first-summer male similarly killed there on 27 April 1958 (wing 106mm., weight 29.2grs.) (Ash *in litt.*); several trapped on Farlington Marshes between 14 April and 18 May 1956 (103–106mm.) and one trapped at Hengistbury on 19 October 1957 (C.H.O.S.G.). There are many more sight records which quite probably were of this race but proof is lacking.

A first-winter bird ringed 16 August 1965 at Gilkicker recovered in Morocco on 20 September 1965 (*B.B.* 59. 476).

132

312. Desert Wheatear. *Oenanthe deserti**: The first record for the county and the fourteenth for Britain was seen at Farlington Marshes from 4 to 19 November 1961 (Billett, Clay *et al. − B.B.* 55. 577).

313. Black-eared Wheatear. *Oenanthe hispanica**: One, the first record for the county, at Farlington Marshes on 18 September 1954 (Le Brocq *et al. − B.B.* 48. 130).

317. Stonechat. *Saxicola torquata*: K & M say: 'A common resident in all parts of the county and Wight but numerous only where furze abounds'. Today it breeds commonly in the New Forest, is reasonably well-spread on the heaths of the north and east and along parts of the coastal belt, but is scarce on the Isle of Wight and the mainland chalklands. Numbers show serious declines after hard winters, but they recover well in a year or so. About October/November there appears to be some dispersal from breeding areas to water meadows, the coast and parts of the Island not frequented in the breeding season; the return takes place in February/March. Details of these points are outlined in the following paragraphs.

Breeding: In the New Forest at least 102 pairs bred in 1957 of which 21 were on the eastern part of Beaulieu Heath; corresponding numbers for 1958 were 130 and 29; for 1959 they were 143 and 46, figures which were described as unprecedented, yet in 1961 a census of the New Forest showed a total of 262 pairs in the breeding season (*H.* 22. Part 2); following the cold winters of 1961/2 and 1962/3, the breeding population of the Forest and the western heaths was cut to 25 pairs, but in 1966 172 pairs were found in 15,120 acres of New Forest heath and bog, half the area of such vegetation in the New Forest (*H.* 1966). In the northern and eastern heaths, 33 pairs were found in an exhaustive search of suitable habitat in 1966 (*H.* 1966) and 14 pairs were found in Hampshire heaths along the Surrey border in 1971 (*H.* 1971). No breeding reported on the Island for three years following the 1962/3 winter, but pairs recorded in two or three localities each year before and after that period (e.g. at Headon Warren, St. Catherine's Point and Tennyson Down). A full account of fluctuations in the Forest and the reasons for them is contained in *The New Forest* (Tubbs, 1968, Chapter 12).

October movements: 22 at Hengistbury on 20 October 1968 (*H.* 1968) and 21 there on 3 October 1970 (*H.* 1970) are indications of the numbers involved. They have been seen at St. Catherine's Light at this time.

Spring movement: 18 at Hengistbury on 24 March 1967 (*H.* 1967) and 10 there on 12 March 1968 (*H.* 1968).

One ringed 22 August 1959 near Christchurch was killed at Noisy-les-Bains (Algeria) on 7 February 1960, the first British-ringed Stonechat to be recovered in Africa (*B.B.* 54. 483).

318. Whinchat. *Saxicola rubetra*: K & M say: 'A summer visitor in all parts but nowhere plentiful'. Today it is a regular breeding species only in the New Forest where, in the years 1956/71, the most recorded in any one year was 13 pairs in 1965 (*H.* 23. Part 3), though in 1966 nine pairs were located in a survey that covered 50 per cent of the Forest heath and bogland, i.e. 15,120 acres (*H.* 1966). The only breeding *proved* elsewhere in the last decade was one pair in the north in 1967 (*H.* 1967) and one pair at Longstock in 1969 (*H.* 1969), though there have been a few reports of birds present in the breeding season. Meinertzhagen recorded three pairs breeding at Mottisfont in the nineties but none between 1935/45, supporting the view that it has decreased since K & M.

Spring passage is usually very small. The earliest recorded date is 9 March (1938) when Ringrose saw three at Keyhaven (*B.B.* 31. 382), though March birds are scarce and the first are normally seen from the second week of April. 40 coming in at Hengistbury in April/May 1962 (*Bird Migration* 2.3.174) and 50 plus at St. Catherine's Point on 9/10 May 1958 were quite abnormal numbers for spring; in 1969, for instance, there were only four spring records for the county (*H.* 1969).

Autumn passage is much larger, from July onwards with the peak in late August and September. 35 in the Titchfield Haven/Warsash area on 27 August 1957, 35 at Hengistbury on 22 August 1971, 32 at Eling on 11 September 1963 (*H.* 23. Part 1) and 30 on the cliffs at St. Lawrence on 13 September 1960 (*I.o.W.* 5. Part 5) have been the largest recent counts but gatherings in the 20s are not unusual. November birds are scarce, the latest being one at Titchfield Haven on 28 November 1948 (Suffern). The species has been recorded at St. Catherine's Light and 43 were killed there between 1905/8 in April, May and September (*I.o.W.* 1922).

There are two cases of presumed wintering, one at Brook (I.o.W.) on 2 January 1959 (*I.o.W.* 5. Part 4) and one at Hengistbury on 30 January 1961 (Southampton N.H.S. report).

A first-winter female ringed 6 September 1956 at Fair Isle found dead at Petersfield just over a month later (*B.B.* 50. 479).

320. Redstart. *Phoenicurus phoenicurus*: K & M called it fairly plentiful in the New Forest, but not very common in other parts of the county or in the Isle of Wight. This would describe it reasonably well for most recent years though on the Island and parts of the mainland chalk it is scarce, if not rare, as a breeding species. Cohen gave just one breeding record for Isle of Wight since K & M, a pair by the Medina about 1948 (Mrs. Seabroke), and a pair with young at Newtown on 22 June 1964 was said to be the third breeding record for the Island (*H.* 23. Part 2); another pair bred at Osborne in 1968 (*I.o.W.* 6. Part 3). There have been other suspected cases of breeding on the Island.

The New Forest is its headquarters in the county, numbers varying from year to year. In 1956 it was abundant there, and the species was exceptionally numerous in 1968 (*H.* 1968). Disaster seemed to hit the Redstart somewhere overseas on its migration over the 1968/9 winter, for in common with so much of Britain, numbers were very low in 1969 when a survey of one patch of old woodland in the New Forest showed an 85 per cent decrease from 1968 (*H.* 1969). Declines have been recorded before, and there seems to have been a serious decline in breeding numbers during the first half of the present century, especially between 1925 and 1945, with some recovery in the middle fifties.

Away from the Forest, the north and north-east seem to hold reasonable numbers, e.g. five singing males found at Bramshill in 1959 (*H.* 21. Part 3); 10 singing males at Crookham in 1961 (*H.* 22. Part 2); 24 singing males in the Bordon/Liphook area in 1964 (*H.* 23. Part 2); nine pairs on the Hampshire heaths along the Surrey border in 1971 (*H.* 1971). Over parts of the chalk it seems to be absent and the *Atlas* survey failed to prove breeding in the majority of 10-kilometre squares away from the Forest.

Attempts by the Hampshire and Isle of Wight Naturalists' Trust to attract Redstarts with nest boxes have met with very little success, 100 boxes in 1961 and 1962 failing to attract a single pair (*B.o.H.* 220).

The earliest date is 13 March 1967 when a bird was at Brading (*I.o.W.* 6. Part 2); the latest, the 24 November 1939 at St. Catherine's Point, though November records are very few in number. On spring and autumn migration, the species is much more widespread and some heavy passage has been recorded at times, e.g. *ca.* 70 at St. Catherine's on the nights of 14/15 and 16/17 September 1958 and 40 plus at Latchmore Bottom (New Forest) in late August/early September 1956 and 1958 (Ash). 133 were killed at St. Catherine's Light from 1905/8, nearly all in May and

September.

A male ringed 23 April 1960 near Christchurch found dead in Inverness-shire about 10 May 1960 (*B.B.* 54. 483). A male ringed 17 April 1960 near Christchurch found long dead in the desert SE of Tata (Morocco) on 15 April 1962 (*Ringers' Bulletin* Vol. 2, No. 1). One ringed 1 May 1960 at Hengistbury caught Beira Alta (Portugal) about 17 October 1962 (Wise). A nestling ringed 29 May 1968 in Herefordshire controlled E. Boldre on 23 August 1968 (*B.B.* 62. 429). A nestling ringed 4 June 1968 at Fordingbridge recovered at Aoulef (Algeria) on 7 April 1969 (*B.B.* 64. 176).

Redstart

321. Black Redstart. *Phoenicurus ochruros*: Of the 20 or so mentioned in K & M nearly all were shot. The latest nineteenth century record was one in January/February 1897 at Mottisfont (Meinertzhagen).

It was reported with increasing frequency both in the south of the mainland and in the Island from October to April, even before the Second World War when it bred in the county for the first time — two pairs at Southampton both in 1943 and 1944, one pair in Portsmouth in 1945, and one pair at Bartley near Cadnam in 1943 (*B.B.* 39. 208/9).

Since World War II records have been much more frequent, mostly from the Island (especially St. Catherine's Point and the Needles downs) and the mainland coast, with a few from scattered inland mainland localities. No further breeding has been proved but up to three pairs in Portsmouth during 1965 (including two singing males) may have bred (*H.* 1965). Apart from those, an analysis of sightings from 1959 to 1970 (making every possible allowance for double-counting individuals) gives the following monthly totals: January, eight; February, three; March/May, *ca.* 70 with very few in May; June, one; July, none; August/September, very few; October/November, *ca.* 120 mostly in October; December, 10.

322. Nightingale. *Luscinia megarhyncos*: As in K & M's time, a common summer resident in most suitable localities including the Isle of Wight and in good seasons almost abundant in some areas in the central and northern parts of the county, notably in the Upper Test Valley and in the vale-country running from Kingsclere to Eversley (*per* P. E. Brown). 1947 and 1957 were particularly good years. There are reports of decreasing numbers from some parts, however. It is being driven out of some haunts by building and industrial development, for instance in the Island, in the SW coastal belt, and along the west shore of Southampton Water. Orr thought (1961) that it was declining all over the SW part of the county and Ash stresses the decline in the Damerham area in the early sixties. On the Island, the first years of the *Atlas* survey showed an absence in the eastern third, where birds used to be in the past; a deliberate search in that area during 1971 failed to reveal any (Stafford).

Pratt found some 30 singing males holding territory between Fleet and Aldershot in mid-May 1961 (*H.* 22. Part 2).

Two were caught at St. Catherine's Light on 10 September 1956 and between September 1905 and June 1908, 18 were killed there, all in April.

324. Bluethroat. *Cyanosylvia svecica*: K & M mention four in the Island and one at Eastney, giving the *Zoologist* of 1866, 1867, 1889 as the authority for the first three. Subsequent reports of one near Bembridge in 1929 and one of each race (*C.s. svecica* and *C.s. cyanecula*) also at Bembridge in about 1938/9 do not appear to be sufficiently substantiated.

Two were recorded in 1956, a first-winter female at Farlington Marshes on 9/10 September and one at Damerham on 11 October (*H.* 19. Part 3). Subsequently, an analysis of the years 1958/70 shows the species recorded every year except 1960, the total number of individuals being 20 (possibly 23 since it is not certain whether some records concerned the same individual on different dates or more than one individual). Four (possibly five) was the most in any one year, and seven years had only one bird each. 12/15 were in September, one in August and five in October. The only spring records were one at Southsea on 26 March 1958 (*H.* Supplement) and a male of the Red-spotted race *svecica* at St. Catherine's Light on the night of 24/25 April 1959 (*H.* 21. Part 2). All others save two *cyanecula* were not identified by race. Most of the records came from the mainland coast, with four/five from the Island, and one inland on the mainland (at Yateley gravel pit on 3 October 1965 — *H.* 1965).

A first-winter female ringed 7 September 1958 at Stanpit, killed by high-tension cables near Fonz (Spain) on 9 November 1958 was the first recovery of a British-ringed Bluethroat (*B.B.* 52. 475).

325. Robin. *Erithacus rubecula*: A widely distributed and very common resident; no evidence of any change in status in this century. 22 pairs were found in 1.4 square miles of woodland at West Walk in 1968 (Carpenter). The Continental race (*E.r. rubecula*) has been taken at St. Catherine's both in spring and autumn in the years 1907/9 (*B.B.* 2, 3, 4 and 5). 11 (race not specified) were killed there at the Light in spring and autumn between 1905/8 and there have been notable influxes there in recent years, e.g. 30/40 passed N. with thrushes in the early morning of 2 March 1958; in October 1968, 40 were present on 25th, 100 on 26th, *ca.* 200 at the Light on the night of 26/27th, and 60 on 27th — all this associated with an influx of Wrens and Blackbirds — *H.* 1968. Such influxes, and birds occurring at unusual coastal localities, point to regular movements, particularly noticeable in autumn.

Four recoveries of birds ringed in winter between 1949 and 1958 all show westerly movement, thus: Winchester to Salisbury (*B.B.* 44. 296), St. Mary's Bay (Kent) to Andover (*B.B.* 46. 324), Ewell (Surrey) to Bordon (*B.B.* 50. 68), and Sandown to near Cardiff (*B.B.* 53. 494). One ringed 4 September 1960 near Christchurch found dead at Ranuhec (NW France) 18 days later; many more British-ringed Robins than usual were recovered abroad that year (*B.B.* 54. 484). One ringed 24 April 1963 at Spurn Point (Yorks) found dead Christchurch on 27 August 1964 (*B.B.* 58. 570). One ringed 29 November 1966 at Sway and controlled there 3 March 1967 and 8 December 1967 found dead at Gainsborough (Lincs.) on 20 May 1968 (*B.B.* 62. 431). Juvenile ringed 16 July 1968 near Hareid (Norway) recovered Southampton on 28 September 1968 (*B.B.* 63. 252).

326. Cetti's Warbler. *Cettia cetti* *: The first one for the county was caught by Carter in a mist-net at Titchfield Haven on 19 March 1961; it was first seen by Suffern on 4 March and stayed until early April (*B.B.* 55. 577).

The *Handbook* gives only three previous records for England, all in Sussex between 1904 and 1916, and these have now been rejected among the 'Hastings Rarities' (see *B.B.* 55. 366).

327. Grasshopper Warbler. *Locustella naevia*: K & M say: 'found in all parts of the County and Isle of Wight, though plentiful only in a few districts and but sparingly distributed over the larger area.' There seems to have been a marked increase in the middle 1960s so that today it is widespread and reasonably common in suitable localities as a breeding species, notably in parts of the New Forest and the heaths in the east and north. *B.o.H.* said it was generally scarce or absent on the chalk (though breeding in young plantations on the chalk at Damerham — Ash), but the *Atlas* survey and general observations from the past few years show that it is found all over the chalklands where suitable habitat exists, e.g. in the scrub at Shedden Oak (near Winchester), though absent from the open chalk field areas of course. It is also plentiful in parts of the river valleys. Information from the Island suggests that it is less common there.

It is one of the regular warblers recorded at St. Catherine's Light on both spring and autumn migration since the area has been well-covered by observers from the early 1950s onwards. 25 were killed there in April, August and September between 1905/8.

The earliest date is 4 April (1967); the latest 26 October (1968).

329. Savi's Warbler. *Locustella luscinioides* *: One singing in a reed bed from 11 May to 21 June 1969 was the first ever for Hampshire. It was accepted by *British Birds* Rarities Committee. There was no indication that it found a mate but the locality and observer's name are being withheld as it is a very possible breeding site.

331. Moustached Warbler. *Lusciniola melanopogon* *: The first for the county were seen on Eling Great Marsh on 13 August 1951 by C. Ballantyne and G. E. Wooldridge who watched two at close quarters for a total of about three hours. The birds had gone the next day without other local ornithologists having a chance to see them, but the very full description was accepted by *British Birds* (45. 219) where all details are given in full.

332. Great Reed Warbler. *Acrocephalus arundinaceus*: K & M give one shot in 1884 and another shot in 1900.
 One, Titchfield Haven, 18/24 May 1960 (*B.B.* 54. 191).
 One, Frensham Pond, 29 May/9 June 1966 (*H.* 1966).
 One, Fleet Pond, 24 May 1970 (*H.* 1970).
 The last two were accepted by *British Birds* Rarities Committee.

333. Reed Warbler. *Acrocephalus scirpaceus*: A common summer resident where reed beds are numerous. Munn, just after the First World War, said that this species had extended its range considerably up the valleys of the Test and Itchen. K & M stated that it was not found in the Test valley above Bransbury Common and if that were so it has certainly extended its range considerably. It breeds now near Basingstoke above the 250 foot contour, a relatively high situation for the species in Britain. Reports certainly suggest that it has increased its numbers this century. Examples of breeding numbers recorded recently give an idea of how common the Reed Warbler is: Fleet Pond, *ca.* 30 pairs, 1970; Stanpit, 44 pairs, 1969; Longstock, *ca.* 100 pairs, 1967; Brading and the western Yar, *ca.* 40 pairs each, 1966 — not many suitable localities on the Isle of Wight; Nursling gravel pit, 1963, 26 pairs; Titchfield Haven, *ca.* 30 pairs, 1962 (all figures from *H.* for the year in question). Occasionally local declines are reported, e.g. a marked decline to 30 pairs at Bembridge in 1967 (*H.* 1967).
 First date, 31 March 1960 at Stanpit (*H.* 22. Part 1). Last date, 1 November 1969 at Farlington Marshes (*H.* 1969), apart from one incredibly late bird at Stanpit on 5 December 1970 (*H.* 1971). Very few have been recorded during watches in recent years at St. Catherine's Light but 13 were killed there in the months May, August and September between 1905/8. The largest movements reported have been in autumn from late July onwards, e.g. over 200 ringed at Stanpit/Hengistbury in 1963 (*H.* 23. Part 1).
 A nestling ringed 13 June 1949 at Winchester recovered 20 miles N. on 8 August 1949 (*B.B.* 43. 315). A young bird ringed 14 June 1952 at Slough (Bucks) recovered Petersfield on 5 August 1952 (*B.B.* 46. 324). One ringed 19 July 1959 at Stanpit retrapped there 5 July 1963 (C.H.O.S.G.). One ringed 16 August 1963 killed at Estremadura (Portugal) on 28 September 1964 (*B.B.* 58. 572). One ringed Slapton Ley 1 September 1968 controlled at Alverstone (I.o.W.) on 5 July 1969 (*H.* 1969). One ringed 13 June 1971 in Christchurch Harbour found dead at Burgos (Spain) on 20 August 1971 (*H.* 1971). One ringed 12 August 1971 in Christchurch Harbour controlled at Weymouth on 6 September 1971 (*H.* 1971).

334. Marsh Warbler. *Acrocephalus palustris*: A rare summer visitor. Meinertzhagen says one or two pairs bred regularly at Mottisfont in the 1890s; K & M knew of two clutches taken in the 1860s. In this century, two pairs apparently bred in the south-east in 1907 (*B.B.* 1. 296/7) and Miss Popham found a pair nesting at Mudeford in 1940.
 Otherwise, the total of birds since K & M (1905) is as follows: a male killed at St. Catherine's Light on 7 June 1912 (*B.B.* 6. 344); isolated records in 1931, 1935, 1939 (one killed at St. Catherine's Light on 19 May — *B.B.* 33. 115), 1943 and 1946; one trapped at Stanpit on 6 August 1960 (*H.* 22. Part 1); a male in full song on 2 June 1963 in the Avon valley, not seen or heard on later dates (Orr); two ringed at Hengistbury in the autumn of 1963 (Wise); one trapped at Christchurch Harbour on

16 August 1964 (*H.* 23. Part 2); one at Porchfield for seven days from 12 May 1969 in full song, the third Island record since K & M (*H.* 1969).

K & M thought the species was overlooked. However, the paucity of records in recent years, when observer coverage has been so much increased, leaves no doubt that it really is very rare in the county.

337. Sedge Warbler. *Acrocephalus schoenobaenus*: As in K & M's day, a common summer resident in all suitable mainland localities and probably also in the Island from where, however, there is less available data. In 1969, numbers were low, as if some disaster had occurred on migration (see Redstart and Whitethroat), and numbers were still below normal in 1970.

The earliest date is 17 March 1963 when one was singing at Stratfield Saye (*H.* 23. Part 1). The latest date is 9 November 1963 when a first-winter bird was caught at Winchester (*H.* 23. Part 1).

Numbers are seen at St. Catherine's Light on both migrations, larger numbers than usual occurring in 1958 — 80/100 on the night of 9/10 May and about 50 on 9/10 September. In the years 1905/8, no fewer than 226 were killed there in April/June and August/October. Considerable passage is recorded at other points, e.g. *ca.* 75 at Titchfield Haven on 16 April 1959, whilst no fewer than 567 were ringed at Stanpit in 1965, and 500 were caught there from 23/26 August 1971.

Sedge Warbler

There are not many detailed breeding counts but the following suggest the numbers present: Winnall, 1967, 45 pairs; Longstock, 1967, *ca.* 60 pairs; Gins, 1970, 19 pairs; Timsbury, 1970, 20 pairs.

One ringed 28 July 1963 at Stanpit controlled at Abberton (Essex) on 22 April 1964 and on several subsequent days (*B.B.* 56. 572). One ringed 30 July 1963 at Stanpit found dying at Albufeira (Portugal) on 17 November 1965 (*B.B.* 59. 479). One ringed 19 April 1964 at St. Catherine's Point controlled at Attenborough (Notts) on 24 April 1964 (*B.B.* 58. 572). Two ringed in Christchurch Harbour in August 1971 were controlled a few days later at Chichester, and another ringed there on 28 August 1970 controlled in Isle of Man on 3 May 1971.

338. Aquatic Warbler. *Acrocephalus paludicola*: K & M record three (one in the Appendix), all killed, in September 1876, September 1897 and September 1905. Between then and 1956 there were only two records, a young male at St. Catherine's Point on 17/18 August 1909 and a male there on 17 August 1912 — the latter went to the Osborne College collection (*B.B.* 6. 344).

But, beginning in 1956, the species has been recorded in every year (apart from 1963 and 1966) up to and including 1971. At least 35 birds were involved, possibly over 40, all in the period August to October with August having the most and only three occurring in October. The vast majority were on the mainland coast, especially in the Stanpit area where several have been trapped, five were on the Island, and only one was from inland on the mainland — at Latchmore Bottom on 15 September 1956 (*H.* 19. Part 3). The birds are all recorded in *H.* for the years in question.

It seems that this species must have been overlooked in the past and has been revealed as a very scarce but regular autumn migrant by the increase in observer coverage and particularly by ringers at Stanpit and Farlington. It would be interesting to see what widespread ringing in all suitable localities would reveal.

339. Melodious Warbler. *Hippolais polyglotta* *:
One, Keyhaven, 2/3 September 1961 (D. Wooldridge, *B.B.* 55. 578).
One, St. Catherine's Point, 31 August/1 September 1963 (*I.o.W.* 1963/4).
One, Titchfield Haven, 2 September 1963 (*H.* 23. Part 1).
Three, St. Catherine's Point, 12 September 1964, and one there 13th (*H.* 23. Part 2).
One, Needs Oar, 17 October 1964 (*H.* 23. Part 2).
One, Hurst, 25/26 September 1965 (*H.* 23. Part 3).
One, Farlington Marshes, 14 September 1968 (*H.* 1968).
One, St. Catherine's Point, 7 and 14 September 1968 (*I.o.W.* 6. Part 3 and *H.* 1969. p.36).

340. Icterine Warbler. *Hippolais icterina*: The first record appears in the Appendix to K & M, a young female taken at St. Catherine's on 29 September 1905.
One, caught at St. Catherine's Point, 14 Septembr 1956 (*H.* 19. Part 3).
One, Hengistbury, 10 September 1966 (*H.* 1966).
There is a report in *The Field* (26.1.67) by Doris Barron of one singing, answered by another, at Fritham on 6 September 1966. The bird remained for a few days and was seen settled on a clothes line. No details were sent to the Hampshire societies, however, so the record cannot be considered as fully substantiated.

339/340. Melodious/Icterine Warbler. *Hippolais* warblers that were one or other of these species have been:
One, St. Catherine's Point, 22 August 1959 (*B.B.* 53. 425).

One, Crookham, 24 June 1961 (*H.* 22. Part 2).
One, Gilkicker, 15 September 1962 (*H.* 22. Part 3).
One, Farlington Marshes, 3 September 1963 (*H.* 23. Part 1).
One, Farlington Marshes, 7 September 1964 (*H.* 23. Part 2).
One, Winchester, 9 July 1965 (*H.* 1965).
One, St. Catherine's Point, 12 September 1965 (*I.o.W.* 5. Part 10).

343. Blackcap. *Sylvia atricapilla*: A generally distributed and fairly plentiful summer resident in most parts of the county and the Isle of Wight. Many observers consider it to be commoner than the Garden Warbler (e.g. EC for parts of southern Hampshire) but others consider the reverse to be true in particular areas. Very few details of breeding numbers are available but some counts have been made, viz. — 55 singing males in the Alice Holt area in 1947 (A. F. Mitchell), and in 1967 12 pairs in Nightingale Wood and eight pairs in Lord's Wood (both near Southampton — *H.* 1967).

The first appear in March but it is impossible to give earliest and latest dates because of wintering birds. Every Hampshire Bird Report from 1960 to 1970 inclusive (except 1968) records examples of birds in winter, often visiting bird tables and sometimes remaining in one locality for some length of time. Up to four visited a bird-table in New Milton from 21 December 1969 to 18 January 1970, for instance (*H.* 1969, 1970).

A dramatic 'fall' occurred at St. Catherine's Light on the night of 20/21 September 1963 when it was one of the most abundant species present. 29 were caught and ringed and *ca.* 80 were in the surrounding area the following day, numbers falling to six by 22nd (*H.* 23. Part 1). 76 were killed at the Light in April, May and August/October between 1905/8 (*I.o.W.* 1922).

A female ringed 9 September 1958 at St. Catherine's Point shot near Tetuan (Spanish Morocco) on 28 April 1959 (*B.B.* 53. 495). A male ringed 12 April 1957 at Portland found dead at Totton on 16 June 1958. A female ringed 1 November 1964 at Niton (I.o.W.) found dead at La Chapell, Loire-Atlantique (France) 15 June 1965 (*B.B.* 59. 480). One ringed 12 September 1965 at Hengistbury killed at Bilbao (Spain) 17 May 1966. One ringed 13 July 1967 at East Boldre found dead at Villafranca (Spain) 3 October 1967 (*H.* 68. p.44).

345. Barred Warbler. *Sylvia nisoria* *: One at Farlington Marshes on 16 October 1965 (Renyard — *H.* 1965).

346. Garden Warbler. *Sylvia borin*: A summer resident in almost all parts of the county and the Isle of Wight. K & M stated that: 'It is nowhere so plentiful as the Blackcap and in some localities it is scarce.' It may still be scarce in some districts and less plentiful than the Blackcap in many southern parts, but in many places it is common and not only as plentiful as the Blackcap but even more so. This is particularly true of some areas in the NE of the county, around Alice Holt Forest (90 singing males plotted by A. F. Mitchell in 1947 compared with 55 Blackcaps) and in the Basing/Bramley area, for example. It therefore seems highly probable that the species has increased, at least in some areas, during the present century (most of the above written by P. E. Brown).

The first date was one at Netley on 1 April 1961 (*H.* 22. Part 2). The heaviest passage appears to be in early May, e.g. a considerable fall occurred at Hengistbury on 7 May 1962 (*H.* 22. Part 3), and seven seen at St. Catherine's Point on 9 May 1965 indicated a large fall in the area (*H.* 1965). In autumn, 22 at Hengistbury on 11 August 1968 were exceptional (*H.* 1968), whilst considerable numbers occurred at

St. Catherine's Point on the night of 20/21 September 1963 and 50 were seen in the area the next day (*H.* 23. Part 1). The latest date was one at St. Catherine's on 10 November 1968 (*H.* 1968), a remarkably late date for October birds are not very common.

142 were killed at St. Catherine's Light in April, May, August and September between 1905/8 (*I.o.W.* 1922).

One ringed 5 August 1964 at East Boldre controlled at Portland on 16 August 1964 (*H.* 23. Part 2). Adult ringed 20 July 1964 at Winchester controlled at Dungeness on 7 May 1965 (*B.B.* 59, 480). One ringed 31 August 1966 at Benacre (Suffolk) found dead at Chandlers Ford on 13 September 1966 (*B.B.* 60. 466).

347. Whitethroat. *Sylvia communis*: This appears to have been the species most severely hit by whatever catastrophe overtook several species of summer migrants during the spring passage of 1969 (see Redstart and Sedge Warbler). Many observers remarked on the extreme scarcity during passage and in the breeding season, an 89 per cent decrease being reported from Hengistbury compared with spring passage in 1968 and a 20 per cent decrease in breeding numbers around Silchester. Some observers reported *all* sightings during 1969 which in some cases did not amount to more than a dozen records (*H.* 1969). There was some recovery in 1970 and 1971 but numbers were still well below normal.

Up to then, a common summer resident on the mainland and Island, possibly rivalling the Willow Warbler as the commonest warbler of that time. There is little information on detailed numbers breeding but A. F. Mitchell found 120 pairs at Alice Holt in 1947.

Spring passage has been *very* heavy on occasions. There were enormous waves of migrants at Farlington Marshes in 1955, about 500 on 26 April and some 800 on the 29th when they were 'not only in every bush but on the seawalls and even in the saltings' (*H.* 19. Part 2). At St. Catherine's Light on the night of 9/10 May 1958, about 500 were seen, mostly females (*H.* 21. Part 2).

Likewise, autumn passage has also been very heavy, e.g. at St. Catherine's Light on 10 September 1956 about 100 were caught in five and a half hours, and 'phenomenal numbers were moving from W. to E. through the beam all the time' (*H.* 19. Part 3). A peak of 70 at Hengistbury on 20 August 1967 (*H.* 1967) was quite normal.

501 were killed at St. Catherine's Light in April, May and August/October between 1905/8, 67 of these on the two days of 29 and 30 September 1907, and 30 on each of the dates 5 and 9 May 1908, so the species was equally numerous early in the century. 78 were killed as late as the night of 4/5 May 1967 despite preventative measures by the R.S.P.B.

The earliest date was one on 17 March 1968 at Farlington Marshes; the latest date was one at St. Catherine's Point on 9 November 1968 (*H.* 1968) apart from an adult female trapped at Basingstoke sewage farm on 15 December 1959 (*H.* 22. Part 1, p.31).

A nestling ringed 13 June 1968 at Anglesey controlled at Portsmouth on 20 August 1968 (*B.B.* 62. 434).

348. Lesser Whitethroat. *Sylvia curruca*: A summer resident, widely but thinly distributed throughout the county and Island. E. L. Jones finds it not uncommon on the chalk of the NW, but the first four years of the *Atlas* survey showed several 10-kilometer squares in the north with no records and several observers have described the species as scarce in that area, e.g. a special search round Stratfield Saye and Bramshill in 1963 failed to reveal a single pair (*H.* 23. Part 1). An inconspicuous species with an inconspicuous song, it has been suggested that it may often be overlooked, but it seems almost certainly the rarest of the 10 migrant warblers which breed regularly, as it apparently was in K & M's time (most of the above by P. E. Brown). Only the Winchester College N.H.S. reports for 1931, 1949 and 1965 respectively say: 'Definitely common; often overlooked', 'Not as scarce as is often thought' and 'apparently increasing'. The *Atlas* survey showed a denser distribution on the southern mainland than elsewhere, whilst recent Island Reports list breeding localities which suggests a fairly sparse population.

Earliest dates, one at Swaythling in poor condition on 7 March 1971 (*H.* 1971), and one at Butser on 6 April 1959 (*H.* 22. Part 3). Passage numbers suggested by the following peaks: 10 at Hengistbury on 4 May 1969; 12 at Hengistbury on 12 September 1969 (*H.* 1969); 16 at Farlington Marshes on 19 September 1966 (*H.* 1966). Latest date, one at Keyhaven on 21 October 1971 (*H.* 1971).

59 killed at St. Catherine's Light in May, August and September from 1905/8 (*I.o.W.* 1922).

One ringed 5 July 1967 at East Boldre killed at Bergame (Italy) on 10 September 1968 (*B.B.* 62. 434).

352. Dartford Warbler. *Sylvia undata*: This species, whose breeding headquarters in the county are in the New Forest, has more marked ups and downs than most other species. Its 'ups' result from dull and wet breeding seasons when there are fewer heath fires and from mild winters when the existing population can survive to breed in the following season; conversely drought, fires, hard winters and egg collectors cause set-backs, sometimes serious. In 1931, 1936, 1937, 1957, 1960 and 1961 it did well; in 1938, 1939, in the winter of 1946/7 and in 1955 it fared very badly. In the New Forest at least 56 pairs bred in 1956, 67 in 1957, 98 in 1959 and 152 in 1960 plus at least eight pairs (an unusually high number) in the east. It would appear that numbers were at a peak in about 1925 and a trough came between 1947 and 1950 (Watson), but as a result of mild winters there was a new peak of some 200 pairs in the county in 1961 (*H.* 22. Part 2). Numbers were much reduced by the cold winter of 1961/2 (*H.* 22. Part 3), and then came the terrible winter of 1962/3 which took such a toll that only six pairs were known to breed in the Forest in 1963 (Orr) and none were seen in the north or on the Island — an all-time low for the county. Recovery has been slow but steady. 50 to 60 pairs were located in the New Forest and surrounding heaths in 1971 and at least 70 pairs in 1972 (Orr).

In the east of the county it has always been scarce, eight pairs being located in 1960 (*H.* 23. Part 1). A few pairs were breeding at a handful of Island localities before the 1962/3 winter (perhaps four/five pairs at three localities in 1961 and 1962 — *I.o.W.* 5. Parts 6 and 7), but following the severe cold, birds were not located in suitable breeding habitat until 1965/6, and the first proved resumption of breeding was one pair in 1967 (*I.o.W.* 6. Part 2).

Although afforestation of new areas and ploughing of its gorse/heather habitat to provide more pasture for Forest ponies and cattle reduces the area available for its breeding, it has a long way to go before the areas left to it are occupied to saturation point, but these two activities and planned rotational or malicious haphazard burning are a nuisance in that new breeding sites have repeatedly to be found as the birds are driven from the old.

For a full account of the species in the New Forest, the reader should go to Chapter 12 of *The New Forest* (1968) by Tubbs, and for an account of the species in Hampshire to a paper by the same author in *B.B.* 56.

Before the 1962/3 winter, and to a lesser extent in the past few years, birds were not infrequently seen from July onwards into winter on or near the mainland coast in places where they do not breed (e.g. Gilkicker, Hengistbury, Needs Oar and Pennington) suggesting some dispersal from the Forest. Similar occurrences have occurred at St. Catherine's Point.

There is even some small evidence of either immigration or emigration, e.g. one at Farlington Marshes in April 1958 and one caught at St. Catherine's Light on 14 April 1958 (*I.o.W.* 5. Part 3), though these might have been dispersal birds returning from the nearby coast. No birds of this species were included in the totals killed at St. Catherine's Light from 1905/8, and the above bird is the only one caught there in recent years despite a full coverage by observers.

One strange record was of a bird freshly dead at Burlington Arcade, in the middle of Bournemouth, on 5 August 1969 (*H.* 1969).

354. Willow Warbler. *Phylloscopus trochilus*: Common and widely distributed summer resident all over the mainland and Island; no evidence of any change of status since K & M, being indisputably the commonest warbler in Hampshire since the recent decline in numbers of its chief rival, the Whitethroat. A. F. Mitchell found 276 pairs in the forest area of Alice Holt in 1947.

Large migratory movements occur every spring, the peak usually being in the third and fourth weeks of April. St. Catherine's Light has attracted the largest numbers, e.g. 'many hundreds' passed through the beams during the night of 18/19 April 1966 and about 250 were found in the immediate surrounds the following morning (*H.* 1966). 497 were killed at the Light in spring and autumn between 1905/8. Counts such as 60 at Pennington on 16 April 1966 (*H.* 1966) are typical peaks in spring from other places on the coast.

Apart from one winter record in January 1913 (*B.B.* 8.273), the earliest date is 24 February 1961 when one was at Newtown (*I.o.W.* 5. Part 6), the only February record for Hampshire. The latest date is 30 October 1964 when one was at Needs Oar (*H.* 23. Part 2).

Ticehurst exhibited six specimens of the northern race, which he referred to as *P.t. eversmanni* at the British Ornithologists' Club in October 1908, all obtained in Hampshire (*B.B.* 2. 234/5). Since then, a specimen of the northern race (*P.t. acredula*) was taken at St. Catherine's Light on 26 May 1911 (*B.B.* 6. 323), another was caught there on the night of 10/11 May 1957 (*H.* 20. Supplement), and one was trapped at Hengistbury on 23 April 1966 (C.H.O.S.G.).

One ringed 21 April 1960 at St. Catherine's recovered on 2 May 1960 at Williton (Somerset) (*B.B.* 46. 445). One ringed 21 April 1960 near Christchurch controlled at Bardsey (Caernarvon) on 23 April 1961 (*B.B.* 55. 533). One ringed 17 April 1966 at Hengistbury found dead at Partington (Cheshire) on 30 April 1966 (*B.B.* 60. 467). A juvenile ringed 15 July 1967 at Winchester controlled at Lerma (Spain) on 3 October 1967 (*H.* 68. p.44).

356. Chiffchaff. *Phylloscopus collybita*: Generally distributed as a summer resident throughout the mainland and Island, less common than the Willow Warbler but plentiful in places (i.e. the north, east and parts of the Forest). *B.o.H.* said it was rather scarce in some parts but this must have been due to lack of coverage for this does not seem to be the case today. A. F. Mitchell found 139 pairs in the Alice Holt area in 1947.

Each of the last few years has regularly produced records from November to February, so some apparently overwinter and survive. There were fewer such records for the years before 1960 which may have been due to fewer observers or to a real increase in wintering birds since then.

Some large migratory movements occur in the spring and autumn, e.g. very numerous at St. Catherine's Point in a fall at dawn on 15 April 1967, birds still arriving during the first hours of daylight (*I.o.W.* 6. Part 2); very numerous at St. Catherine's Light on the night of 20/21 September 1963 (*I.o.W.* 1963/4) and 100 there on the night of 26/27 September 1970 (*H.* 1970). 144 were killed at the Light from March/May and September/October between 1905/8 (*I.o.W.* 1922).

One of Scandinavian form (*P.c. abietinus*) caught at St. Catherine's on 15 April 1907. Two of this race or *tristis* (Siberian form) were there in the springs of 1956 and 1957 (*H.* 20. Supplement). One of the race *abietinus*, at St. Catherine's again, was caught on 31 August 1963 (*I.o.W.* 1963/4).

One ringed 11 September 1961 at Sandown controlled at Dungeness on 20 September 1961 (*B.B.* 55. 533). One ringed 24 September 1962 at Steep Holme (Somerset) found dead at Gurnard on 12 April 1963 (*I.o.W.* 1963/4). Juvenile ringed 18 July 1965 at Winchester controlled at Beachy Head on 5 September 1965 (*B.B.* 59. 483). First-winter bird ringed 7 September 1965 at East Boldre killed in Badajoz Province (Spain) on 12 October 1965 (*B.B.* 59. 483). One ringed 19 September 1965 at Totton recovered near St. Malo (France) on 23 March 1966 (*B.B.* 60. 468). One ringed 24 August 1969 at Christian Malford (Wilts.) controlled Hengistbury on 12 April 1971 (C.H.O.S.G.). One ringed 14 August 1969 at Connah's Quay (Flint) controlled Hengistbury on 18 April 1971 (C.H.O.S.G.).

357. Wood Warbler. *Phylloscopus sibilatrix*: A not uncommon summer resident but very local in distribution. Most numerous in parts of the New Forest where it is sometimes abundant in certain inclosures (e.g. 1946, 1948 and 1950), though absent from others which look equally suitable (EC). It is also numerous in the north and

Wood Warbler

east of the mainland, especially on or adjacent to the greensand tracts, but generally speaking it is uncommon on the chalk because of the scarcity of suitable habitat (e.g. the *Atlas* survey failed to find any Wood Warblers in some 10-kilometer squares in central Hampshire). There are very few records of breeding in the Island.

A. F. Mitchell located 41 pairs in the Alice Holt area in 1947, but said there were none there in 1961. As there is no evidence of any decline, this is likely to be the result of annual variations rather than a real drop in numbers.

The earliest date is 29 March 1965 when one was at Thornhill (*H*. 1965). The latest date is 29 September 1964 when one was at Winchester sewage farm (*H*. 23. Part 2). There are *very* few coastal records on either spring or autumn passage (e.g. only four birds seen at St. Catherine's Point, all in spring, for the years 1959/71 inclusive). 19 were killed at St. Catherine's Light, however, in May from 1906/8 inclusive.

A nestling ringed 15 June 1956 at Lyndhurst reported from Teolo, Padova (Italy) on 15 August 1956 (*B.B.* 50. 481).

360. Yellow-browed Warbler. *Phylloscopus inornatus**: Doubt was cast (*B.B.* 38. 160) on one reported at Ringwood on 24 October 1943 (*H*. 16). One on board the *Queen Elizabeth* between Cherbourg and Southampton was last seen 10 to 15 miles from St. Catherine's Point on 12 October 1959 (*B.B.* 53. 426).

The first acceptable bird was one at Avington on 30 November 1959 (*B.B.* 54. 178). One caught and ringed at East Boldre on 10 October 1967 (Pullen — *H*. 1967). One at Downs View (I.o.W.) on 18 October 1967 (Angell — *H*. 1967 — in September/October 1967 this species visited England in unprecedented numbers, *B.B.* 60. 536).

361. Pallas's Warbler. *Phylloscopus proregulus**: One at St. Catherine's Point on 27 October 1963 (Duffin, Williams, Wiseman — *B.B.* 57. 274). There were only seven previous records for Britain though the above was the first of six in the country in October/November 1963.

364. Goldcrest. *Regulus regulus*: Breeds throughout the county and the Isle of Wight, becoming really numerous in many areas where larch, yew and other conifers are plentiful, but almost scarce in places where such habitat is lacking. Its numbers are often drastically reduced by severe winters; after the cold of 1962/3, for example, it was missing from some areas where it was previously common (e.g. Silchester), decimated in others (e.g. breeding population at Crookham in 1963 estimated to be only 10 per cent of 1962 numbers), and even migrants were few (e.g. one at Hengistbury on 1 April 1963 the only record there for the whole year) (*H*. 23. Part 1). Within a few years, numbers were back to normal.

In some winters numbers are swollen by immigrants and the period September/November often sees such influxes. At Hengistbury, for example, there were peaks of 30 on 26 September 1965, 40 on 12 October 1969, and 120 plus on 14 October 1970; similar peaks occur elsewhere on the coast, e.g. 45 at St. Catherine's Point on 4 October 1970 (*H*. for those years). At that time of year, birds are seen in unusual coastal localities and numbers have been seen arriving over the water at the two localities mentioned. Such arrivals have also been seen in March/April when coastal areas again experience peaks, though *usually* smaller than the autumn ones, e.g. 40 at Hengistbury on 28 March 1971 (*H*. 1971) and up to eight at St. Catherine's Point.

Apart from temporary changes after severe winters, there is no evidence of any change in status since K & M, although with the increase in conifers an expansion of

146

the population might be expected.

One ringed 1 November 1950 at Towcester (Northants) recovered at Ringwood on 12 January 1951 (*B.B.* 44. 294). A female ringed 20 October 1956 at Dungeness recovered at Headley Down (Bordon area) on 27 October 1956 (*B.B.* 50. 481). A female ringed 10 November 1967 at Sandwich Bay (Kent) found dead at Waterlooville on 9 March 1968 (*B.B.* 62. 436).

The Continental race (*R.r. regulus*) has been taken at St. Catherine's between 26 October and 4 November of the years 1908 and 1910, in both of which years autumn movement of the species was considerable (*B.B.* 4. 337 and 6. 322).

365. Firecrest. *Regulus ignicapillus*: K & M admitted four, the last in 1887. Now a regular spring and autumn migrant in *very* small numbers; a few pairs have nested since at least 1962 and there are occasional reports of birds in winter. This increase since K & M, especially marked in the last 20 years or so, must in part be due to the greater number of observers, but the increase is so marked that it must be partly real.

An analysis of the period 1959/70 shows the following:

Spring passage: Over 60 recorded, mostly in March/April with very few in May. Birds were recorded every spring, never more than five per year apart from 1969 (perhaps 20) and 1970 (10 plus). Nearly all were on the coast, especially at Hengistbury and St. Catherine's Point.

Breeding: Unless stated otherwise, all in the New Forest. Adams watched four singing males and a female in May/June 1961 for some 40 hours but had no proof of breeding. However, they returned in April 1962 and at one time there were six singing males. Later, Adams watched fledged young being fed in three localities. Breeding has occurred in each subsequent year, as many as 23 singing males being found on 8 June 1969 (*H.* 1969), and a full account of the early events appears in *B.B.* 59. 6. In 1971, Adams found three singing males at a locality in the north of the county.

Autumn passage: Over 65 recorded, mostly in October/November but with a few in September. Birds were present every autumn with 13/20 in 1967 the most for one year. Nearly all were coastal birds, mainly at Hengistbury and St. Catherine's, with seven at the former place on 5 November 1966 (*H.* 1966) the most at one place on one day.

Winter: Most winters in this period produced a record but the total of individuals was only around 22.

In 1971, outside the period analysed above, numbers at Hengistbury reached a peak of 11 on 28 March (*H.* 1971).

366. Spotted Flycatcher. *Muscicapa striata*: A common summer visitor, widely distributed throughout the mainland and the Island. No evidence of a change in status since K & M. The earliest dates are 5 April 1960 (three at West Walk — *H.* 22. Part 1) and 8 April 1961 (two at West Walk — *H.* 22. Part 2), but the first is not normally seen until late April or even early May. The last are usually seen in early October, the latest being a bird at Longdown (New Forest area) on 29 October 1961 (*H.* 22. Part 2) and one at Freshwater on 28 October 1946 (*B.B.* 40. 158). Normally, only small concentrations are seen at times of passage, but larger numbers have occurred on occasions, e.g. up to 40 have been seen at St. Catherine's Point in the second week of May, and 30 around mid-September (both peak passage times); 50 were at Hengistbury on 22 September 1963 (*H.* 23. Part 1); bushes at East Boldre were 'alive with them' on 23 September 1965 (*H.* 1965).

Few breeding counts are available but 35 pairs were found on Southampton Common in 1963 (*H.* 23. Part 1).

A nestling ringed 14 June 1960 at Christchurch found dead at Madrid on 27 September 1964 (*B.B.* 58. 576). A juvenile ringed 1 August 1968 at Winchester killed at Higuera de Arjona (Spain) on 15 September 1968 (*H.* 1968).

368. Pied Flycatcher. *Muscicapa hypoleuca*: A regular passage migrant in spring (*very* small numbers) and autumn (moderate to small numbers). There are two breeding records. An analysis of passage for the years 1959/70 showed spring passage in April/May (with the annual total never reaching double figures), and autumn passage from July (once) to October (very few), the vast majority being in August/September with annual totals varying from eight to 50 plus (1968). Nearly all records were from the mainland and Island coasts, especially from St. Catherine's Point and Hengistbury, but a few were from scattered localities well inland.

The earliest date is 5 April 1970 when one was at Shanklin (*H.* 1970). The latest date is 21 October 1967.

Mostly, these passage records are of singletons or small parties, but larger concentrations have occurred, e.g. at St. Catherine's Light, a maximum of 77 in three and a half hours on the night of 10 September 1956, about 100 on the night of 20/21 September 1957, and about 85 on the night of 14/15 September 1958 (*H.* 19. 20 and 21); 38 at Hengistbury on 10 August 1968 (*H.* 1968). 20 were killed at St. Catherine's Light between 1905/8.

Possibly the largest spring influx was when six males arrived at Mottisfont on 19 May 1895 and stayed for five days (Meinertzhagen).

Pied Flycatcher

K & M list five breeding records but without any reasonable documentation. Breeding was alleged at Micheldever in 1915 but cannot be confirmed, and breeding records at Romsey in 1943 and Alton in 1944 (*H.* 16. 210) were discounted by EC in

148

B.o.H. However, single pairs bred successfully in the New Forest in 1954 (*H.* 19. Part 1) and 1968 (*H.* 1968), the latter birds being photographed by Orr (*H.* 1968). Birds have also occurred in June at Newtown in 1962 (Mrs. Seabroke), and in the New Forest in 1963 (*H.* 23. Part 1). With the spread of the species elsewhere, it could possibly nest more often in Hampshire in the future.

One ringed in Finland on 26 August 1966 was controlled at East Boldre on 18 September 1966 (*B.B.* 61. 75), the first British recovery of a Finnish-ringed Pied Flycatcher.

370. Red-breasted Flycatcher. *Muscicapa parva* *:
Male, Southsea, 1 May 1944 (*B.B.* 38. 174).
Male, Newtown, 12 October 1950 (Mrs. Seabroke).
Male and first-winter bird or female in a Farlington garden, 14 September 1953 (*H.* 18. 361).
Male, Newport, 19 June 1960 (*I.o.W.* 5. Part 5).
Female or immature male, St. Catherine's, 25 September 1960 (*I.o.W.* 5. Part 5).
Male, Shanklin, 7 May 1962 (*I.o.W.* 5. Part 7).
Male, Pennington, 2 October 1968 (*H.* 1968).

371. Dunnock. *Prunella modularis*: A very common resident. No evidence of change in status.

There is evidence of some movement in autumn; for example, a remarkable and sudden increase in numbers was noted at Farlington Marshes on 15 November 1953 (*H.* 18. Part 3); on 26 October 1956 two came in from the sea at St. Catherine's Point and left to the north, and there was a large influx there on 1 November 1959 (*H.* 21. Part 3); a peak of 25 at Gilkicker on 17 September 1967 was exceptional for the area; 40 at Hengistbury on 14 October 1970 was a peak (*H.* 1970).

There have been some large gatherings in kale fields during winter, e.g. a remarkable concentration was found in a kale field at Sopley during the last week of February 1960 when Clafton and Ash ringed no fewer than 40 (*H.* 22.); in similar habitat, 50 were in a field at Needs Oar on 26 December 1961, and 40 at the same place on 17 November 1962 (*H.* 22. Parts 2 and 3).

372. Alpine Accentor. *Prunella collaris*: One in K & M — shot. Three during 'a howling blizzard from the SSE' from 19 to 21 January 1926 at Beaulieu were recorded as 'probable' in *B.B.* 20. 107 but, as the *Handbook* gives four for Hampshire, the editors must have definitely accepted these three. The description in *B.B.* is certainly quite convincing.

373. Meadow Pipit. *Anthus pratensis*: In K & M's time, a common resident in all suitable parts of the mainland and Island. There seems to have been a considerable decline since then, at any rate in the north of the county where it is scarce or even absent in some habitats that appear suitable (P. E. Brown). It is still common on the New Forest heaths, and reasonably common in the rougher coastal areas, on the heaths of the north and east (33 pairs located on heaths along the Surrey border in 1971), and in wilder tracts amongst the intensively cultivated chalklands.

In winter, some of the breeding grounds are almost deserted (e.g. the New Forest heaths) and birds appear in localities where they do not breed (e.g. flocks in stubble, in parts of the major river valleys and in watercress beds). Winter numbers are increased by immigrants.

Spring passage from St. Catherine's Point, the mainland coast and inland points is in a generally northwards direction, though some coasting movements are seen.

From March to early May, hundreds have been seen coming in off the sea at St. Catherine's, Hengistbury and Gilkicker, e.g. 1,000 at Gilkicker from 24 March to 19 April 1970 (*H.* 1970), 2,200 at Gilkicker from 21 March to 20 April 1967 (*H.* 1967) and 235 at St. Catherine's on 4 April 1966 (*H.* 1966). Inland movement has also been marked at times, e.g. over 500 flew north in two hours at Hampton Ridge (New Forest) on 21 March 1966 (*H.* 1966).

Passage from late August to early November is very complicated involving emigration southwards, coastal movements to both east and west, and immigration off the sea in a generally northwards direction. To quote from *H.* 19. Part 3, 'the bulk of the movement (in 1956) during September was E. with some coming in from the sea to the N., but during October, while numbers to the N. increased the majority were moving to the W. (*cf.* a similar switch noted under Swallow).' Examples of such movements are: 800 flew east in three and a half hours at St. Catherine's Point on 15 September 1956 and 810 flew east there on 22 September 1956; 530 flew SE at Hurst and 625 flew ESE at Gilkicker on 23 September 1961 (*H.* 22. Part 2); 890 flew south from Hengistbury on four dates between 29 September/10 October 1968 (*H.* 1968); 230 flew NE off the sea at St. Catherine's and coasted east on 19 September 1966 (*H.* 1966).

One ringed 8 September 1960 at Hengistbury controlled at Anglet, Basses-Pyrenées (France) on 13 October 1961 (*per* Wise). One ringed 6 November 1962 at Dungeness recovered at Fawley on 27 January 1963 (*B.B.* 57. 575). One ringed 2 August 1967 at Frensham (Surrey) found moribund at Yarmouth on 10 December 1967 (*I.o.W.* 6. Part 2).

374. Richard's Pipit. *Anthus richardi**: A bird picked up dead near Totland Bay late in 1938 and accepted at the time (*H.* 14. 376) was subsequently proved to be an abnormal Skylark.

Two, Titchfield Haven, 16 April 1955 (Bowers, Rees and Suffern — accepted by *B.B.* but not published — Ferguson-Lees *in litt.*).

One, Needs Oar, 4 October 1960 (Dennis — *H.* 22. Part 1).

Two, St. Catherine's Point, 29 September 1970 and one there 10 October 1970 (*H.* 1970).

One, Keyhaven, from 14 October to 21 November 1970 (*H.* 1970).

These were all accepted by *B.B.* but one at Farlington Marshes on 27 October 1959 reported in *H.* 21. Part 3 was rejected by them.

375. Tawny Pipit. *Anthus campetris*: K & M admit one, shot in 1879.

One, Needs Oar, 3 September 1963 (*B.B.* 57. 275).

One, Gilkicker, 8/11 September 1965 (*B.B.* 59. 296).

One, Gilkicker, 17 September 1967 (*B.B.* 61.354).

One, Silchester, 13/19 September 1969 (*B.B.* 63. 288).

The two reported at Gilkicker on 5 September 1961 (*B.B.* 54. 447) were later found to be 'unacceptable' (*B.B.* 55. 583).

376. Tree Pipit. *Anthus trivialis*: A summer resident on the mainland, quite numerous in suitable habitats such as the heaths of the New Forest (50 pairs in 2,000 acres of the Matley/Denny area in 1960 — *H.* 22. Part 1), and the heaths of the north and east (137 pairs found on the Hampshire heaths adjoining Surrey in a heathland survey in 1971, making it the commonest species there — *Hants/Surrey Border Bird Report*, 1971). A. F. Mitchell found 36 singing males at Alice Holt in 1947. Very local on the chalklands of the centre and along the coastal belt, the *Atlas* survey showing some 10-kilometer squares in those areas having no Tree Pipits. On the

Island, although breeding has been suspected in one or two places, there are no proven cases of nesting for some 20 years at least, Island bird reports making statements such as 'recorded only on migration' (*I.o.W.* 5. Part 7 for 1962).

Small spring passage (earliest date one at Titchfield Haven on 18 March 1970 — *H.* 1970), birds seen flying N. off the sea at places such as St. Catherine's Point and Hengistbury, e.g. daily peaks in 1968 were 12 on 21 April (St. Catherine's) and 12 on 22 April (Hengistbury). Occasionally, a few are recorded at St. Catherine's Light such as on the night of 2/3 May 1968 (*H.* 1968), and 18 were killed there in April/May and August/September between 1905/8.

Autumn passage is generally to the south, e.g. 30 flying south at Keyhaven on 16 August 1969 (*H.* 1969) and 64 seen to fly south-east out to sea at St. Catherine's Point on 27 August 1960 (*H.* 22. Part 1) but directions are somewhat confused by birds coasting, these latter movements being mainly to the west (e.g. 37 flying west at Hengistbury on 15 August 1970) but some being to the east (e.g. 12 flying east at St. Catherine's on 19 September 1966). The latest date was one at St. Catherine's Point on 9 November 1968 (*H.* 1968).

The species is said to be partial to stubble fields on autumn passage (Ash and Jenkins).

379. Rock Pipit. *Anthus spinoletta petrosus*: K & M said 'a common resident on the coast, particularly plentiful on the Isle of Wight shores.' Certainly no longer common on the mainland coast, breeding proved in only two 10-kilometer squares during the first four years of the *Atlas* survey. The two main sites are Hurst (eight/10 pairs in 1963 the most — *H.* 23. Part 1) and Hengistbury (one/two pairs at best). Breeding on the Island is also very local today, the main area being the stretch between Freshwater and the Needles where 15 singing males were located on 21 June 1970 (*H.* 1970) and 10 pairs estimated in 1954 (*H.* 19. Part 1).

From September to April, widespread along the coast, e.g. 15 at Portchester Castle on 1 January 1970 (*H.* 1970), 26 in two and a half miles at Pennington on 22 December 1968 (*H.* 1968) and 20 at Stanpit on 27 December 1961 (Orr). This winter population is associated with quite marked influxes in autumn, e.g. 30 appeared at Farlington Marshes on 10 October 1957. Return passage reported much less often.

Very scarce inland.

379. Scandinavian Rock Pipit. *A.s. littoralis*: One 'possible' at Farlington Marshes on 30 March and 2 April 1956 (Rees in *H.* 19. Part 3). One trapped at Stanpit on 28 February 1971 (*H.* 1971).

379. Water Pipit. *A.s. spinoletta*: K & M admit one killed in 1865. Now a regular but very local winter visitor in small numbers from October to April or even early May, and a regular spring migrant (also in small numbers). It must have been overlooked before Johnson drew the attention of ornithologists to the species (*Bird Study* 17. 297), so it is uncertain to what extent the large number of recent reports represents a real increase since K & M.

The main localities for wintering birds are the coastal marshes (especially upper Southampton Water and the lower Test valley), watercress beds in the chalklands (especially those of the Itchen system), and to a lesser extent, sewage farms. The largest counts have been: 14 on 28 December 1971 in a census of the Itchen watercress beds from Headbourne Worthy to Bishop's Sutton (JHT and Thelwell); 10 at Farlington Marshes on 4 March 1961 (*H.* 22. Part 2); eight at Farlington Marshes on 27 March 1960 (*H.* 22. Part 1); eight in the Lower Test Marshes late in 1965 (*H.*

1966 p.44); The two March counts above probably refer to migrants whereas the count from the Itchen watercress concerned wintering birds for they had been on the cress-beds all through winter. Otherwise, up to six have been recorded at one locality but generally reports have been of one or two birds. Spring migrants appear mostly along the coast.

A real search for this species in winter may well reveal an unexpectedly high number.

380. Pied Wagtail. *Motacilla alba yarrelli*: *B.o.H.* notes a *possible* decline in breeding numbers since K & M but it is widely distributed throughout the county today and not at all uncommon.

Some sizeable roosts have been recorded, a few examples being as follows. In January 1950, Crook and Goater mapped routes of birds going to roost near Cadland Woods and in the Totton reed-bed, counting 117 on the 8th, about 800 on the 11th and 442 on the 14th. In the winter of 1957/8, a roost developed in the greenhouses of a carnation grower near Sway and did so much damage fouling flowers that the owner contrived to lure them all into one house which he then closed for four days; 325 were picked up dead when the counting stopped but he estimated that there were nearer 600 (*B.B.* 53. 315); in 1966, when the roost built up again, B.T.O. ringers caught 148 and released them in Tring (Herts) and Shoreham (Sussex), but birds from both these localities were subsequently retrapped in the same glass-house. 1,000 plus roosted at Basingstoke sewage farm on the 12 November 1961 (*H.* 22. Part 2). 500 plus at Testwood on the 15 November 1967 were in reeds, as so many roosts are, but they have been in gorse, thorn bushes and a variety of vegetation. For further examples, see *H.* 1970, 1967, 1966.

Considerable movement has been recorded in autumn (far less in spring) from the mainland coast and St. Catherine's Point. In *B.o.H.* EC said autumn movement was W. to E. in the latter half of September but mainly E. to W. in October (similar reversal of direction being noted for Swallows and Meadow Pipits). Further observation has shown the movement to be more complicated than that and directions are not fully understood, but between September/November birds coast east and west (e.g. 68 flew east at St. Catherine's Point on the 4 October 1959, most coming in from the sea from the SW — *H.* 21. Part 3; 167 flew SE out to sea at Gilkicker and 215 did likewise at Hurst on the 7 October 1962 — *H.* 22. Part 3; at St. Catherine's Point in 1963, 67 flew west on the 28 September and 71 flew west on the 12 October — *H.* 23. Part 1) and southerly passage was noted in 1969, 71 flying south at Hengistbury on the 19 October (*H.* 1969).

One ringed 14 December 1937 at Winchester recovered at Glen Feshie (Inverness) on 29 March 1940 (*W.* 1946). A young bird ringed 9 July 1952 near Settle (Yorks) recovered at Sandown on 10 January 1953 (*B.B.* 46. 326). A nestling ringed 8 June 1951 in Northumberland recovered at Basing on 27 February 1954 (*B.B.* 48. 495). A nestling ringed 11 June 1964 at Winchester recovered in Portugal on 23 November 1964 (*B.B.* 58. 577). An adult male ringed 17 July 1964 at Stanpit recovered in Portugal in January 1965 (*B.B.* 59. 486). One ringed 3 October 1965 at Winchester recovered Loire-Atlantique (France) on 10 November 1965 (*W.*). A juvenile ringed 4 July 1968 at Bickershaw (Lancs.) recovered at Romsey on 14 October 1968 (*B.B.* 62. 438).

380. White Wagtail. *M.a. alba*: Almost all reports of this race are between March/May (earliest date 5 March), mostly from the mainland coast (or a few miles inland) and St. Catherine's Point. Passage is usually moderate or small, the largest numbers recorded in recent years being: 30 at Keyhaven on 20 April 1966 (*H.* 1966);

a total of 50 seen at Farlington Marshes between 5 and 21 April 1959 (*H.* 21. Part 3); 32 seen to leave Titchfield Haven to the north between 18 and 20 April 1959 (*H.* 21. Part 3). There have been two June records in recent years and then only a handful in August/November with one on 17 December 1967 at Bembridge (*I.o.W.* 6. Part 2), this paucity of records from late summer onwards being due to identification difficulties.

There are two unconfirmed breeding reports from the Island in the 1920s in addition to the one in K & M. A pair breeding at Bartley in 1951 was square-bracketed in the Hampshire bird report; the nestlings were ringed by R. Elmes. In 1957, a male Pied was said to have mated with a female White (which may, however, be a pale-backed variant of British stock — see *B.B.* 42. 194 for B. W. Tucker's ideas on the subject) at Brading, rearing two young.

A first-winter bird ringed 13 September 1958 at St. Catherine's Point recovered at Ondárroa, Vizcaya (NE Spain) on 22 March 1959 (*H.* 21. Part 2).

381. Grey Wagtail. *Motacilla cinerea*: A comparison with K & M suggests that there has been a considerable spread in the distribution of this species. It probably breeds by almost all suitable streams on the mainland though the pairs are well spaced and it could not really be called common. Munn, part author of K & M, had noticed a pronounced increase by 1914 (*B.B.* 7. 228) and again by 1919 (*H.* 8. Part 3). An idea of numbers can be obtained by a full survey in the New Forest where 28 pairs were found in 1960 — Orr finding another nine in W. Hampshire (*H.* 22. Part 1); in the severe cold of the 1962/3 winter the species was much reduced in numbers but it had fully recovered by 1969 when another survey of the New Forest revealed 32 pairs (an excellent paper by Mrs. Tyler, organiser of the 1969 survey, appears in *H.* 1969, describing the breeding biology of Forest Grey Wagtails in detail).

K & M gave no records for the Island but the species did breed at a few localities before 1962/3. The first breeding record from Wight following that winter was not until 1966 (*I.o.W.* 6. Part 1), and the Island bird reports for 1967 and 1968 said that there were no records of the species other than wintering or passage birds (*I.o.W.* 6. Parts 2 and 3) so at best it is a rather scarce breeding species there today.

Coastal observations in August/October since 1954 show that birds move both E. and W., numbers involved being small as the following *annual peaks* show: 25 flew SE at Gilkicker on 18 October 1969 (*H.* 1969); in 1968, 12 flew E. at St. Catherine's Point on 7 September and 16 flew SW at Hengistbury on 8 September (*H.* 1968). Very little spring movement has been observed.

In winter, it is a typical bird of the chalkland watercress beds. A roost of 81 birds was found at Testwood on 5 January 1967 (*H.* 1967).

One ringed 5 August 1959 at Holwell (Dorset) recovered at Alresford on 6 January 1960 (*B.B.* 57. 16). A nestling ringed 7 May 1969 at Brockenhurst recovered at Poitiers (France) in December 1969 (*B.B.* 64. 182).

382. Yellow Wagtail group *Motacilla flava*:
Yellow Wagtail. *M.f. flavissima*:
'A summer visitor in much smaller numbers than formerly. Between the two world wars this species was plentiful in parts of the Test valley and tributaries, especially between Whitchurch and Stockbridge, and certainly not uncommon in the Itchen valley and in other suitable areas' (P. E. Brown's summary). It still breeds in some numbers in parts of the main river valleys, particularly the Test, but fishing activities make much of this habitat inaccessible so numbers present today are not really known; it can safely be said, however, that it is nothing like as abundant as it was and in some areas it has disappeared as a breeding species. It also breeds in

several suitable localities along the mainland coast, the following counts from recent years giving an idea of numbers involved: Calshot, six pairs (1970); Dibden Bay, 10 pairs (1969); Farlington Marshes, eight pairs plus four on the islands in Langstone Harbour (1968); Stanpit, seven pairs (1970). In other coastal areas the species does not breed, none having been found in the Needs Oar area in 15 years of intensive coverage.

The Island position is obscure. The last reference to breeding in the bird report was in 1953, and at best it is very scarce there today. Similarly, the far north of the county is shown by the *Atlas* survey to hold very few pairs.

The main arrival in spring is from mid-April/early May, the earliest record being two flying N. at Gilkicker on 10 March 1968 (*H.* 1968). Males arrive about a fortnight before the females. Movement in recent years has been rather small but Meinertzhagen, writing of the 1890s (i.e. before the decline) reports a strong movement up the Test valley in April with often up to 100 birds in one meadow and

Yellow Wagtail
Blue-headed Wagtail

an estimate of about 500 every April, already paired. This would mean that the males had waited for the females before moving together to inland breeding grounds. On occasions, they have been seen at night around St. Catherine's Light, where five were killed in May and September between 1905/8.

Autumn passage is much heavier, especially in the coastal belt where flocks associate with grazing cattle. The main departure takes place in August and the first half of September with stragglers occurring in October; the latest date is the 1 November but there have been wintering records, e.g. on 8 December 1957 (Suffern in *H*. 20) and 27 February 1938 (*H*. 14. 259). As with so much autumn passerine passage, direction is varied, birds moving east, south and west and in all directions in that arc, and occasionally birds have been seen to come in off the sea at St. Catherine's Point and fly north. Examples of autumn movement are: 436 flying W. and 32 E. at St. Catherine's in August 1959 (*H*. 21. Part 3); 117 flying SE out to sea at St. Catherine's on 27 August 1960 and 230 flying south on the same day at Hurst Castle (*H*. 22. Part 1); 110 flying S. at Hengistbury on 20 August 1967 (*H*. 1967).

During this autumn movement, considerable roosts develop in reed beds, mostly on the mainland coast but also at places such as Yarmouth and at one or two places inland. Gatherings may reach a few hundred at one such roost, 1,000 at Wick from 6/15 September 1971 being the largest in recent years (*H*. 1971).

One unusual movement was on 6 June 1963 when 73 were moving SE at Gilkicker, coincidentally with a large number of Swifts, all apparently seeking to avoid an advancing thunderstorm (*Bird Migration*. 2. 5. 314).

Six birds ringed in Hampshire on autumn migration have been recovered in Portugal and one in Spain, five of them recovered later in the same autumn that they were ringed. An adult male ringed 3 September 1962 at Fordingbridge found dead at Casablanca (Morocco) on 11 March 1967 (*H*. 68. p.44). One ringed 3 September 1961 at Jersey caught at the Stanpit roost on 18 July 1963 (*B.B.* 57). A juvenile ringed 11 September 1966 at Vannes (France) controlled at Christchurch Harbour on 19 July 1967 (*B.B.* 62. 21).

382. Blue-headed Wagtail. *M.f. flava*: Birds of this race have been satisfactorily identified in spring on a number of occasions; a few have been reported in autumn when identification problems are considerable, e.g. one trapped at Stanpit on 11 August 1964 (*H*. 23. Part 2).

E. L. Jones saw three pairs on Chilbolton Common in 1955, 1956 and 1957 of which the cocks were typical *flavissima* and the hens *flava*, but B. W. Tucker suggests (*B.B.* 42. 194) that such hens *may* be variants of the British race (*flavissima*). The male of a pair breeding at Keyhaven in 1966 had all the characteristics of the Blue-headed race (Wiseman in *H*. 1966).

[**382. Grey-headed Wagtail.** *M.f. thunbergi*: A bird of the Grey-headed race was recorded at Britford in the 1936 Hampshire report. However, Britford is in Wiltshire and the error is perpetuated in *B.B.* 31. 94 and again in the *Handbook* where it is recorded as 'probable' for Hampshire.]

Citrine Wagtail. *Motacilla citreola**: Two at Stanpit on 15 October 1966 were accepted by *British Birds* Rarities Committee (C.H.O.S.G. — *B.B.* 59. 439).

383. Waxwing. *Bombycilla garrulus*: To the occurrences quoted in K & M can be added that of eight birds at Mottisfont from Christmas Day 1897 to New Year's Day (Meinertzhagen).

There were no reports for the next 20 years and none between 1920 and 1931. They occurred in six years in the thirties, five in the forties and four in the fifties, mostly in ones or twos but with some larger counts, e.g. 20/30 at Bembridge from late October to early November 1937 (*I.o.W.* 1937); about 75 during the 1946/7 winter in the heaviest invasion to that date for the whole country (see *B.B.* 41.34 for details of the invasion); 20 plus near Godshill (I.o.W.) in late November 1954; 45 'in off the Solent' on 13 January 1960 (*H.* 22. Part 1).

An analysis of records for the years 1960/71 inclusive shows the typical 'irruptive' character of the species. Three years had no records (1962, 1968 and 1969). Four years had a combined total of 10 birds (1961, 1963, 1964 and 1967). 1960 had the single flock of 45 mentioned above. The other years experienced irruptions. In the winter of 1965/6, over 300 individuals were seen, several of the flocks contained 20 or 30 birds with 47 at Farnborough the most at one locality. These birds started to arrive in late November and many were in the county by the end of 1965, remaining in strength through January with quite a few left in March and the last straggler occurring on the 29 April 1966 (*H.* 1965, 1966). Records came from all over the mainland and Island. Then again in 1970 at least 60 individuals appeared in November/December, nearly all of them in the latter month, and a minimum of 130 were seen in the first three months of 1971 (*H.* 1970, 1971).

384. Great Grey Shrike. *Lanius excubitor*: A regular winter visitor in small numbers to the mainland; rare on the Island where there have only been two occurrences this century, at Brading on 3 November and 7 December 1963 (*I.o.W.* 1963/4) and at Headon Warren on 24 October 1968 (*I.o.W.* 6. Part 3).

On the mainland, only one or two a year were recorded until more intensive watching from 1960 revealed the true picture. In the winters from 1959/60 to 1969/70 inclusive, a minimum of 108 individuals was reported, the lowest total for any one winter being six (1959/60) and the highest being *at least* 22 (1966/7). The majority of records came from the New Forest but reports were widespread with some localities such as Woolmer having fairly regular occurrences. Some of the birds remained at one locality for most of the winter. The first usually appear in October (on the 10 September in 1966) and the last are seen in April (as late as the 27th in 1967).

An unusual date was one from 4 to 16 July 1938 (*B.B.* 33. 144).

An adult male ringed 31 January 1951 at Fordingbridge recovered in the Netherlands on 4 March 1952.

385. Lesser Grey Shrike. *Lanius minor*: K & M admit two, shot in 1842 and 1900.

One found dead at Holt Pound on 16 May 1967 (Winter), was accepted by *British Birds* Rarities Committee. The skin is in Haslemere Museum (*B.B.* 61. 354).

386. Woodchat Shrike. *Lanius senator* *: K & M must have missed the *Handbook* reference which says: 'said to have nested twice in the Isle of Wight'. One of these times was in 1856 (*I.o.W.* 2. Part 2).

One, Freshwater, early June 1931 (*B.B.* 25. 199).
One, New Forest, 19/20 May 1955 (*H.* 19. Part 2).
A male, Farlington Marshes, 11/12 June 1955 (*H.* 19. Part 2).
One, Bembridge, 12 May 1967 (*B.B.* 61. 355).
An adult, Hengistbury, 19 May 1968 (*B.B.* 62. 485).
An immature, trapped at Hengistbury, 14 October 1970 (*B.B.* 64. 365).
One, Wick Hams (Christchurch), 12 May 1971 (*H.* 1971).

388. Red-backed Shrike. *Lanius collurio*: K & M write: 'found in most parts of the county and the Isle of Wight, but usually not very plentifully. Of late years its range has greatly extended'.

Numbers have since declined disasterously, especially in the 1960s, the decrease being best judged by counts from the species' stronghold of the New Forest since breeding records for the rest of the county are far from complete. In the late fifties, Ash estimated the Forest population as 100 pairs, and he located 60 pairs in 1960. A full Forest survey in 1961 revealed 61 pairs of which 42 nested (35 successfully) and 69 nestlings were ringed (Tubbs *et al.* – *H.* 22. Part 2). By 1966, only 15 pairs were found in a census of 15,120 acres of New Forest heath and bog, half the area of such habitat in the Forest boundary (*H.* 1966).

The rest of the mainland has never been surveyed for the species but isolated reports showed the species to be widely though thinly distributed. In 1949, eight pairs still nested round Winchester, but by 1970 no pairs were seen there in their usual haunts. A few scattered pairs are still reported each year but they are clearly only a remnant of former numbers.

On the Island, the last case of even suspected breeding was in 1954 at Brook (Head in *I.o.W.* 4. Part 9); Mrs. Bannerman considered it only a passage migrant. Six were killed at St. Catherine's Light on one occasion in May at some time between 1906 and 1908, whilst three in spring and three in autumn constitute *all* the Island's occurrences in the years 1958/1968 inclusive.

Locally, birds have left areas because of urban spread (Bournemouth area), road building (Winchester by-pass), and drainage of waste and marginal land. Egg collectors have caused further loss. But the real cause for the decline must be something more widespread, affecting the whole population. Tubbs (*The New Forest*) suggests the cause was a succession of warm wet summers linked to a decline of large flying insects which form the bulk of their food. Certainly such insects are abundant in all those parts of southern Europe where shrikes thrive.

One ringed as a nestling on 22 June 1948 in the Forest was recovered about a month later at Winchelsea, 100 miles to the east (*B.B.* 42. 176). Another Forest nestling ringed 14 June 1959 was recovered 45 miles to the north, in Wiltshire, on 29 July 1959 (*B.B.* 53. 499). The first British-ringed bird of this species to be recovered in Germany was ringed in the Forest by Ash on 17 June 1960 and found dead in Bavaria on 6 November 1960 (*B.B.* 54. 488).

389. Starling. *Sturnus vulgaris*: An abundant resident in all parts, as in K & M's time, and an even more abundant winter visitor.

A number of roosts, some of them only temporary, holding tens of thousands of birds, are reported from time to time, for instance at Swansdale Wood, Wickham in 1951; near Brockhurst, Gosport in 1954 and 1955; and Sowley and Damerham in 1956. Another instance was on the 7 March 1957 at West Park, Damerham, where 'a roost which had numbered tens of thousands during the winter, built up in the previous ten days to hundreds of thousands (perhaps a million). One half roosted in absolute silence but the other half nearby set up a continuous clamour all night. Within the next week practically all had gone' (Ash in *H.* 20. Supplement). Yet another, which reached hundreds of thousands, occupied a wood near Dean (Winchester) late in 1971, whilst a traditional roost numbering several hundreds of thousands at Gosport was broken up by scrub clearance, much altering local flight lines as birds came to the roosts from as far afield as Chichester and Beaulieu (*H.* 1966). By 1970 however, thousands were again seen converging on Gosport in roosting movements (*H.* 1970).

But by far the most spectacular flock was at East Worldham (near Alton) on 9

December 1956. Mr. John Blackwell, Engineer to the Alton R.D.C. estimated that the flock numbered at least a million. He knew the length and width of the field over which they passed and judged the height by electricity poles, and allowing one bird per cubic yard (which, he said, was 'very lean') worked out the size of the flock. They flew off west at about 15.30 but no roost was known in the neighbourhood (*H.* 19. Part 3). There are references to flocks of a million birds or more in *Yorkshire Birds* (Chislett) and in *Birds of Lancashire* (Oakes).

That at least part of these vast numbers is composed of immigrants from Eastern Europe is shown by ringing recoveries. Nine ringed in Germany, Russia, Latvia, Sweden and Denmark have been recovered here in winter, whilst 22 Starlings ringed in Hampshire in winter have been recovered in seven European countries to the east, mostly on their presumed breeding grounds or on their way to them. The three longest journeys were to Kazakhstan (Russia), 2,620 miles to the east and by far the most easterly recovery of a British-ringed Starling (ringed 29 January 1954 at Fordingbridge and killed by a raptor on 23 September 1960), to Brest Litovsk (Russia), 1,200 miles to the east in 91 days, and to Kaunas (Lithuania), about the same distance and found carrying nesting material some 13 months after ringing. A juvenile ringed 21 June 1957 at Southampton and probably of British origin was recovered in S. Sweden on 3 June 1958, an unusual date (*B.B.* 52. 480). An interesting double recovery was that of an adult ringed 15 October 1960 at St. Catherine's, controlled at Swansea on 8 February 1961, and killed at Friesland (Netherlands) about 30 June 1963 (*B.B.* 57. 577).

There are a number of recoveries in other parts of Britain of Hampshire-ringed Starlings but no conclusions can be drawn from their scatter.

Ringing shows where some of the birds come from but it is not only ringing which shows that our resident population is swollen by great numbers of immigrants in winter. Large scale immigration has been observed on the coast, e.g. 1,700 coming in off the sea at St. Catherine's Point and flying north on 12 November 1961, and on the same day, 2,240 flying north from the sea at Hurst (*H.* 22. Part 2). Other coastal movements have been to the west, e.g. 10,000 flying west at Titchfield Haven on 14 November 1961, and these northerly and westerly movements are parallelled on a smaller scale inland. Sometimes the movements are nocturnal e.g. they were numerous at St. Catherine's Light on the night of 25/26 October 1963, and 3,000 which were still there the following morning flew off to the west (*H.* 23. Part 1). Like so much autumn movement however, directions taken are very varied and SE movement at this time of year of up to 500 a day has been observed at Hengistbury and St. Catherine's Point. Generally however, movement is to the west or north, or somewhere between these two points, indicating immigration from the Continent, and occurs regularly from late September to early December with the bulk in October/November.

These movements are distinct from hard-weather movements when birds, local or immigrant, move in a generally westerly direction to escape the cold. 145,000 flew west at Gilkicker in massive flocks in such a movement on 1st January 1962 (*H.*22. Part 3), and 40,000 flew west in one hour at Farlington Marshes on 9 December 1967 (*H.* 1967).

All the above movements are, of course, only a selection of such records showing the high numbers that can be involved. There are many examples of similar movements concerning smaller numbers.

390. Rose-coloured Starling. *Sturnus roseus*: K & M quote eight between 1841 and 1896. There were apparently no more until 1925, but from then down to 1959 six were reported, three from the Island, two from the SW of the county and one for which no locality was given. One was in March, two were in June, and there was one each for July, August and October. Four were accepted by *British Birds*. Subsequently, there have been:

One, Newport, 26 July 1966 (*B.B.* 61. 363).
One adult, Fleet, 13 June 1968 (*H.* 1968).

391. Hawfinch. *Coccothraustes coccothraustes*: K & M describe it as a sparingly distributed resident with a considerable increase in numbers in autumn and winter and say that in the Isle of Wight it has occurred only in winter. They quote Meade-Waldo as saying that: 'in winter I have seen frequently as many as two hundred individuals collected together in a kind of straggling flock — it is certainly very far from scarce at the present day'; this probably refers to the early years of this century.

Hawfinch

In *The Hawfinch* (Collins 1957), Mountfort says: 'Widely distributed in small numbers throughout the county, probably most numerous as a breeding species in the Winchester area and in the north-west towards the Wiltshire border. Population seems to be increasing. Small flocks are not uncommon in winter and there is an exceptional record of 300 seen in the New Forest during the last war.'

Although it is an elusive species, there seems little doubt that both Meade-Waldo's and Mountfort's descriptions will not do today. With observer coverage better than at any time, reports from recent years suggest that the species is thin on the ground in most places, though widely distributed on the mainland. The New Forest is perhaps its Hampshire headquarters, 14 pairs in 1960 and five pairs in one square mile in 1962 (Adams) giving a slight idea of numbers. The *Atlas* survey in its first four years proved breeding in only three 10-kilometer squares, showed suspected breeding in three more and birds present in a further 12. As for winter flocks, the years 1959/70 inclusive showed only four places to have gatherings reaching double figures and at three of those the flock was seen on one day only. On the Island there have been few records this century, with one or two breeding pairs up to 1919 and only three birds (one dead) in the years 1958/68 inclusive.

Perhaps the best way of summing up its status today is to say that any ornithologist in Hampshire would pause to look at a Hawfinch when one is found.

392. Greenfinch. *Chloris chloris*: A very common resident as in K & M's time. Winter flocks of up to several hundred are found in such habitat as kale or stubble on the chalklands, in parts of the river valleys, or on the tideline near spartina flats where the seeds of the plant are washed ashore, and in the most favoured localities, flocks may exceed 1,000. Ringing has shown that many birds breeding in Hampshire do not move very far from their nesting areas in winter, but it has also shown that birds come to us in winter from counties to the north and east. Birds ringed in Hampshire during winter have been found between spring and autumn in Cambridgeshire, Derbyshire, Essex, Hertfordshire, Kent and Surrey; birds ringed in summer or autumn in Essex, Kent and Sussex have been found in late autumn or winter in Hampshire.

This direction of autumn movement is supported by visual records of passage, for in October/November (especially around the middle of that period) movement on the mainland coast and at St. Catherine's Point is mainly towards the west, peak movements exceeding 1,000 per day. Examples of such movements were 2,674 flying west at Brownwich between 25 October and 1 November 1959, and 460 flying west at St. Catherine's Point on 1 November 1959 (*H.* 21. Part 3).

Occasional hard-weather movements are seen, mainly to the west (6,900 flew west past Hengistbury on 31 December 1961) but also to the east (3,000 flew east past Gilkicker on 1 January 1962, the day after the above movement at Hengistbury).

393. Goldfinch. *Carduelis carduelis*: There are numerous reports of increase from nearly all parts throughout the years since K & M and none of decrease save a small and short-lived decline in a few places following the 1962/3 winter. The Goldfinch can now be considered reasonably common as a breeding species but scarce in the winter months, flocks such as the 100 which stayed at Fleet from late December 1968 to February 1969 being unusual (*H.* 1968, 1969).

Flocks are most often seen in September and sometimes into October (200 plus were at Winchester sewage farm on 23 October 1969). An exceptional date for the largest flock which has been reported was 26 June 1949 when up to 600 adults and juveniles were counted in one six-acre meadow (probably near Petersfield — *H.*

17. Part 3).

Very considerable movement has been observed on the mainland coast and at St. Catherine's Point in autumn and spring. The directions of both passages are very mixed, not only to east and west between late March/mid-May and in October/November, but — most unexpectedly — also out to sea at St. Catherine's in May, as well as off the sea in a generally northerly direction in both spring and autumn. Numbers involved may exceed 1,000 in one day: 1,172 flew east at Eastney between 5 and 9 October 1959; 1,156 flew west at Brownwich between 25 October and 1 November 1959; 1,130 flew west at St. Catherine's on the 1 November 1959 and 1,750 flew east there on 3 November 1963; 1,740 flew south at Gilkicker between 7 October and 3 December 1962 and 2,250 flew south or SE there between 5 and 19 October 1962. Spring numbers are smaller.

Cold-weather passage is occasionally seen in winter, e.g. 1,700 flew west at Brownwich on 31 December 1961.

A first-winter bird ringed 11 August 1964 at East Boldre controlled at Fuenterrabia (Spain) on 1 May 1965 and shot in Les Landes (France) on 8 November 1965 (*B.B.* 59. 487). A juvenile ringed 25 July 1967 at East Boldre found dead at Tolosa (Spain) on 14 October 1967 (*H.* 1968. p.44). One ringed 12 September 1969 at Farlington Marshes found near Bilbao (Spain) on 25 October 1969 (*H.* 1969).

394. Siskin. *Carduelis spinus*: K & M say: 'A winter visitor: never occurring in any numbers'. Now a widespread winter visitor in moderate numbers and a scarce and local breeding species, so apparently it has increased since K & M.

Winter flocks occur from October to April. They usually number up to 50 but in recent years flocks of 200 (Wellow, November 1968), 150 (Fleet Pond, December 1970; Frensham Great Pond — Hampshire area — December 1961) and 100 (Stratfield Saye, January 1959; Fleet Pond, November 1968; Marlborough Lines sewage farm, November 1965) have been reported. In 1971, flocks of 100 or more were reported from several areas. Flocks occur particularly in the New Forest, in Alder patches along the river valleys and in the area north of the chalklands. On the Island, smaller winter parties have been seen quite frequently — especially in Alder — the largest in recent years being 36 at Ryde on 29 November 1959 (*I.o.W.* 5. Part 4).

A moderate autumn passage has been noticed since the 1950s, particularly on the Island coast but also on the mainland. As with most passerines, directions are very varied; thus 40 flew east at St. Catherine's Point on 11 October 1970, 30 flew north at Alum Bay on 26 October 1969, 44 flew west at St. Catherine's Point on 5 November 1961 and 20 came in off the sea from the south at the Foreland on 28 October 1961. October/November sees most of this passage (*H.* for full details). Spring movement in April is shown by more widespread flocks.

In 1953, Day found the first nest in the New Forest (*B.B.* 47. 209). Since then, birds have probably bred in the Forest every year, breeding being proved in several years. 10 pairs there in 1960 were the most reported during summer (*H.* 22. Part 1). On two or three occasions, pairs have bred or have been suspected of breeding in other parts of the mainland.

395. Linnet. *Carduelis cannabina*: A common breeding species in all parts of the mainland and Island, as in K & M's time. Only two detailed surveys are available in recent years: 60 pairs bred on the eastern half of Beaulieu Heath in 1967; Ash found 119 nests in the Fordingbridge area in 1953, and of the 87 whose ultimate fate was known, the young probably flew from 48 (55.2 per cent), 16 were deserted and 23 were robbed.

Outside the breeding season, flocks of several hundred are quite commonplace, especially in kale fields where Fat Hen occurs, and smaller numbers occur quite frequently on the tide line where Spartina seeds collect. Some of these winter flocks on farmland may number a few thousand, e.g. 7,000 in a kale field at Martin in cold weather during January 1960, 5,000 in kale near Cheesefoot Head (Winchester) in December 1971, and 2,000 in kale at Danebury in January 1960.

Considerable spring passage has been reported from coastal areas, when birds are often seen flying north or coasting in both easterly and westerly directions, the latter direction being the more usual. Any sea-watch in spring at St. Catherine's Point is likely to record Linnets moving along the cliff edge, sometimes a few hundred passing in one morning.

Autumn movements, mostly in October/November, involve larger numbers and as has been said under so many species already, flight directions are varied, e.g. at St. Catherine's Point, 2,810 flew east on 24/25 October 1965 (*H.* 1965) but 2,100 flew west there on 11 October 1970 (*H.* 1970); at Gilkicker directions seem more constant, flights being generally to the east or south-east, 4,100 moving in those directions from 28 September to 19 October 1969 (*H.* 1969) and 2,790 moving SE on 19 October 1963 alone (*H.* 23. Part 1). Presumably these directions are influenced by weather but research is badly needed on the subject in Hampshire so that it can be properly understood.

Cold-weather movements can be enormous but again varied in direction, e.g. on 31 December 1961, 15,000 flew ESE at Gilkicker whilst a few miles away, 2,000 flew west at Needs Oar and 9,200 flew west at Hengistbury (*H.* 22. Part 2). In another cold-spell movement, 10,000 flew east at Gilkicker on 1 January 1962 (*H.* 22. Part 3).

Five birds ringed in the county have been recovered in the SW of France in October of the year in which they were ringed, whilst others ringed at Stanpit have been recovered in the same year or in later years in the same area of France and in Spain. One ringed 27 August 1963 in Northumberland was controlled at Stanpit on 20 October 1963.

396. Twite. *Carduelis flavirostris*: K & M give four for the mainland and one for the Island. The next report is of a flock of about 20 which appeared near Bournemouth in hard weather in December 1938, staying for a day or so (Hayward). After another gap of 14 years, eight or nine were recorded on 22 December 1952 at Farlington Marshes (P.G.).

Every winter from 1956 has produced flocks of varying size from the mainland coast. The largest have been 150 at Farlington Marshes on 24 October 1959 (50/60 still there in December — *H.* 21. Part 3) and up to 80 at Dibden Bay from 23 January to 6 March 1960 (*H.* 22. Part 1), but flocks do not usually exceed 30 and some winters have failed to produce a double-figured count (e.g. winter 1968/9, maximum six; winter 1969/70, maximum six). Birds might appear at any place on the mainland coast where there is marsh or spartina-flat, but Farlington Marshes and Dibden Bay (before reclamation) have been particularly favoured whilst other localities have only produced isolated records.

The first Island report since K & M was one at Newtown on 9 October 1958 (Mrs. Seabroke — *I.o.W.* 5. Part 3). Since then, every year from 1963 onwards (except 1968) has produced odd records of up to four birds but never from more than one locality per year.

Inland records from the mainland are very scarce but birds have been seen in the New Forest and at Damerham, Woolmer, Blashford and Beaulieu on isolated occasions.

The first generally occur in the second half of October (earliest date, 6

September 1960 — *H.* 22. Part 1) and apparently some of these are just passing through for birds disappear at some localities after appearing in October. The last are generally seen in March (latest date, 2 April 1966 — *H.* 1966).

397. Redpoll. *Carduelis flammea*:
Lesser Redpoll. *C.f. disruptis*:
Continental Lesser Redpoll. *C.f. cabaret*:
Mealy Redpoll. *C.f. flammea*:

K & M describe the Lesser as appearing in all parts in winter, sometimes fairly plentifully on spring and autumn migrations, and say 'A few remain to breed.' This would describe the mainland position today apart from the quote at the end, for as a breeding species it seems almost rare. A pair bred at Selborne in 1966 (*H.* 1967. p.37) and four pairs apparently bred in the New Forest in 1960 (*H.* 22. Part 1), but otherwise there have only been suspected cases of breeding since 1960. The first four years of the *Atlas* survey (1968/71) showed suspected breeding in only three 10-kilometer squares and birds present in five others. Apparently, it has never been proved to breed on the Island.

Flocks of up to 50 (occasionally around 100) are seen not infrequently in winter in all parts of the mainland, especially to the north of the chalklands, in the New Forest and the river valleys, sometimes in association with Alder and Birch. The largest gathering recently was in a field of kale at Sopley in late February/early March 1960; no less than 250 were ringed, and 61 examined by Ash consisted of 44 British (*disruptis*), 15 Continental (*cabaret*) and two Mealy (*flammea*) (*H.* 22. Part 1). Two *disruptis* were recovered later on their breeding grounds near Ingleton (Yorks) and near Scarborough (Yorks), and a Mealy was found dead in Östergötland (Sweden) on 7 September 1962 (*B.B.* 56. 521). Winter records from the Island have been rather few and concern *much* smaller numbers — most Island records refer to passage birds.

Movement in spring and autumn — reported mainly but not exclusively from the coast — is shown by larger and more numerous flocks (sometimes at 'migration points', e.g. 60 at Hengistbury on 17 October 1970 and 110 there on 1 November 1969) and birds seen moving along the coast (e.g. at St. Catherine's Point, 31 flying west on 12 November 1967 and 20 flying east on 17 October 1970). The autumn movement — mainly in October but also in September and November — is the larger of the two.

K & M admitted three Mealy, and Meinertzhagen records a flock of 20 at Mottisfont on 24 December 1898 which stayed for nine days. Three were 'secured' as specimens.

400. Serin. *Serin canarius*: The first recorded in England was procured at Eastney in April 1852 (K & M). The next was a male on Farlington Marshes on 4 November 1961 (Sharrock — *B.B.* 55. 582). With the spread of the species in Europe, reports have been more frequent, viz. —
A male, Totland, from 17 February to 1 March 1963 (*I.o.W.* 1963/4).
A male (possibly two females), Beaulieu, 7 March 1965 (*H.* 1965).
Two, Hengistbury, 15 October 1966 (*B.B.* 60. 330).
One, Farlington Marshes, 30 October 1967 (*B.B.* 61. 357).
One, Christchurch Harbour, 27 October and 5 November 1969 (*H.* 1969).
One, St. Catherine's Point, 26/27 April 1969 (*H.* 1969).
A male, St. Catherine's Point, 24 May and 14 June 1970 (*H.* 1970).
A male, Stanpit, 13 December 1970 (*H.* 1970).
A male singing, near St. Catherine's Point, 1 April 1971 (*H.* 1971).

401. Bullfinch. *Pyrrhula pyrrhula*: A widespread and quite common resident despite instances of persecution: for instance, 39 pairs bred on the Mottisfont estate in 1897 although over 60 were shot, and in the following year it was estimated that 44 pairs bred (Meinertzhagen); again, about 60 were shot in a small garden in N. Hampshire in 1954 (Ash). Indeed, there have been several reports of increase in recent years from widely separated localities, sometimes in areas where it *is* persecuted. It was apparently quite un-affected by the very severe weather of 1962/3.

Though mainly sedentary, it does move a little. Birds have been involved in autumn passerine movement on the coast, moving past St. Catherine's Point and other places, though numbers involved have been *very* small (e.g. four flew west at Main Bench on 27 October 1962 and a few were seen passing several localities in 1961 — *H.* 22. Part 2). The species has also been involved in cold-weather movements, again in small numbers (e.g. 80 flew east at Gilkicker on 1 January 1962 and 25 flew west at Needs Oar on 31 December 1961 — *H.* 22. Parts 2 and 3). Ringing also shows short-distance movements (e.g. 48 miles from Bournemouth to Basing and 12 miles from Cosham to Warnford).

402. Scarlet Grosbeak. *Carpodacus erythrinus**: None in K & M. A male at Titchfield on 13 August 1913 seen and described by Spear Smith was accepted as a 'probable' in *B.B.* 7. 179 and was admitted without question by Witherby in the *Handbook.* 1913 was an 'invasion year' for this species.

403. Pine Grosbeak. *Pinicola enucleator*: One example of this species was admitted by K & M quoting an article by Gurney in the *Zoologist* for 1890 in which 'he remarks that the specimen is among the four most authentic examples recorded'. It was supposed to have been killed in the neighbourhood of the New Forest many years before 1876. It is not mentioned in the *Handbook* which, however, only details the 'most recent records' beginning in 1890.

404. Crossbill. *Loxia curvirostra*: K & M describe it as an irregular and uncertain visitor chiefly between mid-summer and February, which has frequently nested on the mainland. Since then it has nested nearly every year, chiefly in the New Forest where numbers have varied enormously from one season to another, perhaps depending partly on whether or not an 'irruption' occurred the previous year, e.g. 100 pairs bred in the Forest in 1960 (*H.* 22. Part 1) following an 'irruption' in 1959 and unprecedented numbers in the early months of 1960, but in other recent years very few pairs have been found breeding. It has nested elsewhere on the mainland, e.g. Ashford found over 20 nests in Bournemouth in 1931 (*H.* 13. 172), and Gosnell found 16 nests in NE in 1936 (*H.* 13. 272). The *Atlas* survey showed no breeding proved away from the SW quarter of the mainland. Apparently it has not bred on the Island.

As a visitor its numbers depend much on 'irruptions'. These occurred in 1909, 1927, 1929, 1935, 1953, 1958, 1959, 1962, 1963 and 1966. The birds first appear in late June/July but go on arriving and moving into October. In such 'irruptions' flocks may reach or even exceed 50 (70 in Amberwood Inclosure — New Forest — on 26 July 1966), and numbers are seen moving (e.g. 103 flew W. or SW at Binstead — Isle of Wight — from 5 to 23 July 1966 and 83 flew SE at Hengistbury on 18 September 1966). Following 'irruptions', more parties than usual are likely to be seen in winter, the parties often being much larger than in non-irruption years.

Years when numbers have been low were 1933, 1937, 1952, 1965, 1968 and 1970.

For details of recent 'irruptions' see *H.* 1962 and *H.* 22. Part 3 for the picture in Hampshire, and *B.B.* 59. 351, *B.B.* 57. 477/501 and *Bird Migration* 2. 252/260 for the picture in the country as a whole.

Crossbill

Parrot Crossbill. *Loxia pytyopsittacus**: About 10 or 12 birds were identified at Studley Wood (New Forest) on 27/28 August 1966 by Mr. and Mrs. Brice. Two were males, the remainder females or immature birds (*H.* 1966).

406. Two-barred Crossbill. *Loxia leucoptera*: K & M admit two procured in the Island about 1838. None since.

White-throated Sparrow. *Zonotrichia albicollis**: Sharrock (*B.B.* 58. 230) records that four birds of this species arrived in October or November 1958 on a Cunard ship from North America and that they were all placed in the East Park Aviary (Southampton) where the last survivor died in January 1964. He also saw one at Needs Oar on 19 May 1961 (*B.B.* 54. 367). Durand records a bird of this species travelling from New York to Southampton about the same time as the Needs Oar bird on R.M.S. *Queen Elizabeth* (*B.B.* 54. 439), so the two records could possibly have concerned the same individual. See also the *Note* at the end of this Systematic List.

407. Chaffinch. *Fringilla coelebs*: *Very* common in all parts with occasional indications of increase; for instance, Meinertzhagen estimated the number of breeding pairs on the Mottisfont estate at 135/150 in the nineties and 200/215 in 1939 and 1945. In winter large flocks occur, the biggest in recent years being 1,000 at Dibden Bay on 31 January 1960 (probably due to cold weather) (*H.* 22. Part 1).

700 at Morestead Down on 31 January 1971 (*H*. 1971), and 635 in kale at Moorcourt on 8 December 1963 (*H*. 23. Part 1).

As with most passerines, there is a certain amount of movement from late September to early November, especially in coastal areas on the mainland and at St. Catherine's Point. As with most small-bird autumn movement direction is varied but it would seem that most of the birds come from the east. This is confirmed by ringing recoveries. Five birds ringed in Holland and Belgium in the first half of October in five different years were recovered in the south of the county, the recoveries being in November of the same year (one), January (one) and March (one) of the following year, March 17 months later (one) and February 28 months later. Birds ringed in Hampshire during winter have been recovered in the breeding season in NE Germany (one) and SE Germany (one), the first proof of *hortensis* wintering in the south of England (Ash), and two of the nominate race *coelebs* were caught in different places in S. Sweden the following summer (Ash). Others ringed in Hampshire in winter have been recovered later — but not in the breeding season — from Belgium and the Netherlands. Ringing also shows individuals who move very little, one colour-ringed by EC at Sway on 25 February 1951 was last seen on 13 April 1961 when it must have been at least 11 years old, and a female ringed at Fordingbridge on 7 June 1951 was retrapped there on 11 December 1960 (Ash).

Some considerable cold-weather movement occurs at times, e.g. 6,000 flew east at Gilkicker on both 31 December 1961 and 1 January 1962; 2,300 flew *west* on the latter date at nearby Hengistbury (*H*. 22. Part 2), showing how complex the direction of cold-weather movements can be.

408. Brambling. *Fringilla montifringilla*: A regular winter visitor, numbers varying very much from year to year, ranging from plentiful to rather scarce. The first are nearly always recorded in October (on 28 September in 1963 — *H*. 23. Part 1); the last nearly always linger into April, flocks of up to 80 being seen during that month in recent years (in 1910, the last two were reported from Basingstoke as late as 4 May — *B.B*. 4. 20). Flocks of up to 100 are recorded quite frequently in good years, and gatherings of 200 have been seen on at least five occasions in the years between 1959/70. On occasion even larger flocks occur, e.g. 500 near Preshaw on 19 November 1970 (*H*. 1970) and 300 plus at Corhampton on 22 December 1966 (*H*. 1966), whilst Jourdain said there were 'certainly not less than 1,000' in the Bournemouth area in December 1938 (*H*. 14. 253). These winter birds are likely to occur all over the mainland, and the species is now recorded each year from the Island, though reports are far less frequent than from the mainland and numbers are usually smaller. However, in a cold spell during the winter of 1925/6, they were 'all over the Island, even in the middle of Shanklin' (*Proc. I.o.W. N.H.S*. 1. Part 7. 458).

They are sometimes involved in westerly passerine passage from the mainland and south Island coast in October/November, and some take part in cold-weather movements (e.g. 230 flew *west* at Hengistbury and 50 flew *east* at Titchfield Haven on 31 December 1961). A less usual spring movement was 720 flying east past Gilkicker on 4 March 1965.

One ringed 14 October 1933 in South Holland recovered in Hampshire on 10 December 1935 (*B.B*. 33. 65). A juvenile female ringed 28 October 1952 at Aachen (Germany) found dead at Botley in February 1954 (*B.B*. 58. 596). A juvenile ringed 8 September 1968 at Kaldholelva (Norway) recovered at Swanmore on 2 January 1970 (*B.B*. 64. 500). 1 ringed 8 March 1970 at East Worldham recovered at Wiesbaden (W. Germany) on 13 March 1971 (*H*. 1971).

409. Yellowhammer. *Emberiza citrinella*: K & M describe it as an abundant resident in all parts of the county and the Isle of Wight. It could hardly be called 'abundant' today, but it is a common resident in most parts of the mainland and Island. For instance, it is one of the characteristic birds of the chalk (perhaps the commonest species in some patches), and it is also very common on heathlands to the north of the chalk (131 pairs were located in 1971 on heaths along the Surrey border). In the New Forest its distribution is rather patchy; on heaths bordering surrounding farmlands it breeds in reasonable numbers (Palmer found 29 pairs on East Beaulieu Heath in 1957), but it is scarce on many heaths deeper into the Forest. It breeds freely along the coastal belt and over much of the Island.

There is little detailed evidence of breeding numbers such as the two already given, but 62 singing males were found in the parish of Silchester on 4/7 July 1966 (*H.* 1966) and Meinertzhagen reported 27/37 pairs at Mottisfont between 1935 and 1945 compared with 36/51 pairs in the 1890s.

Decreases, ascribed to the excessive burning of gorse, were reported all through the forties from Petersfield, Burghclere, Appleslade (New Forest) and the SE of the Island. On the other hand it was described as common in the Bournemouth area in 1936/9 (Hayward), as an abundant resident in the Alton area in 1949, as widespread and common around Winchester in 1950 (Burton) and common on the downs round Damerham in 1960 (Ash).

From the above, it appears that there have been decreases in some areas since K & M whilst in other areas it has held its own.

Winter flocks may reach or exceed 100 on occasions, viz. — the largest flocks in recent years were 150 plus at Crondall on 14 February 1970, 150 at Fernie Bottom (I.o.W.) on 15 February 1970 (*H.* 1970) and 100 at Butser on 27 March 1955 (*H.* 19. Part 2). Males in breeding plumage may keep in flocks well into spring, e.g. about 50 on stubble at Butser on 19 April 1954 (Rees). 40 (sex-composition not known) were at Brangsgore in a flock as late as May in 1949 (Miss Popham).

Small numbers occur in spring and autumn finch movements, and in cold-weather movements. Sudden influxes have occurred at Farlington Marshes in November; in 1953, numbers rose from three on the 27th to 60 on the 28th and none the next day; similarly in 1959 there was an influx on the 1st, 20 on the 8th and about 70 on the 22nd (*H.* 21. Part 2). A similar increase was observed in 1961.

At Titchfield Haven on 20 October 1956, Bowers saw about 30 in a mixed flock with 25 Corn, 12 Cirl and six Reed Buntings (*H.* 19. Part 3).

410. Corn Bunting. *Emberiza calandra*: K & M called it resident and fairly plentiful in all suitable localities in the county and the Isle of Wight. Since then it has certainly decreased. It disappeared from the Island in the early twenties (*I.o.W.* 1. Part 4 and 2. Part 3), although most years from 1957 have produced a small number of birds outside of the breeding season (mostly October/November) and very recent years have seen singing males in a few suitable breeding localities (*I.o.W.*). Munn himself, writing in 1918/19, said that it had perhaps decreased, but it was never a very plentiful species in the county (*H.* 8. 3). It has decreased in the north around Sherborne St. John, Basing, Tunworth and neighbouring areas, where it bred in fair numbers before the Second World War (P. E. Brown); now only one or two pairs breed at Sherborne St. John and Tunworth. In the coastal belt, a few pairs remain but building has destroyed much suitable habitat. Its stronghold today is in the chalklands of the mainland where, although local in its distribution, it is still quite common in places (e.g. the King's Somborne, Stockbridge and Winchester area). The *Atlas* survey showed proved or suspected breeding in almost all the mainland 10-kilometer squares other than those covering the New Forest where it is understandably absent.

Winter roosts tend to use the same area year after year; Clafton found a roost of 26 on Hengistbury Head on 28 November 1958 and in subsequent years numbers have reached 100 (*H.*); JHT found 80 roosting in reeds at Winnall in October/November 1956 (*B.B.* 51. 126), a roost which is still in use today with 160 on 3 October 1971. Titchfield Haven and Avington are other areas that have been used as roosts, 100 roosting in reeds at the latter locality on 1 March 1955 (*H.* 19.. Part 2). These roots obviously mean that winter flocks often use the same feeding areas year after year, so that visitors to places such as Danebury in winter are almost certain to find a Corn Bunting flock at the time of writing, possibly containing over 100 birds (e.g. *H.* 22. Part 1). There is a tendency for some flocks to be seen in coastal areas in winter, and the species has been recorded in coastal movements in spring, autumn and cold weather. Winter flocks have assembled by September and may still be found in April or even May (e.g. 42 were at Titchfield Haven in May 1970).

[**413. Red-headed Bunting.** *Emberiza bruniceps* *: An adult male was seen at Keyhaven on 2 July 1961 by Butler, Oddie and Whitehouse (*B.B.* 55. 582 where, however, it is stressed that many 'are imported annually into Britain and other West European countries and it is certain that all, or almost all, British records refer to escaped birds').]

415. Cirl Bunting. *Emberiza cirlus*: K & M call it a local resident throughout the county and Island and a highly characteristic bird of the southern parts and the coastal strip all along from Christchurch to Southampton Water; and also in *The Birds of Milford* (1913) by Kelsall and Coles, it is called 'one of the most characteristic birds of this coast'.

Without doubt it has declined appreciably since then although it is an elusive species and one of those about which we know least insofar as its distribution is concerned. *H.* over the last few years has noted any breeding reports sent in by observers, always a sign of some scarcity. Information suggests that it is now local and rather scarce, being found more in the southern half of the mainland than the north with a few breeding records each year from Wight (particularly at Osborne). The decline seems to be continuing for it has disappeared from some areas in the last few years and the *Atlas* survey showed breeding proved or suspected in only about a third of the mainland 10-kilometer squares. Back in 1954, E. L. Jones found 30 singing males within seven and a half miles of Andover and Jenkins located eight to 10 pairs on 1,000 acres at Micheldever. In 1961, Orr found 15 pairs in the SW of the county and the same observer located 14 pairs in the W. of the county in 1963 (*H.* 22. Part 2 and 23. Part 1). These give some idea of numbers that have been proved in the *better* areas.

Orr, who has probably found more pairs in recent years than any other observer, says that they are found in three main types of habitat in Hampshire, viz. —

1. the *sides* of main river valleys such as the Avon, a view supported by Terry Jones on the Test at Leckford.

2. The chalk downlands where there are trees and hedgerows.

3. The area behind the low cliffs between Christchurch and Lymington, although they are being driven out of this habitat by building and the species is no longer one of the characteristic birds of the coastal belt as it was in K & M and *B.o.M.* In some 600 visits to the coast between Lymington and Calshot, JHT has not seen a single bird.

It can be found in well-used areas, e.g. it nests regularly on Southampton Common, up to five pairs breeding in recent years.

416. Ortolan Bunting. *Emberiza hortulana**: K & M rejected the only report they had, one at Freshwater in August 1867, on grounds of insufficient evidence. They did not know that Meinertzhagen obtained an adult male at Mottisfont on 7 April 1897. Subsequent records:

A juvenile, caught at St. Catherine's Light, 10 September 1956 (Marr).

Two, Damerham, 17 September 1956 (Ash — *H.* 19. 352). There was an influx at Portland about the time of these two.

One, Needs Oar, 15 October 1961 (Sharrock — *H.* 22. Part 2).

One, St. Catherine's Point, 10 October 1965 (*I.o.W.* 5. Part 10).

Ortolan Bunting

[**420. Little Bunting.** *Emberiza pusilla*: One on 27 October 1959 at Farlington Marshes, reported in *H.* 21. Part 3, was rejected by *British Birds* Rarities Committee. None in K & M.]

421. Reed Bunting. *Emberiza schoeniclus*: K & M's description of it as a fairly plentiful resident in the county and the Isle of Wight where there are suitable habitats fits its status today. 'Suitable habitats' include quite dry areas of gorse and bracken on the New Forest heaths. Palmer made censuses on East Beaulieu Heath in 1957, 1958 and 1959 and found that the numbers breeding in boggy and dry places were respectively 13 and eight, seven and three, seven and 11. There are few such censuses to indicate numbers but from the Island 12 pairs bred round Yarmouth in 1953, at least 25 pairs bred in the West Yar valley in 1958 (Adams in *H.* 21. Part 2), and 20 pairs bred at Brading in 1966 (*I.o.W.* 6. Part 1).

Considerable passage occurs from September to early November, mainly to the west and mostly along the coast. Unusual numbers occur at such times (e.g. counts at

Titchfield Haven rose from 30 on 25 September 1959 to about 150 on the 27th — *H. 21. Part 3* — and 120 were at Hengistbury on 9 October 1966 — *H.* 1966) and numbers are seen moving (e.g. 321 flew west at Brownwich between 25 October and 1 November 1959 — *H. 21. Part 3*).

The species also appears in cold-weather movements (e.g. 184 flew west in cold weather at Hengistbury on 31 December 1961 — *H. 22. Part 2*).

Winter flocks occur from September and some are still together as late as April. They occur in kale fields, on the coast, on stubble and a variety of habitat where seed is available, often in mixed flocks with other finches (e.g. Mr. and Mrs. Tucker saw 200 with Bramblings, Redpolls, Tree Sparrows and various other species at Stratfield Saye on 17 January 1960 — *H. 22. Part 1*). They have also been found (since 1962) to flock in the New Forest, sometimes appearing to feed on fallen heather seed. Usually these Forest flocks number less than 200 but a remarkable gathering in New Millersford plantation reached 1,500 on 8 January 1967, 1,000 on the 14th and 750 plus on the 15th (Ash in *H.* 1967). Another large gathering was a roost at Fleet Pond which reached 341 in late 1971.

Proof of 'commuting' between Suffolk breeding grounds and Farlington Marshes in winter is shown by several ringing controls at both places. Two ringed at Chichester have been recovered on the mainland in October and one ringed at Stanpit on 28 January 1962 was killed near Rugby on 5 April 1962.

422. Lapland Bunting. *Calcarius lapponicus*: Two in K & M 1891 and 1893. Meinertzhagen records one on plough at Mottisfont on 4 January 1898.

A male was at Hayling Island on 23 December 1953 (Rees and Tubbs). One flew high to the NW over Damerham on 18 September 1956 (Ash) and another was on Farlington Marshes on 8 October 1956 (these coincided with a rush of this and other species at Portland — *H.* 19. 353). One was at Langstone Harbour on 1 March 1958 (PG).

Better observer-coverage over recent years has shown this to be a fairly regular but very scarce winter visitor. An analysis of records for 1959/70 showed the species to be present in all but three years. No year had more than seven individuals and all birds were on the coast between September and March, few staying for any length of time. Four at Newtown from 23 October to 2 November 1959 were the first ever recorded from the Island (*I.o.W.* 5. Part 4), and remain the only Isle of Wight birds to date.

423. Snow Bunting. *Plectrophenax nivalis*: K & M call it 'a winter visitor, usually to the coast of the mainland, less frequently to the Isle of Wight, and still more rarely to our inland districts. Arriving in October and departing in March or April.'

Since 1955, around 300 have been recorded with particularly high totals in 1959 (about 30), 1960 (about 70) and 1962 (50/60, but most of these in one flock). Some years have produced very few (e.g. one in 1966 and none in 1965).

The vast majority of these birds have been on the mainland coast. Most records are of single birds or *very* small parties but Sharrock saw about 20 in the Southampton Dock area on 27 October 1956 (*H.* 19. Part 3) and 15 plus at Needs Oar on 27 January 1960 (*H.* 22. Part 1), whilst S. L. White saw 22 at Warsash on 1 December 1961 (*H.* 22. Part 2).

Island records are fewer. Apart from 30/40 at Shanklin on 1 January 1962 (*I.o.W.* 5. Part 7 — the largest flock seen in Hampshire in recent years), 13 birds were seen between 1958/70, mostly at Newtown.

Some 20 birds have been seen inland including a flock of seven which remained at Mottisfont for a week in December 1894 (Meinertzhagen). The last inland bird was

170

at Basingstoke in 1960 (*H.* 22. Part 1).

There is a tendency for records to concentrate in October/November, indicating that some birds are on passage through Hampshire rather than appearing as winter visitors.

424. House Sparrow. *Passer domesticus:* An abundant resident except on open heaths and in the forests. Local increases or decreases have been attributed to various causes but no significant change in status seems to have occurred since K & M.

Small spring and considerable autumn movements have been seen in the last three or four years by watchers on the mainland coast and at St. Catherine's Point where two were seen to fly north off the sea on 4 May and where there was 'some evidence' of spring movement in April. 1959 gave evidence of autumn movement, 97 flying east at St. Catherine's on 4 October, 700 flying west at Brownwich on 25 October and 604 flying west — also at Brownwich — on 1 November (*H.* 21. Part 3). Much smaller movements have been recorded in some subsequent years.

A juvenile ringed 24 August 1961 at Maidstone (Kent) was controlled at Fareham on 14 October 1961 (*B.B.* 55. 541). An adult ringed Selsey Bill (Sussex) on 23 April 1962 found dead at Bitterne on 8 May 1966 (*B.B.* 60. 474).

425. Tree Sparrow. *Passer montanus:* K & M write 'A resident species but plentiful only in winter in most districts in the county and not so common in the Isle of Wight. As a breeding species it is distinctly rare, and even unknown in many parts. The nest has been found in the New Forest, at Bursledon and Laverstoke'. Meinertzhagen knew of two colonies of about eight pairs each at Mottisfont in the nineties.

From 1905 until 1957 reports are extremely sparse and mostly of one or two birds; for instance, in 1954, Suffern, Ash and EC did not see a single one in their various districts, nor P. E. Brown in 1955 round Basingstoke. The only breeding reported was near Portsmouth in 1950/2 (but the nests were robbed each year), round Old Basing (two or three pairs in most years from 1945/53, P. E. Brown), two pairs annually in the parish of Fyfield near Andover in 1960/3 (Brigadier Simson) and in the Island in 1953 and 1954 (*I.o.W.* 4.9. 347). And, earlier, 'Pamber Forest used to have one or more colonies in old oak trees' (Wallis *in litt.* 8 January 1906 to Munn). There appear to be no other reports of breeding down to 1962 inclusive.

But beginning in a small way in 1957 (50 at Southampton, 20 at Stratfield Saye, seven on Farlington Marshes — *H.* 20. Supplement) and, omitting 1958, again in 1959, and 1960/2, flocks outside the breeding season have suddenly come into the picture. E. L. Jones saw none in the NW from 1950 to 1957 but he has seen parties of up to 45 since then. In 1959 (*H.* 21. Part 3) there was a considerable autumn influx at the same time as one of Siskins, Redpolls, Bramblings and Snow Buntings; 97 passed W. at Brownwich and 125 NNW at Weston, near Southampton, on 1 November on which day there were also 10 at St. Catherine's Point. From 5 December onwards there were small parties totalling 100 or more in kale — a favourite habitat in winter — with other finches in the Damerham district where Ash had only once seen a single one previously. There were also about 200 at Stratfield Saye from 11 November to 13 December (Taylor) and some 200 at Basingstoke sewage farm on the 15th (Lee).

In 1960 (*H.* 22. Part 1) the species was involved in hard weather movements in January, for example 40-odd at Hurst Castle on the 9th, 300 at Stratfield Saye and 100 at Titchfield Haven on the 17th, and numbers rising at Basingstoke sewage farm from 200 in January to 500 on 16 March (Lee). There were also 10 at St. Catherine's Point on 9 January (Truckle) and three on 11 April (E. Williams).

Tree Sparrow

1961 again saw much westerly movement along the coast involving thousands of birds between mid-October/mid-December, though the maximum of 1,000 at Gilkicker on 14 October were flying east. Wintering flocks in 1961/2 reach 500 plus at the Gins in a kale field with Fat Hen (*Chenopodium album*), 400 at Titchfield Haven, and hundreds in the Fordingbridge-Whitsbury-Damerham area from January to the end of March, Ash describing the species as 'the commonest small bird over a wide area.'

Subsequent years have produced a similar picture and today it can be said that the species occurs in some numbers on the mainland during winter, especially in kale fields, flocks occurring on the coast and inland (800 plus at Crondall on 12 December 1970 the largest). Reports from the Island are far fewer and almost always concern very small numbers. Apart from wintering flocks, the species is also seen in the small bird movements that occur mostly in October/November, reports coming mainly from St. Catherine's Point and the mainland coast.

This revival in the fortunes of the species in Hampshire must in part be due to the better observer coverage we have today, but it is also a real increase as witnessed by the above comments from reliable observers who saw none or very few in the years before 1957.

As a breeding species, it is still rather scarce and completely absent from many parts. The *Atlas* survey showed breeding to be more frequent in the northern half of the mainland with a very patchy distribution in the south (missing from the south-west), whilst Island bird reports for 1958/68 list only one case of breeding, a pair with young at Calbourne in 1962. In one or two areas, small 'colonies' have been found, e.g. 10 pairs near Odiham in 1965 (*H.* 1965).

So the position has come back to that of K & M, with breeding a little more frequent than in their day.

Note

No fewer than four North American species which had travelled in a wild state on board the R.M.S. *Mauretania* were still on board when she berthed at Southampton on 14 October 1962. They were: 1 Slate-coloured Junco (*Junco hyemalis*), two White-throated Sparrows (*Zonotrichia albicollis*), one Song Sparrow (*Melospiza melodia*) and one Wood Pewee (*Contopus virens*) or possibly a Yellow-bellied Flycatcher (*Empidonax flaviventris*) (A. L. Durand *per* J. Wright). Mr. Wright tells me that Mr. Durand, who is a bank official stationed over the past year or two on liners plying between Southampton and America, is a very conscientious and reliable ornithologist. For a note by him on North American birds crossing the Atlantic on board the R.M.S. *Queen Elizabeth* see *B.B.* 54. 439/40.

Appendix I

This appendix shows maximum counts of the more common wildfowl species at their main waters since the Second World War. It is included to give an idea of the numbers involved in recent years, though it must be remembered that some of the counts were made in unusual weather conditions and so are abnormally high.

G.P. = Gravel Pit

Mallard

Alrebury	250	Bickton	300
Alresford Pond	800	Bishop's Dyke	600
Avington Lake	795	Brading Marsh	230
Avington (river)	530	Colgrims Mead	210
Avon Village	100	Dibden Bay	600+
Baffins Lake	440	Gins area	535
Bembridge	540	Harbridge/Blashford	1,500
Bishop's Dyke	200	Hurst area	400
Blashford (river)	350	Langstone Harbour	1,123+
Blashford G.P.	430	Lee G.P.	200
Brading Marsh	200	Millbrook	200
Braishfield	400+	Newtown	728
Bramshill	312	Northington	153
Broadlands (Romsey)	160	Sowley Pond	800
Christchurch Harbour	100+	Stone Point	200
Dibden Bay	146	Stratfield Saye	524
Eling Marsh	420	Timsbury	120
Gins area	620	Titchfield Haven	2,300
Gins — Sowley Pond	910	Warsash	183
Harbridge area	500	Woolmer	75/100
Hursley Park	200+		
Hurst/Pennington	215	**Wigeon**	
Langstone/Farlington	150	Ashlett Creek	105
Longstock	1,000	Avington	100
Marsh Court	100	Black Point (Chichester Hbr.)	660
Milford Lake	100+	Broadlands (Romsey)	150+
Newtown	400	Chichester Harbour	1,030
Northington	1,250	Christchurch Harbour	1,000+
Nursling G.P.	353	Dibden Bay	1,000+
Sowley Pond	1,000	Eling Marsh	900
Stratfield Saye	1,700	Gins area	2,000+
Test (river by Timsbury)	400+	Harbridge/Blashford	1,800
Timsbury Lakes	600+	Hurst/Pennington	500+
Titchfield Haven	700	Langstone Harbour	1,700+
Tundry Park (Dogmersfield)	150	Newtown	550/600
Warnford Park	173	Redbridge	1,011
Winchester Sewage Farm	300	Sowley Pond	700
Winnall	150	Stratfield Saye	160
Woolmer	300+	Timsbury	100+
Yateley G.P.	192	Titchfield Haven	1,600

Teal

Alresford Pond	270	**Shoveler**	
Ashlett Creek	1,400	Alresford Pond	45
Avon Village	200	Avington Lake	25
		Christchurch Harbour	100+

Gins area	75
Harbridge/Blashford	230
Hurst/Pennington	80
Langstone/Farlington	30
Newtown	52
Northington	46
Sowley Pond	140
Timsbury	32
Titchfield Haven	224
Yarmouth	15

Tufted Duck

Alresford Pond	28
Ashlett Creek	54
Ash Vale G.P.	65
Bembridge	40
Blashford/Ibsley	60
Bramshill	14
Christchurch Harbour	50+
Ewhurst	16
Fawley	169
Fleet Pond	41
Gins area	127
Kimbridge	73
King's Pond (Alton)	38
Langstone Harbour	60
Marsh Court	20
Milford Lake	15
Northington	35
Redbridge	428
Sinah G.P. (Hayling)	100+
Sowley Pond	109
Stratfield Saye	25
Timsbury	55
Titchfield Haven	300
Tundry Park (Dogmersfield) ..	34
Winnall	29
Woolmer	28
Yateley G.P.	117

Pochard

Alresford Pond	54
Ashlett Creek	36
Ash Vale G.P.	57
Badshot Lea	51
Bembridge	163
Blashford G.P.	300+
Christchurch Harbour	40
Fawley	100
Fleet Pond	74
Gins area	80
Harbridge	200
Hatchet Pond	50
Kimbridge	95
Milford Lake	10
Mottisfont	40
Newtown	30

Northington	52
Redbridge	257
Sinah G.P. (Hayling)	100
Sowley Pond	274
Stratfield Saye	110
Timsbury	107
Titchfield Haven	400
Tundry Park (Dogmersfield) ..	13
Walhampton	54
Winnall	75
Yateley G.P.	150

Canada Goose

Aldershot Camp Sewage Farm ..	89
Ash Vale G.P.	69
Bramshill	161
Elvetham Lake	220
Farnborough North G.P.	63
Fleet Pond	200
Gins area	110
Heath Pond (Petersfield) ..	68
Sowley Pond	91
Stratfield Saye	520
Tundry Park (Dogmersfield) ..	300+
Yateley G.P.	170

List of Observers and Correspondents named in Systematic List

Adams, M.C.
Alexander, H.G.
Alexander, W.B.
Andrews, C.W.
Angell, B.J.
Arnold, A.
Ash, J.S.
Ashby, E.
Ashford, W.J.
Atkins, H.
Avery, G.
Bacon, A.F.L.
Ballantyne, C.B.
Bannerman, Dr. & Mrs. D.A.
Barnes, J.R.
Barraud, Miss E.M.
Batchelor, Miss E.
Betts, F.N.
Bidmead, Miss H.A.
Billett, D.F.
Blackwell, J.
Blagg, F.E.
Blank, T.H.
Boswall, J.
Boutflower, J.
Bowers, J.K.
Boyd, H.J.
Boys, J.V.
Brewer, W.E.
Brice, T.E.
Britton, P.L.
Brotherton, Miss H.A.
Brown, K.
Brown, P.E.
Brown, R.
Brown, W.D.H.
Bryant, M.
Bulson, P.S.
Bundy, G.
Burton, J.
Butler, R.W.
Buxton, E.J.M.
Buxton, H.
Buxton, J.
Cadman, W.A.
Campbell, B.
Carpenter, R.J.
Carter, M.J.
Champion, N.G.S.
Chawner, Miss E.M.

Cheke, R.A.
Cheverton, J.M.
Christie, H.H.V.
Clafton, F.R.
Clarke, S.
Clay, G.H.
Cobb, Mr. & Mrs. D.
Cohen, E.
Conchie, J.
Cook, R.
Cram, F.
Crewe, P.R.
Crook, J.H.
Cundall, R.J.
Curber, R.M.
Curtis, W.P.
Davies, Miss M.G.
Davison, J.R.
Day, P.L.
Dennis, R.H.
des Forges, C.G.
Dilke, Mrs. R.
Donaldson, R.P.
Draper, J.C.
Duffin, B.S.
Durand, A.L.
Elmes, R.
Everett, J.J.W.
Ferguson-Less, I.J.
Fisher, Miss C.
Fisher, G.H.
Fisher, J.
Forster, G.H.
Fox, R.H.
Gladstone, N.
Goater, B.
Gobbett, D.
Goddard, F.J.
Godfrey, D.J.
Gooch, G.B.
Goodall, J.M.
Goodhart, J.
Gosnell, H.T.
Grant, P.J.
Green, G.P.
Griffiths, C.
Grove, E.A.
Gunston, D.
Gurney, J.H.
Hack, Miss K.M.B.

Harrison, M.
Harvey, M.
Hayward, L.W.
Hazelwood, A.
Heal, C.H.
Heath, B.A.
Henry, A.
Henson, N.
Henty, C.J.
Heycock, C.W.
Highway, Mrs. F.G.
Hill, A.G.
Hobby, P.
Hollom, P.A.D.
Holme, H.C.
Honner, F.J.
Hook, O.
Hopkinson, H.C.
Hunter, Miss M.L.
Hurcomb, Lord.
Jackson, R.J.
Jeffreys, P.
Jellicoe, Miss M.
Jenkins, D.
Johnson, I.G.
Jones, Miss D.V.
Jones, E.L.
Jones, T.
Jourdain, F.C.R.
Kinsey, G.G.
Klamborowski, Miss.
Knowlton, D.
Lack, D.
Le Brocq, P.F.
Lee, S.L.B.
Longstaff, T.G.
Lorenz, K.
Lyon, A.D.
Machin, R.J.
Mann, P.D.
Marr, B.A.E.
Martin, S.
Martin, T.M.
Mead-Waldo, E.G.B.
Meinertzhagen, R.
Meyrick, Sir G.
Miller, Mrs. E.M.
Mills, J.
Minchin, C.
Minton, C.D.T.

Mitchell, A.F.
Mitchell, O.H.
Mitford, R.S.
Mole, D.C.
Monk, J.F.
Moody, A.
Moreau, R.E.
Mountfort, G.
Munn, P.W.
Murton, R.K.
Newton Dunn, Miss D.
Nicholl, A.M.C.
Nicholson, E.M.
Nisbet, I.C.T.
Normanton, Earl of.
Norton, W.J.E.
Oddie, W.E.
Orr, N.W.
Paddon, C.
Palmer K.H.
Parrinder, Mrs. E.
Parsons, R.
Paulson, C.W.G.
Payn, A.W.
Pearce-Smith, A.
Pearce-Smith, N.
Peart, D.E.M.
Penrose, Miss F.E.
Penrose, F.G.
Phillips, D.H.
Phillips, D.T.
Pickess, B.P.
Pierce, G.G.
Pierce, G.W.
Pilkington, J.L.L.
Pitman, C.R.S.
Ponchaud, A.J.
Poole, H.F.
Popham, Miss C.
Portal, M.
Powell, R.
Praed, C.W.M.
Pratt, N.H.
Presst, I.
Pullen, N.D.
Pumfrett, D.G.
Radford, Mrs. M.C.
Rees, G.H.
Renyard, B.W.
Riddick, E.P.
Ridpath, M.G.
Ringrose, B.J.
Robertson, A.W.P.
Rogers, A.M.
Rogers, Mrs. M.
Rogers, N.R.
Rooke, K.B.

Rowan, W.
Rycroft, Sir Newton
Scott, P.M.
Seabroke, Mrs. M.
Searle, A.
Seth-Smith, Mr.& Mrs. L.M.
Seymour, C.G.
Shackleton, K.
Sharland, R.E.
Sharrock, J.T.R.
Shaw, C.A.
Shelley, H.
Simond, F.A.
Simmonds, J.
Simson, E.C.L.
Smallwodd, J.R.
Smith, C.
Smith, K.D.
Smith, K.S.
Spear Smith, K.
Spencer, R.
Sporne, S.H.
Staffel, T.E.
Stafford, J.
Standring, K.T.
Suffern, C.
Summers-Smith, D. & M.
Taverner, J.H.
Taylor, M.W.
Terry, M.H.
Thelwell, D.A.
Thomas, W.J.
Thornycroft, Miss B.
Ticehurst, C.B.
Troubridge, Sir T.H.C.
Truckle, W.H.
Tubbs, C.R.
Tucker, B.W.
Tucker, Mr. & Mrs. M.W.
Tyler, Mrs. S.
Venables, Miss M.
Venning, F.E.W.
Walker, A.
Wallis, H.M.
Watson, J.B.
Waydelin, F.J.
Webber, G.L.
White, E.H.
White, S.L.
White, Miss W.P.
Whitehouse, D.A.
Williams, E.J.
Williams, R.E.
Winter, T.G.
Winterbottom, R.H.
Wise, A.J.
Wiseman, E.J.

Witherby, H.F.
Wolfe-Murray, D.K.
Woods, H.E.
Wooldridge, D.B.
Wooldridge, G.E.
Wren, Miss L.I.
Wright, J.
Wynne, J.F.
Yorke-Norris, A.

Index

English names mentioned in Systematic List. Heavy type denotes a Plate number.